THE BOFFINS BAFFLED

What chemistry, we are often asked, takes place in the succulent bosom of the sherry casks where The Macallan lies slumbering for a decade (at least) before it is allowed out to meet the bottle?

The fact is, we do not know.

It is a <u>matter of history</u>, of course, that someone in the last century discovered that whisky ages best in oaken casks which have previously contained sherry (and that today The Macallan is the *last malt whisky* exclusively to be so matured).

And it is a <u>matter of fact</u> that in goes the translucent stripling spirit. And out comes amber-gold nectar positively *billowing* with flavour.

But let us take our cue from a party of scientists whom we once invited to explore the matter. '*Magic!*' they exclaimed, swigging their drams in a most unboffinly manner. 'But magic is merely undiscovered science and we'd like to take some home *for further investigation*.'

To join our small (but devoted) band of merry malt sippers, please call 1-800-428-9810.

THE MACALLAN. THE SINGLE MALT SCOTCH.

The Paris Review

Founded in 1953.

The Paris Review is published quarterly by The Paris Review, Inc. Vol. 39, No. 142, Spring 1997.
Business Office: 45–39 171 Place, Flushing, New York 11358 (ISSN #0031-2037). Paris Office:
Harry Mathews, 67 rue de Grenelle, Paris 75007 France. London Office: Shusha Guppy, 8 Shawfield
St., London, SW3. US distributors: Random House, Inc. 1(800)733-3000. Typeset and printed in
USA by Capital City Press, Montpelier, VT. Price for single issue in USA: $10.00. $14.00 in Canada.
Post-paid subscription for four issues $34.00, lifetime subscription $1000. Postal surcharge of $10.00
per four issues outside USA (excluding life subscriptions). Subscription card is bound within magazine. Please give six weeks notice of change of address using subscription card. *While The Paris
Review welcomes the submission of unsolicited manuscripts, it cannot accept responsibility for
their loss or delay, or engage in related correspondence. Manuscripts will not be returned or
responded to unless accompanied by self-addressed, stamped envelope.* Fiction manuscripts
should be submitted to George Plimpton, poetry to Richard Howard, The Paris Review, 541 East
72nd Street, New York, N.Y. 10021. Charter member of the Council of Literary Magazines and
Presses. This publication is made possible, in part, with public funds from the New York State Council
on the Arts and the National Endowment for the Arts. Periodicals postage paid at Flushing, New
York, and at additional mailing offices. **Postmaster:** Please send address changes to 45-39 171st
Place, Flushing, N.Y. 11358.

"How many a man has dated a new era
in his life from the reading of a book."

HENRY DAVID THOREAU

• • •

Crawford Doyle Booksellers

1082 Madison Avenue

New York City 10028

212 288 6300

• • •

Neighborhood Bookstore

Special Orders • Searches • Modern Firsts

BENNINGTON WRITING SEMINARS

MFA in Writing and Literature
Two-Year Low-Residency Program

A. BLAKE GARDNER

FICTION
NONFICTION
POETRY

For more information contact:
Writing Seminars, Box PA
Bennington College
Bennington, VT 05201
802-442-5401, ext. 160
Fax 802-442-6164

The James Jones Literary
Society
is pleased to announce that
the 1996 First Novel Fellowship
of $2500
has been awarded to
Greg Herbek
for his novel-in-progress
The Hindenburg Crashes Nightly

Petaluma
1st. Ave. at 73rd. St., New York City
772·8800
©1987 John Fischer

The
Paris
Review

Editorial Office:
541 East 72 Street
New York, New York 10021
HTTP://www.voyagerco.com

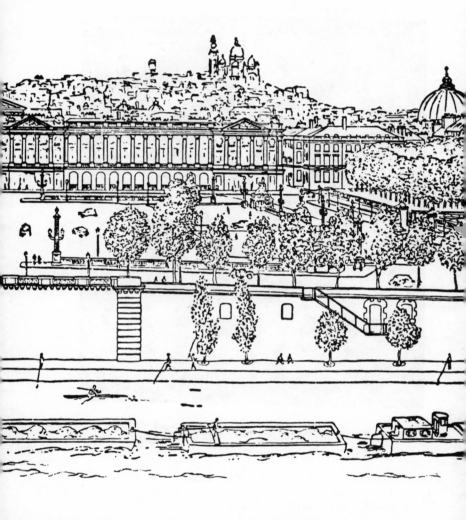

Business & Circulation:
45-39 171 Place
Flushing, New York 11358

Distributed by Random House
201 East 50 Street
New York, N.Y. 10022
(800) 733-3000

BLACK RIDER '90

Robert Wilson, *The Black Rider*, color pencil, graphite on
Fabriano paper.
Frontispiece by William Pène du Bois.

Number 142

NOTICE

While *The Paris Review* has published a number of interviews on the craft of playwriting over the years (Samuel Beckett, Tom Stoppard, Arthur Miller, Tennessee Williams among others) it has not offered its readers the stuff of the theater itself—plays, theatrical sketches, verse drama, whatever. One reason is that so often the lines of a play seem flat on the page without the agency of actors to give them life. Not that we haven't had the opportunity to publish plays. In the early years of the magazine Edward Albee sent us a playlet entitled *The Sandbox*. The undersigned accepted the work but made the mistake of offering a suggestion or two about one of the characters—that the grandmother might be toned down a bit. This so miffed Albee that he had the work withdrawn. He said about the play later (indeed, in a *Paris Review* interview): "I'm terribly fond of *The Sandbox*. I think it's an absolutely beautiful, lovely, perfect play."

Perhaps the ongoing reticence to publish plays goes back to this unfortunate experience—the thought that playwrights are far more sensitive to editorial suggestions than fiction writers.

In any case, last autumn the editors of *The Paris Review* put aside their qualms and offered a two-thousand-dollar prize for the best verse play. The response was extraordinary. Over one thousand plays in verse of varied forms were received . . . as well as over a hundred plays sent in by writers unaware of the "verse only" stipulation. The quality of the latter was such that it was determined to accept these as well—the final choices for this issue being two dramas and one verse play. *The Cripple of Inishmaan* by the brilliant young Irish playwright, Martin McDonagh, gives readers the longest selection this magazine has seen since the publication of Philip Roth's short novel, *Goodbye, Columbus*.

The submissions, of course, ranged in style and content

across an entire spectrum — from the radically "experimental" to the overtly political ("issue" plays), from domestic comedy through bedroom farce to tragedy. Many of the verse plays were based on Greek tragedies or Shakespeare, i.e., a sequel to *Romeo and Juliet*.

There were the oddities. Two plays by different playwrights centered on jars of formaldehyde sitting on stage, one of which contained a baby, the other the foot of a man who has murdered the protagonist's father. Those who enjoy such things will be delighted to find among the contents of this issue a poem about General Daniel Edgar Sickles, the Union officer who lost a leg at Gettysburg, had it preserved, put in a box and donated to the Smithsonian, which he would visit on occasion to pay it his respects.

—**G.A.P.**

Alcestis: A Bedroom Comedy

Karl Kirchwey

The setting is the master bedroom of a city apartment. The time is the early 1970s. A queen-sized bed, with a gold silk quilt on it. Next to the bed is a plate with crumbs remaining, an empty glass of milk and a pile of books; the volume on top is Bertrand Russell's Unpopular Essays.

There are three speaking voices, the parts divided among them as follows:

A: The Doctor, Alcestis, Heracles
B: Charun, Admetus
C: Eumelus, The Serving Maid, The Servant of Admetus

There are also matched choruses of Neighbors and Relatives.

This is a work in progress, which incorporates the writings of Ellen Douglas Kirchwey (1922–1972).

"I gave you my heart, and my body which was its case,
slim and ardent, almost as in its first youth.
I even sealed the smooth wrappings with my tears
and bound the entire gift in ribbons of laughter.
In return for this, I ask only for acceptance.
This is the dearest debt that lovers know."

•

Theonoë: *For all men, in the world below and in the world*
above must pay for acts committed here. The mind of those
who have died, blown into the immortal air, immortally has
knowledge, though all life is gone.
— Euripides, *Helen* (Richmond Lattimore tr.),
1013-1016

A. (The Doctor)

I want to say, in this matter, that I am blameless.
Malpractice insurance rates being what they are,
one may not take lightly even an accident of timing.
Still, the hospital's being unable to reach me
to authorize an ambulance for this unfortunate woman
should have no bearing on the facts of the case, which are
   these:
I saw no irregularity in the heart when I examined her
in the fall of that year. Her affliction was . . . middle age.
I was on vacation, it is as simple as that.
Forty-nine years old, largely sedentary;
perhaps it was inevitable she should suffer a coronary.
Her husband traveled a lot. I met him once or twice:
another outgoing, friendly American,
completely out of place in our gray Confederation.

B. (Charun)

So for once you will not argue with me over this?
She is mine; and when she is being prophetic and weird,
in a dark Scots mood, with a bit of drink inside her,
she has augured that she will be dead before fifty.

As to the cause of death—let the certificate
say that she died of a broken heart, induced by
twelve family moves. Or say whatever you like.
Such a history has its own inexorable logic,
and she was, at the end, completely deracinated.
It is never I who cause the struggle, anyway;
it is life itself. And she has grown tired of life.
But she will mean more to me if you keep her out of your
    shambles.
Do not cut her, trying to keep unwilling life inside.

A. (The Doctor)
No cardiac massage?

C. (Eumelus, a child)
       What they do is plunge through the sternum.
He told me there had been some cutting, trying to save her
    life;
that I might want to remember her as I had seen her
just the weekend before. At age sixteen, what did I know?
At least in his case there was closure. There is no mistaking
that absolute stillness which will never move again.
But she—

B. (Charun)
      No. And let her be laid out in that grass-green suit,
the pilled one, with perhaps a golden brooch.

C. (Eumelus)
              By the waters of Leman
I did not, at that time, weep, the lake's fathoms green
and imperturbable under the long steel jetty,
the limit of visibility twenty-one meters
in the month of February, 1891, as measured by
a white disc of twenty-one centimeters in diameter
suspended there, like the dust that makes a screen.
The service was in a chapel down by the shore.

I poured him out, at last, like arborio rice
from a kitchen canister, a gray plume smoking into the water
and then he was gone.

B. (Charun)
For those who are considering cremation,
here is what you should know: a 140-pound body,
after fifty minutes in a reverberating furnace
(which attains temperatures of 2000 degrees)
is reduced to four pounds of ash, essential salts.
Her body rested in a light pine shell,
and clothed, not asked to stride naked through the fire
as she was when she first came crying to this earth.

A. (The Doctor)
Practiced more widely in Europe than in America,
to be sure; but what about disfavor after the Holocaust?
You will not get that brooch, not with the sumptuary laws
under Augustus, for death must not put the value
of any real property beyond the reach of the State.
Apropos, there were certain accounts, dormant since '39,
which the State used to reimburse businessmen for their losses
following the nationalization of industries in Hungary. . . .

Chorus of Neighbors
The foreigners—something has gone wrong behind closed
　　doors.
The silence is suspicious. Where is the boy's loud music?
What has happened? The woman drinks, we know. And the
　　husband's accent!

C. (Eumelus)
My mother was wearing an engagement ring when she died,
a band of rubies, which was never seen again.
My father didn't give it to his third wife.
I suppose the hatchet-faced ambulance drivers palmed it.

B. (Charun)

As to the alternative—you had better have kept up
your cemetery payments, or else—bingo!—after ten years
the coffin is rudely broken up like so much kindling,
bones clapped in a jar, and everything else (clothes, shoes)
leaves by the chimney. No time to be sentimental
about old Aunt Lil. It's pay up or get out: no space.
I had this from a friend working in the Protestant Cemetery.
And when the wind blew the wrong way and the furnace was
    running—

B. (Admetus)

I wanted her to get out of bed and dress for the day.
The boy had left for school. The sunlight in its
passages lay across the furniture. She must get up,
get dressed, take a walk beside the sober lake
or ride the bus into Centre Ville for lunch
at the American Women's Club, or her conversation class.
Anything but these three-day passages of stale bedclothes,
tomato-and-mayonnaise sandwiches and reading all night.

A. (Alcestis)

"The sunlit boy's eyes, warm on me for no reason. . . ."
But there is no sun today! When the clouds gather
in a rolled muff on the crest of the Jura, then
the north wind will blow for weeks at a time, and squalls
will appear with their black grains on the face of the lake.
[*with a Vaudois accent*] Le joran qui suit le vent
                    Tient la bise par la man [*pause*]
What time is it? You mean it's only morning? [*weeps*]
And I still have the whole day to get through.
I had hoped that it might be afternoon already. [*pause*]
"Wake; stay; or depart: milder than milk my indifference."
But you alone brought me to this life of utter stasis,
obedient, always obedient to someone else's whims.

Chorus of Relatives

I'm tired of people who are stubborn and contrary enough
not to obey "doctor's orders." She will always have a cough

as long as she smokes. At the Shadow, she had such a severe
  bronchitis
it was almost pneumonia, and she was left weak and
  susceptible.

A. (Alcestis)

May I bore you, briefly? I was seventeen,
a friend and I were picnicking
and generally inviting our souls with large and small talk
somewhere in the Ridgefield Hills. The sky was smoke,
the field with its sedge, plumed goldenrod and wild asters
was rust and purple; and in the midst of being quietly serious
and casually clever, I had the abrupt, even apocalyptic
experience of realizing that I was *I*
for the first time. I feel foolish trying to say this,
but please, perhaps, you say it the way you've come
to know it, and that will express it for me, at that time, too.

Chorus of Neighbors

A woman came to lunch, in wheelchair and braces,
and as she was carried back to her car, the boy sang
a song he'd invented which seemed to make him cry,
about a moth which had died in the sewing room
way back in August, which he said had been his best friend.

A. (Alcestis)

As we drove home, we saw the ground mist of twilight mix
with woodsmoke from farm chimneys, and her mother
    met us
at the door with an armful of coppery dahlias.
I never saw my friend again. About three weeks later,
I got a telegram from her uncle saying she was dead
of leukemia. The funeral service was at her house;
the man in front of me had a pimple on his neck
which he picked at while the minister read Yeats
(she had had time to make a few suggestions).
No one but the family went to the cemetery.

The sun came and went; the foliage was brilliant,
and I returned to Vassar with her Ethel Walker roommate
who, after all, having been born with a sense of identity,
went briskly off to the chemistry lab the moment we got back.
But *I* seemed to have lost myself as well as my friend.
I am always trying to be whatever X thinks I should be
or would like me to be, instead of being myself.

Chorus of Relatives

Each of them has matured under disappointment
and pain; each has emerged stronger, finer and surer.
He appears to have kept his sense of human trust
despite the injury done him, and she, being high-spirited,
needs and wants a firm guiding hand, which she has
    never had.
His hand has been tender, sympathetic and loving
but she longs for it to be directive and masterful.

C. (Eumelus)

[*sings*] On top of Old Smokey
Lay poor little Moth-y
All withered and dead.

A. (Alcestis)

I tried to keep myself busy on that frozen hilltop,
the first year of our marriage, alone with the child.
My parents' place was called "The Shadow"; this was called
    "The Dump."
You were away on business for almost a month.
The car got stuck on the last rise of the long hill.
The old gardener had to tow it out with his truck,
and Mrs. Flynn the laundress—

C. (The Serving Maid)

Why is he so careful with the sand? Why always so careful?
You'd think he was putting salt and pepper on his egg!
What does he care how much sand he uses?
Not that I don't disapprove of waste, you know.

A. (Alcestis)

I painted the downstairs bathroom—too bright a shade
of yellow for such a space—and I made curtains,
miscalculating the required ninety-inch length;
with pleats, which you must understand are the complete
   Eleusinian
Mysteries to me—

B. (Admetus)

Wednesday and Thursday nights at the
   Alameida;
(or you may want to send letters ahead to the Roger Smith),
and the 25th at the Statler.

A. (Alcestis)

I developed a *thing*
about having at those curtains, after the first
curiosity-inspired fine careless rapture,
because it took me so dismally back to Michigan,
that autumn before I went to Reno, so the measuring and
   pinning,
the sewing machine and I swathed in bolts of material,
through a queer condensation of time, evoked that wretched
   period.
At last I tried to make matching shirts for you and me
out of madras we had brought back from Bermuda,
but the cloth's smell reminded me of our honeymoon, and I
   had to stop.

B. (Admetus)

For the dead, time stops. There is nothing past death.
Her life simply ended; there was no subsequent experience.
A "dreamless sleep," as I described it to him once,
after another death, as we sat in the parked car
in the shopping center, before I got out to do
whatever unimportant errand it was I did.

A. (Alcestis)

Tina the black Lab bitch, asleep on the hearthrug:
twitches and whimpers . . . Suddenly Miss Beanbag
rolls over, the more lazily to enjoy the modicum
of affection she is vouchsafed—and, to my horror,
her radish looks inflamed. I undertake
a clinical-minded inspection, and on the basis
of my shaky knowledge, I conclude that she isn't yet
about to embark on the alarums and excursions
   of puberty . . .

B. (Admetus)

                  I met a cardiologist on vacation
on Lemnos the summer after it happened. One evening
we drank and talked, and he said, from the sound of it,
that she would not have survived, even if the ambulance
had come sooner. The smell of sewage they used to water
the abundant gardens mingled with the parched smells
of wild thyme and sage from the hills. It was August. My son
made friends with a pretty English girl his own age
whose father was a director of some repute.
I felt both his longing and his ignorance.
In this way life continued, as it had to do.

A. (Alcestis)

We had her fixed—I with feelings of injustice,
warmly and fully, if queerly, thinking, She is female,
as I am. If some other Power had done that to me,
were to do that to me. . . . And this was three years before
my new thing about at last only wanting to be with
and do for and teach and learn from my own children,
dozens of them, darling: which was my earth-mother phase.

B. (Admetus)

A story from almost twenty years ago. The dog died.

A. (Alcestis)

A botched spaying. Painful. Bandaged at the hips. *C'est fait,*
c'est fini, I know. I took them off with lighter fluid,
a harrowing experience for all concerned. She almost bit me.

Chorus of Relatives

She seems very twirled up with nerves—heaven knows why—
high blood pressure (she told me it was *210*
before she started on this new snakeroot wonder herb
from India), and also, I think, King Bottle.

A. (Alcestis)

But what match are my ego, my restlessness for perfection,
mercurial humanist curiosity and enthusiasms,
for all that it is not a tranquil mixture,
against your granite integrity, your tolerance
(with small exceptions, sympathized with, for small people,
not sympathized with), your quiet perceptive mind,
that absorbs and analyzes and concludes
so rightly, so compassionately, though the silence
in which it functions is sometimes disconcerting—

C. (Servant of Admetus)

It's Carl lo Stesso calling. From Waltham Sears.
What did you say the catalogue price was on that model?
But buying at the store guarantees you one year's free service,
d'you get me? Well, if things are that tough, little lady,
I'll deliver it myself. The store price? $239.95.
Fine, call me Saturday morning, but—d'you get me?
You might want to surprise the hubby, after all . . .

A. (Alcestis)

—like the time I called you in Chicago late on your birthday.
Someone had said, across the treacherous drifts of music,
that I had never looked better, and my smile answered,
through the blue haze of chagrin and cigarettes.
You were so quiet on the other end, with overtones
of downright orneriness: to be congratulated,
I suppose, for not actually snarling, but I was shaken,
because of the business about "the guy who is sun and moon
and stars to me seems to have just turned himself off:
he almost sounds as though he thought I were boiled

and dancing the Highland Fling on a long table:
as if he neither trusted me nor respected me
nor particularly even loved me at that moment.

B. (Charun)

On the Via Latina, in a residential neighborhood,
there is an unremarkable trapdoor in the sidewalk,
and following the staircase, which leads steeply down,
the temperature rising, and the humidity,
one arrives, a considerable distance under the street,
at a painted suite of Paleochristian tombs:
the peacock, whose flesh was thought to be incorruptible,
and Apollo, who is also Christ and Sol Invictus,
and the hero who leads the veiled woman past the three-
    headed dog.

A. (Alcestis)

I took the boy to school, and noticed, along with the art
on the wall, the room temperature chart, and the lowest
    reading
was seventy-six degrees, and most were in the eighties!
I came home and got on the telephonic warpath.
Honestly, though, it is not healthy, and the only two
other mothers with whom I spoke were as appalled as I.

Chorus of Relatives

My dear, I tell you, such strange rumors make their way
across the ocean—for example, that that man
actually *allowed* her to die, or even killed her!
Who knows? I never liked him, anyway.

A. (Alcestis)

Do you remember, not long after we were married,
a friend of Mother and Daddy's from the dark ages
gave us a set of the nicest clear plastic place mats
and the monogram on them, worked in white and gold,
was EKG, your first initial and mine

flanking the solid majuscule of your surname.
Whatever became of those place mats, I wonder.

Chorus of Relatives
Is there tuberculosis or insanity in the family?
—As her grandmother once asked the future son-in-law,
trying to rattle him. And he answered satisfactorily.

B. (Admetus)
She had seen the doctor a few months before, and the ekg
was completely normal, not a shadow of infarction—

A. (Alcestis)
Two years ago, I was shopping at Selfridge's,
and my hand shook so badly I couldn't sign a check.
The boy saw, and I tried to make light of it,
but his face was grave and still, looking at me.
That black ink is like some kind of autograph.
[*shivers*] I can't get warm. How I long for the white wind
    of July,
the *maurabia*, the wind which ripens the wheat,
or even the snow-eating foehn, which drives people mad.

B. (Admetus)
After so many times when I had implored her and
    cajoled her
and exhorted her to get out of bed and face the day;
after so many evenings with the dinner unprepared,
the house dark, its mistress indisposed, unwell, absent:
as I topped the hill, I would pray to find her up and about.
[*moves to throw open the curtains*]

A. (Alcestis)
"You lie in all my many thoughts like light." [*pause*]
Last night I had such glandular dreams of you.
Once, when we were both younger, I wrote you a letter,
saying that I would love to come visit for the weekend.

You responded, "The word *love*, used in this connection
is frowned upon by grammarians." I thought you were
  kidding,
but I have come to learn that you weren't kidding at all.
I have left parts of myself in every place we lived,
You don't think the traffic with other people comes at no cost,
do you? So well-liked, so affable, so outgoing,
and yet there was a part of you I never touched at all.
Where shall I look for everything I have lost?
In Wayland, with the horsey set at the roaring forge;
silent over a glass of wine at the Peak in Darien,
or at the Barking Dog Luncheonette, around the corner
from 127 East 94th Street, where my parents used to live.
It makes a burning shawl spread over my chest,
the anguish of it, clinging, impossible to shake off —
Ah! Ah! The Doctor! Dark man with your filthy hammer
and your symmetrical step, keep away from me! Keep away!

Chorus of Neighbors
A cry from that apartment — but why? Just the gray-haired
  concierge,
tuning things up with the silent efficiency we expect.

[*the doorbell rings, followed by an unnecessarily loud and
  sustained knocking*]

B. (Admetus)
All right, all right, I'm coming. [*moves downstage to open
  the door*]

A. (Heracles)
[*enters briskly, with a suitcase and a briefcase*]
Why, hello, Dancer, you old Handsome Dan, you,
Chairman of the Senior Prom in '42,
we called you the Tea Dancer. Tell me, are you still a member

of the Turtle Club? Is the card somewhere in your toilet kit,
stained with Vitalis? Remember? "What is it that's round
  and hard
and sticks so far out of a man's pajamas
you can hang a hat on it?" And the answer? The answer?

B. (Admetus)
"His head." Listen—

A. (Heracles)
You haven't forgotten! And what about 322?
[*mimics "Hear no evil, see no evil, speak no evil "*]
No, Dancer, don't look offended and leave the room.
Just remember what Diogenes of Apollonia
tells us: "Life is not worth living for the man
who has not even one good friend."

B. (Admetus)
                    I wish you had called first.

A. (Heracles)
No time to call. Bad weather grounded the plane in Geneva.
Just time for a *croque-monsieur* at the little zinc bar.
And they had a most ingenious device for hollowing frank-
  furter rolls,
a heated spike, a sort of nine-inch lingam
done all in stainless steel: the alimentary French.
Say, Dancer, would there be such a thing as a drink around
  the place?
There's the old monogrammed Steuben cocktail shaker,
but broken and mended with—what is it? Epoxy resin?
A bit slapdash, but old traditions die hard, *n'est-ce pas*?

B. (Admetus)
I don't think—

A. (Heracles)
                    The many glasses you and I have raised
in good times and bad, on several continents,
made me bold in this case, presuming on our friendship
to the extent of arriving unannounced like this,
knowing I could count on you, the consummate host.

B. (Admetus)
But she—

A. (Heracles)
                    Yes, speaking of the moon-driven part of the
    household,
wherever are you hiding the estimable wife?
        "A dog, a wife and a walnut tree,
    The more you beat them, the better they be." [*pause*]
Sorry. They were handing out free splits on the plane.

B. (Admetus)
She's gone, that's just what I've been trying to tell you.

A. (The Doctor)
Consider the case of the Hungarian Michael Kallosy,
recorded in the *Daily Mail* (London) for March, 1927:
who, falling in love with a beautiful Jewess (their wording)
and being rejected, caused a lifelike wax figure
of her to be built and for some time cohabited with it,
until he was induced to take it with him to the asylum.
Then again, the son of Germanicus and Agrippina,
a delightful child, died just as he was reaching boyhood,
and his adoptive great-grandmother, the Empress Livia,
dedicated a statue of him as Cupid
in the Temple of Capitoline Venus, while her husband
    Augustus
had another statue placed in his own bedroom,
and used to kiss it fondly, says Suetonius.

C. (Eumelus)

He called me and told me over the phone she was dead.
I have thought about that decision for a long time.
I think he should have traveled to tell me in person.
An hour's drive, after all, or a little bit over.
Like so much else about him, this decision mingled love and
    remoteness
unbearably. I still don't know at all who he was.
[*on the telephone*] What? What? Please tell me this is a joke.

B. (Admetus)

[*sternly, but full of grief*] No, this is not a joke —

C. (Eumelus)

                                    We had left the village
Where I had spent the stable part of my childhood:
the house, the friends and the familiar landscape.
And not long afterwards, I told him I had the feeling
that this was all a dream, in spite of the trenches
gouged by the moving van's tires in the front lawn;
I told him I kept thinking I would wake up
and once more be among my friends in my familiar place.

B. (Admetus)

I did what I had to. What good would it have done
to let you believe that the change was not irrevocable?

C. (Eumelus)

And he said to me with such harshness — as if the life or death
of the imagination were a personal threat to him,
"This is no dream, and we will not be going back."
I felt my life falling away on all sides of that voice.
What is the use of such a granite integrity
if it makes no allowances for hesitations of the spirit
in those directly affected by the changes it brings on?

B. (Admetus)

Not that I did not weep, but rather I thought
no one should see my weeping. I thought I must be strong.
And how could I save him from this loss or any other?

Chorus of Relatives

I am proud of you in all sorts of ways, but most of all
because you make so many people happy,
and because you have such a wonderful understanding
of just what to do when everything seems in a tangle.
You are so like your grandfather in that—he was such a rock
of refuge and good cheer, and loved by so many people.

C. (Eumelus)

A Wednesday afternoon, our half-holiday at school.
The receiver was a dead weight in my hand.
I put the black thing down and walked down the hall
to knock on the master's door. I heard his Wagner
swelling from inside, and then the suspicious voice
saying, "What is it?" I said, "It's my mother, sir.
She's dead." That got him to open the door in a hurry,
red-faced, in his dressing gown. The rest I hardly remember,
except that I went to a movie with the rest of my class.
How surreal: sitting there in the dark with my mother
    just dead.

B. (Charun)

There may be a third way. In the seventeenth century, I
    once read,
a Florentine physician injected tissues of a cadaver
with a silicate of potash solution, then immersed the body
in a mild acid solution, with the result
that the body turned to stone. And more recently,
although I've lost the source, Spiridon Nicolaon,
a druggist from Argos, achieved similar results
with gum-sandarac in alcohol on a human body
recovered by Heinrich Schliemann from Mycenae.

C. (Eumelus)

And the only time I recall having expressed any emotion
was at table-service: a minor outburst, but the master said,
in front of my companions, "We all know your mother's
   just died,
but you'll have to get a grip on yourself, nonetheless."

B. (Admetus)

I reason with myself. What could I have done to save her?
The doctor was not on call, and the hospital,
with that particular Swiss fondness for bureaucracy,
would not send an ambulance without the doctor's approval.
We lost some minutes there, and she did not die at once.

A. (The Doctor)

This is why the first days after a death
are so important: because the world still remembers
the physical presence of the dead. I mean the streets do,
and the houses, and even the furniture.
After a week or two, this memory is gone.

B. (Admetus)

At some point I came to rely on the anonymity
of hotel rooms, trains, planes and the open road.
Home was sweeter for every departure I made,
and she and I, although opposites, were reconciled
through the intangible medium of regular distance.
Her sentences grew only more euphuistic
in my absence: she needed an audience, a correspondent,
as well as a lover of flesh and blood. So what now?

A. (Heracles)

Once this has happened, the mind begins to consider
whether the dead are not corporeally present elsewhere;
whether they do not, perhaps, inhabit another part

of the world; and whether, for these twenty years,
their lives have not perhaps been going on, parallel
to ours and elsewhere, but nonetheless in consecutive time.
Shall we go? Perhaps in Singapore or Rio . . .
but you know those cities. Is your bag packed, Dancer?

Three Poems by Eleanor Ross Taylor

A Place Apart

Hung, awfully, over the valley
    on this remote escarpment,
a long, unearthly house
    of earth-pink stone,
a sanctum made, an alleluia
    on a rock—the bishop's.

Not a sour monk escaped domestic chains:
    daughters and granddaughters
on the plain storybook swing
    have dangled and disappeared.

Much of God's work—the stinted trees
    and laurels grateful for a cleft.
Much of his wife's—the well-staked
    vortexed lilies that obsess
the hummingbird; potted hydrangeas
    and a rare old door.

Inside, a sylvan mural,
    silver urns, a multipartite service;
Louis chairs in this—
    it cries out, gallery;
slim, satin sofas stressing
    glassed, gouached views.

But first, his poet guest's
    hard put to find his refuge
in vined folds, descents,
    and passes hemlock hung
behind clerestory oaks
    and a world-fending wall.

The bookroom in this bastion
    opens west on flocks of
gathering mountains.
    Book spines soliloquize, they
beckon explorations with no map
    except his musing
azalea aborescens trail
    flicked with goldfinches'
twitter and a sheaf of goldenrod,
    the thin leaves of a testament.

He quotes St. Augustine, talks
    fervently of *Father Sergius*,
is frankly pleased with his stone
    railings (that convent at Amalfi
where bees stole back
    their honey from the *pane fritta*)
his aged brick promenades
    leading to beeches on the bluff—
the Cherokees' sacred groves, still,
    it seems, wringing their hands.

If a night storm drags the valley,
    crawls up and breaks,
the angel of the storm
    loud-swishing in the trees,
he flicks the floodlights on
    iron vines of rainlashed chairs,
the roaming lightning
    and the vast, conclusive dark
wholly manifest, scourging
    his balconied Te Deum.

A fragile man,
    whitehaired and insubstantial,
a handful of evolving sparks
    in a dark room, breakfasting

with existing dark after dreams
   riddled and lanced with glory:
Do thou worship in a place apart,
   go shut the door.
And when you give alms, be it in secret.

What is he, whose polished worldly
   unaccountable Eden's proffered Heaven?
The poet, home, pounds
   his soft, common bed,
and unwords poems.

On Being Worldly

I'll buy that "collage blouse"
   as advertised "prismatic with
faux coins and stones"
   and zigzags of lamé
to run my Visa out of sight.
   No, no. Excess is vulgar . . .
such makings in my attic.

Yes, him, with wheelchair and accordion
   and sheepish dog, faux leg,
I passed on my way home.
   And her, a can of corn and one real
onion, in faux mink.
   The checkers priced us, and I thought
mine rang my diamond up. . . .
   Rejected finery's the story of my attic.

But in this first box there's a fabric collage,
   a patchwork my child sewed at six,
wetting the tip inch of the thread,
   rolling the damp knot off her thumb

like one creating comets;
    these buttons, tacked on,
from my antiques box, two iridescents
    and a peacock eye, hers to learn with
or to waste, at my largesse.

She must have worked their placement
    out with care. Or did she court
the throw of the dice — much like
    the scraps they're sewn to,
and the years
    of new jobs, lovers, bits
of exultant paintings, sudden
    phone calls, and accrued birthdays —

a fading roulette I all by myself
    hold out, interrogate,
and fold back up, and hear
    as nowhere else in the whole house,
the wind from the world terrestrial,
    sweeping the eaves and flicking
the dazzling spiderwebs.

Always reclusive,

I'm constructing my own brierpatch. True,
I'm bleeding from the long canes just dug in;
thorns lash at cultivation, cut both ways,
both in and out; like keeping things
in, more than battling them; that's useful;
I won't try getting out too soon,
say for a tipsy fruit, or reckless stroll.
What I don't spend on tickets I'll apply
on long long-distance calls.

Hunters will come and look into, dogs
panting, feet pointing. I'll like that.
I'll cuddle up and turn the page.

"The blackberry, permitted its own
way, is an unmanageable plant."
Here's a variety called *Taylor*:
"Season late, bush vigorous, hardy . . .
free from rust." That's it.
Don't let my brierpatch rust.

Anne Carson

TV Men: Antigone (Scripts 1 and 2)

Antigone likes walking behind Oedipus
to brake the wind.
As he is blind he often does not agree to this.
March sky cold as a hare's paw.
Antigone and Oedipus eat lunch on the lip of a crater.
Trunks of hundred-year-old trees forced
down
by wind
crawl on the gravel. One green centimeter of twig
still vertical —
catches her eye. She leads his hand to it.
Lightly
he made sure
what it was.
Lightly left it there.

[Antigone felt a sting against her cheek. She motions the soundman
out of the way and taking the microphone begins to speak.]

There is nowhere to keep anything, the way we live.
This I find hard. Other things I like — a burnish
along the butt end of days
that people inside houses never see.
Projects, yes I have projects.
I want to make a lot of money. Just kidding. Next
question. No I do not lament.
God's will is not some sort of physics, is it.
Today we are light, tomorrow shadow, says the song.
Ironic? Not really. My father is the ironic one.
I have my own ideas about it.
At our backs is a big anarchy.

If you are strong you can twist a bit off
and pound on it—your freedom!

Now Oedipus has risen, Antigone rises. He begins to move off,
into the wind,
immersed in precious memory.
Thinking *Too much memory* Antigone comes after.
Both of them are gold all along the sunset side.
Last bell, he knew.
Among all fleshbags you will not find
one who if God
baits
does not bite.

[For sound bite purposes we had to cut Antigone's script from 42
seconds to 7: substantial changes of wording were involved but we
felt we got her "take" right.]

Other things I like: a lot of money!
The way we live, light and shadow are ironic.
Projects? yes: physics. Anarchy. My father.
Here, twist a bit off.
Freedom is next.

OUIJA BOARD

FIVE SCENES

A manuscript page from the author's notebooks.

David Mamet

The Art of Theater XI

*David Alan Mamet grew up in a Jewish neighborhood on
the South Side of Chicago, just a few blocks from Lake Michigan. His father was a labor lawyer, his mother a schoolteacher;
both sides of the family came to Chicago in the 1920s, part
of the city's last wave of central European immigrants. Mamet
was a child actor who attended public schools on the South
Side until his parents' divorce; later, as a teenager, he would*

spend several unhappy years living with his mother in Olympia Fields, a Chicago suburb on the edge of the prairie.

Like many Chicago writers, he claims to have been shaped by the city's peculiar duality, "the admixture of the populist and the intellectual." He would write later of perceiving the city "not as an adversary. . .[but] as an extension of our dream-life."

In 1964 he went off to Goddard College in Plainfield, Vermont, where he was graduated with "no skills, nor demonstrable talents." Over the next several years he pursued a series of odd jobs, including a stint in the merchant marines. With the expectation of becoming an actor, he joined a theater company at McGill University, before returning to Vermont for an instructor's position at Marlboro College.

His first play was staged in 1970, almost by accident. He had won the job at Marlboro by advertising himself as the author of a play, though in fact there was nothing to which he could truthfully lay claim. Upon his arrival he learned that his "play" was scheduled to be performed, so he hastily set about writing Lakeboat, *a one-act drama taken from his experiences in the merchant marines.* Lakeboat *was staged before the year ended; it would set the tone for his later work and eventually become a full-length feature, one that is still performed today.*

He spent only one year at Marlboro before returning to Chicago, where he worked variously as a waiter, a cabdriver and a real-estate salesman. The following autumn, having abandoned acting, he went back to Goddard, which had offered to make him its artist-in-residence. There he formed an ensemble, the St. Nicholas Theater Company, which performed the plays he had written since Lakeboat. *In 1973 he moved back to Chicago, bringing with him a batch of new plays and the means to have them performed.*

He spent the next four years in Chicago, writing, directing and teaching (at Pontiac State Prison and the University of Chicago). After a rough start his plays won the admiration of both critics and audiences. In 1974 he received the Joseph Jefferson Award (given each year to the best new local play) for Sexual Perversity in Chicago. *More prizes followed — two*

Obies in 1976, and in the same year a New York Drama Critics Circle Award for American Buffalo, *which had its Broadway debut in 1977 at the Ethel Barrymore Theatre. In all, nine of his plays — including* A Life in the Theatre, The Water Engine, Prairie du Chien *and* Lone Canoe — *were produced between 1975 and 1978.*

In the eighties, Mamet turned part of his attention to the movies, a genre that had attracted him since childhood. He wrote screenplays for six movies (two of which he directed himself) and received an Academy Award nomination for his adaptation of The Verdict. *He also published* Writing in Restaurants *and* Some Freaks, *both essay collections. New plays continued to appear almost annually, including the revised version of* Lakeboat, Speed-the-Plow, Edmond *and* Glengarry Glen Ross, *which received both the Pulitzer Prize and the New York Drama Critics Circle Award.*

Since 1991 Mamet has lived in New England. At forty-nine he is the author of twenty-two plays, twelve scripts and four collections of essays. His recent work includes the screenplay for Louis Malle's Vanya on 42nd Street, *the novel* The Village *and three plays:* Oleanna, The Cryptogram *and* Death Defying Acts.

—B.R.H.

INTERVIEWER

How was it that you were drawn to the theater?

DAVID MAMET

Freud believed that our dreams sometimes recapitulate a speech, a comment we've heard or something that we've read. I always had compositions in my dreams. They would be a joke, a piece of a novel, a witticism or a piece of dialogue from a play, and I would dream them. I would actually express them line by line in the dream. Sometimes after waking up I would remember a snatch or two and write them down. There's something in me that just wants to create dialogue.

INTERVIEWER
Can you put a date to this?

MAMET
It's always been going on. It's something my mother used to say when I was just a little kid: "David, why must you dramatize everything?" She said it to me as a criticism: why must you *dramatize* everything?

INTERVIEWER
And did you have an answer for her?

MAMET
No, but I found out (it took me forty years) that all rhetorical questions are accusations. They're very sneaky accusations because they masquerade as a request for information. If one is not aware of the anger they provoke, one can feel not only accused but inadequate for being unable to respond to the question.

INTERVIEWER
That happens in your plays a lot. There are a lot of rhetorical challenges.

MAMET
"Why must you always . . ."

INTERVIEWER
One of the things that interests me is how uncompromising you are, both with yourself and the audience. *The Cryptogram*, for example, forces the audience to solve this puzzle that also happens to be troubling the kid in the play. You, as the author, have put the audience and the kid in essentially the same place.

MAMET
Well, that, to me, is always the trick of dramaturgy: theoretically, perfectly, what one wants to do is put the protagonist

and the audience in exactly the same position. The main question in drama, the way I was taught, is always, What does the protagonist want? That's what drama is. It comes down to that. It's not about theme, it's not about ideas, it's not about setting, but what the protagonist wants. What gives rise to the drama, what is the precipitating event, and how, at the end of the play, do we see that event culminated? Do we see the protagonist's wishes fulfilled or absolutely frustrated? That's the structure of drama. You break it down into three acts.

INTERVIEWER

Does this explain why your plays have so little exposition?

MAMET

Yes. People only speak to get something. If I say, "Let me tell you a few things about myself," already your defenses go up; you go, "Look, I wonder what he wants from me," because no one ever speaks except to obtain an objective. That's the only reason anyone ever opens their mouth, onstage or offstage. They may use a language that *seems* revealing, but if so, it's just coincidence, because what they're trying to do is accomplish an objective. "Well, well, if it isn't my younger brother just returned from Australia . . . have a good break?" The question is where does the *dramatist* have to lead you? Answer: the place where he or she thinks the audience needs to be led. But what does the *character* think? Does the character need to convey that information? If the answer is no, then you'd better cut it out, because you aren't putting the audience in the same position with the protagonist. You're saying, in effect, "Let's stop the play." That's what the narration is doing: stopping the play.

Now, there's a certain amount of *essential* information, without which the play does not make sense . . .

INTERVIEWER

And how do you fit that information in?

MAMET

As obliquely as possible. You want to give the people information before they know it's been given to them.

INTERVIEWER

So to you a character is . . .

MAMET

It's action, as Aristotle said. That's all that it is: exactly what the person does. It's not what they "think," because we don't know what they think. It's not what they say. It's what they do, what they're physically trying to accomplish on the stage. Which is exactly the same way we understand a person's character in life: not by what they say, but by what they do. Say someone came up to you and said, "I'm glad to be your neighbor because I'm a very honest man. That's my character. I'm honest, I like to do things, I'm forthright, I like to be clear about everything, I like to be concise." Well, you really don't know anything about that guy's character. Or the person is onstage, and the playwright has him or her make those same claims in several subtle or not-so-subtle ways, the audience will say, "Oh yes, I understand their character now; now I understand that they are a character." But in fact you don't understand anything. You just understand that they're jabbering to try to convince you of something.

INTERVIEWER

So do you end up cutting a lot of material from your earlier drafts?

MAMET

Well, you know, Hemingway said it once: "To write the best story you can, take out all the good lines."

INTERVIEWER

But do you then sometimes find that the audience has a hard time keeping up with you? It seems to me that in this

climate one of the playwright's problems is that the audience
expects things to be explained.

MAMET

I never try to make it hard for the audience. I may not
succeed, but . . . Vakhtangov, who was a disciple of Stanislavsky, was asked at one point why his films were so successful,
and he said, "Because I never for one moment forget about
the audience." I try to adopt that as an absolute tenet. I mean,
if I'm not writing for the audience, if I'm not writing to make
it easier for *them*, then who the hell am I doing it for? And
the way you make it easier is by following those tenets: cutting,
building to a climax, leaving out exposition and always pro-
gressing toward the single goal of the protagonist. They're very
stringent rules, but they are, in my estimation and experience,
what makes it easier for the audience.

INTERVIEWER

What else? Are there other rules?

MAMET

Get into the scene late, get out of the scene early.

INTERVIEWER

Why? So that something's already happened?

MAMET

Yes. That's how *Glengarry* got started. I was listening to
conversations in the next booth and I thought, My God, there's
nothing more fascinating than the people in the next booth.
You start in the middle of the conversation and wonder, What
the hell are they talking about? And you listen heavily. So I
worked a bunch of these scenes with people using extremely
arcane language—kind of the canting language of the real-
estate crowd, which I understood, having been involved with
them—and I thought, Well, if it fascinates me, it will probably
fascinate them too. If not, they can put me in jail.

INTERVIEWER

Going back to your roots in the theater, how did you get involved initially?

MAMET

I was a kid actor. I did amateur theatricals, television and radio in Chicago. Always loved the theater.

INTERVIEWER

You loved it, but I wonder if your plays aren't in some sort of debate with its conventions and what it should be.

MAMET

Maybe, but I always understood that as one of its conventions. Like David Ogilvy said, you don't want to create an ad that says "advertisement." That you will not look at. Concerns of content, concerns of form, it's all the same to me. It's the theatrical event. As for thinking against the sort of conventional narrative formulae of the theater . . . Well, I have the great benefit of never having learned anything in school, so a lot of this stuff . . .

INTERVIEWER

Were you a bad student?

MAMET

I was a non-student. No interest, just bored to flinders. I was like the professor in *Oleanna* who all his life had been told he was an idiot, so he behaved like an idiot. Later on I realized that I enjoy accomplishing tasks. I get a big kick out of it because I never did it as a kid. Somebody said that the reason that we all have a school dream — "I've forgotten to do my paper!" "I've forgotten to study!" — is that it's the first time that the child runs up against the expectations of the world. "The world has expectations of me, and I'm going to have to meet them or starve, meet them or die, and I'm unprepared."

INTERVIEWER

Do you ever feel unprepared?

MAMET

Much of the time. But the prescription for that is to do more, to work harder, to do more, to do it again.

INTERVIEWER

If you hadn't found the theater, what do you think you might have been?

MAMET

I think it's very likely I would have been a criminal. It seems to me to be another profession that subsumes outsiders, or perhaps more to the point, accepts people with a not-very-well-formed ego, and rewards the ability to improvise.

INTERVIEWER

Is that why con men and tricksters appear so often in your plays?

MAMET

I've always been fascinated by the picaresque. That's part of the Chicago tradition: to love our gangsters and con men, the bunko artists and so forth.

It occurred to me while I was doing *House of Games* that the difficulty of making the movie was exactly the same difficulty the confidence man has. For the confidence man it is depriving the victim of her money; for me it is misleading the audience sufficiently so they feel pleased when they find out they've been misled, tricking them so that every step is logical, and at the end they've defeated themselves. So the process of magic and the process of confidence games, and to a certain extent the process of drama, are all processes of autosuggestion. They cause the audience to autosuggest themselves in a way which seems perfectly logical, but is actually false.

You know, also being a very proud son of a bitch, I always thought that the trick was to be able to do it on a bare stage, with nothing but one or two actors. If one could do it like that, then one has done something to keep the audience's attention, make it pay off over an hour and a half, on a bare stage with nothing but two people talking.

INTERVIEWER

Did you read a lot when you were a kid?

MAMET

I always read novels. To me that was "real" writing. I liked all the midwesterners—Sinclair Lewis, Willa Cather, Sherwood Anderson.

INTERVIEWER

Was it just that the Midwest was familiar terrain, or something in the tone?

MAMET

Both. I mean, I loved Dreiser—he talked about streets that I knew and types that I knew and the kinds of people and kinds of neighborhoods that I actually knew. But I also liked the midwestern tone. It was very legato. Perhaps the rhythm of the midwestern seasons—a long, impossibly cold winter, and then a long, impossibly hot summer. It was a vast, impossibly big lake, a huge sea of wheat. It has that same rhythm, the same legato rhythm, moved on like that. Things were going to unfold in their own time, kind of like a French movie, except not quite that drawn out.

INTERVIEWER

You held a number of odd jobs while you were starting in the theater.

MAMET

Yes. After college I worked as an actor, a cab driver, a cook, a busboy—I did all of that. At one point, after I'd been running a theater for a couple years, this guy came up to me at a party and said, "I saw the whole play. I like it very much." I said, "Thank you." He said, "You want to come be an editor at *Oui* magazine?" I said, "Why did you ask me? I have no idea what the job entails, and also, I'm sure I'm unqualified for it." And he said, "You know, I'm not sure what it entails either, but it will be a little bit of this, little bit of that, little bit of this. Make it up. And I'm sure you *are* qualified for it." And I said, "Well, I hate sitting in an office." He said, "Don't. Come in and do the work for however long it takes you, and go home." And I said *hum, hum, hummer.* And he said, "I'll pay you twenty thousand dollars a year." This was 1975. Twenty thousand was a vast amount of money—about three times more than I'd made in my life. So I said okay. I worked there for a while. Before that I was selling carpet over the telephone. Cold calling out of the blue book, absolutely cold.

INTERVIEWER

Do you remember your spiel?

MAMET

"Mrs. Jones, this is"—you always used a fake name—"Mrs. Jones, this is Dick Richards of Walton Carpets. I don't know what you've heard about our current two-for-one special—is your husband there with you now?" "A-buh-buh." "Will he be home this evening?" "A-wah-wah-wah-wah." "Fine, which would be a better time for us to send a representative over to talk to you, seven or nine o'clock?" Because what we wanted to do, it's the same idea as the Fuller Brush men: you get your foot in the door, you offer them something, keep talking, get them in the habit of saying yes, and then you've got them in the habit of accepting what you're giving them.

INTERVIEWER

Were you a good salesman?

MAMET

No, I was terrible. I kept identifying with the people on the other end, which is something you really can't do.

INTERVIEWER

You're much more ruthless as a playwright than you would be as a salesman.

Director Gregory Mosher and David Mamet.

MAMET

I'm a fairly gentle guy. When Greg Mosher directed *Glengarry* we had a lot of salesmen come in to talk to the cast, guys who were making five million dollars a year selling airplanes or industrial equipment. These people were superclosers. There's a whole substratum of people who are *the* closer, like the Alec

Baldwin character in the movie of *Glengarry*. But the most impressive salesman was a saleswoman, a Fuller Brush lady, who came in and showed us how to do the Fuller Brush spiel. It was great. The first thing they do is offer you a choice of two free gifts, and they make sure you take one in your hand. So it's not, "Do you want one?" It's, "Which would you rather have?" And now that you've got one of their free gifts in your hand, how could you not answer their next question, which is also going to be answered—it's going to be yes, and the next question's going to be yes, and the next . . .

INTERVIEWER

Does this follow a rule of drama too, for you?

MAMET

I don't know, but I was fascinated by it. And the idea was, you've absolutely got to stick to the pitch. Have to stick with it. There was a great book called *In Search of Myself* by Frederick Grove, a Canadian novelist, a great writer. Nobody's ever heard of him, but it's a great book. It's about the immigrant experience: coming here with nothing and what America does to that person. And one of the things he becomes is a book salesman who goes from door to door having to sell phony books. Heartbreaking, you know, that he has to do this. Heart-breaking.

INTERVIEWER

Going back to the odd jobs: did you see them as a means to getting your start in the theater, or were you just sort of rooting around?

MAMET

I knew I wanted to be in the theater, but I also knew I was a terrible actor. So I started, by dribs and drabs, forming a theater company that I could direct, because I figured it was something I could do.

INTERVIEWER

When did you start writing plays?

MAMET

I didn't really start writing till I was in my twenties. And I started because the company, the St. Nicholas Theatre, couldn't pay any royalties — we didn't have any money. I was very fortunate, coming from Chicago, because we had that tradition there of writing as a legitimate day-to-day skill, like bricklaying. You know, you need to build a house but you can't afford it, or you need to build a garage but you can't afford a bricklayer. Well, hell, figure out how to lay bricks. You need a script, well, hell, figure out how to write one. There was a great tradition flourishing in Chicago in the early seventies of the theater as an organic unit. The organic theater — in fact, the most important theater at the time was called The Organic Theater — but the organic (small *o*) theater consisted of a company of actors who also directed and also wrote and also designed. Everybody did everything. There was no mystery about it. One week one guy would be the director, the next week the woman would be the director and the guy would be acting, etc. So that was the community and the tradition that I came back to in the seventies in Chicago.

INTERVIEWER

Who were your dramatic influences?

MAMET

Well, primarily Pinter — *The Revue Sketches*, *A Night Out* and *The Birthday Party*. He was my first encounter with modern drama. His work sounded real to me in a way that no drama ever had.

INTERVIEWER

What was a typical drama of the old school that struck you as dead or deadly?

"The Paris Review remains the single most important little magazine this country has produced."

— T. Coraghessan Boyle

THE
PARIS
REVIEW

Enclosed is my check for:

☐ $34 for 1 year (4 issues)

(All payment must be in U.S. funds. Postal surcharge of $10 per 4 issues outside USA)

☐ Send me information on becoming a *Paris Review* Associate.

Bill this to my Visa/MasterCard:

Sender's full name and address needed for processing credit cards

_____
Card number   Exp. date

☐ New subscription ☐ Renewal subscription
☐ New address

Name _____

Address _____

City _____ State _____ Zip code _____

Please send gift subscription to:

Name _____

Address _____

City _____ State _____ Zip code _____

Gift announcement signature _____

call (718)539-7085

Please send me the following:

☐ The Paris Review T-Shirt ($15.00)
  Color _____ Size _____ Quantity _____
☐ The following back issues: Nos. _____

  See listing at back of book for availability.

Name _____

Address _____

City _____ State _____ Zip code _____

☐ Enclosed is my check for $ _____
☐ Bill this to my Visa/MasterCard:

_____
Card number   Exp. date

BUSINESS REPLY MAIL

FIRST CLASS   PERMIT NO. 3119   FLUSHING, N.Y.

POSTAGE WILL BE PAID BY ADDRESSEE

THE PARIS REVIEW
45-39 171 Place
FLUSHING NY   11358-9892

No postage
stamp necessary
if mailed in the
United States

BUSINESS REPLY MAIL

FIRST CLASS   PERMIT NO. 3119   FLUSHING, N.Y.

POSTAGE WILL BE PAID BY ADDRESSEE

THE PARIS REVIEW
45-39 171 Place
FLUSHING NY   11358-9892

MAMET

It was either a Shakespeare, which I wasn't hip enough to understand at that time in my youth, or bad translations of European plays, which were very bad translations, or American poetic realism, which just bored the bloomers off me. People talking too much—I didn't understand those people. They weren't like anybody I knew. The people I knew washed dishes or drove cabs.

INTERVIEWER

Were there advantages to starting in Chicago instead of New York?

MAMET

Being in Chicago was great. It was all happening, all the time, like jazz in New Orleans. We looked at New York as two things: one was, of course, the Big Apple and the other was the world's biggest hick town. Because much of what we saw happening in New York was the equivalent of the Royal Nonesuch—you know, a bunch of people crawling around, barking and calling it theater. But the version in Chicago was people went to the theater just like they went to the ballgame: they wanted to see a show. If it was a drama, it had to be dramatic, and if it was a comedy, it had to funny—period. And if it was those things, they'd come back. If it wasn't those things, they wouldn't come back.

INTERVIEWER

How long were you there?

MAMET

I was in Chicago from like 1973 till 1976 or 1977. And then—whore that I am—I came to New York.

INTERVIEWER

The Cryptogram, can we talk a little about what that was trying to figure out?

MAMET

Well, it was trying to figure out itself, for one. It was trying to figure out what the hell the mechanism of the play was. And I had all this stuff about the kid not going to sleep, and it finally occurred to me, about the billionth draft, well, it's about why can't the kid sleep? It's not *that* the kid can't sleep, but *why* can't the kid sleep? So the kid can't sleep because he knows, subconsciously, that something's unbalanced in the household. But then why is nobody paying attention to him? I thought, Aha! Well, this is perhaps the question of the play.

INTERVIEWER

So you, as the writer inside *The Cryptogram*, you've sort of imagined my questions and led me gradually to revelation. You have certain designs on the audience's mind, you try to persuade them of certain psychological truths . . .

MAMET

No, I'm not trying to persuade them of anything; it's much more basic than that, it's much more concrete. It has to do with those black lines on the white page. Finally it comes down to—maybe this is going to sound coy—it just comes down to the writing of a play. Obviously, the point of the play is doing it for the audience—like the cook who wants to make that perfect soufflé, that perfect mousse, that perfect carbonara. Of course he isn't going to do it if he doesn't think someone's going to eat it, but the point is to cook it perfectly, not to affect the eaters in a certain way. The thing exists of itself.

INTERVIEWER

Is there a moment in one of your plays that you really didn't know was there?

MAMET

Yes. I wrote this play called *Bobby Gould in Hell*. Greg Mosher did it on a double bill with a play by Shel Silverstein over at Lincoln Center. Bobby Gould is consigned to Hell, and he has to be interviewed to find out how long he's going to spend there. The Devil is called back from a fishing trip to interview Bobby Gould. And so the Devil is there, the Assistant Devil is there and Bobby Gould. And the Devil finally says to Bobby Gould, "You're a very bad man." And Bobby Gould says, "Nothing's black and white." And the Devil says, "Nothing's black and white, nothing's black and white — what about a panda? What about a panda, you dumb fuck! What about a fucking panda!" And when Greg directed it, he had the assistant hold up a picture of a panda, kind of pan it 180 degrees to the audience at the Vivian Beaumont Theater. That was the best moment I've ever seen in any of my plays.

INTERVIEWER

What sort of writing routine do you have? How do you operate?

MAMET

I don't know. I've actually been vehemently deluding myself, thinking that I have no set habits whatever. I know that I have very good habits of thought, and I'm trying to make them better. But as for where I go, what I do and who's around when I work — those things are never important to me.

INTERVIEWER

Those habits of thought — how do they govern your writing?

MAMET

It's really not an intellectual process. I mean, as you see, I try to apply all sorts of mechanical norms to it, and they help me order my thoughts, but finally in playwriting, you've got to be able to write dialogue. And if you write enough of it and let it flow enough, you'll probably come across something that will give you a key as to structure. I think the process of writing a play is working back and forth between the moment and the whole. The moment and the whole, the fluidity of the dialogue and the necessity of a strict construction. Letting one predominate for a while and coming back and fixing it so that eventually what you do, like a pastry chef, is frost your mistakes, if you can.

INTERVIEWER

Are you a computer man or a pad-and-pencil man?

MAMET

Pad and pencil. I want to see it, I want to see them all out in front of me, each one of the pencil adaptations, the pencil notations, and the pencil notations crossed out, and the pen on top of the pencil, and the pages . . .

INTERVIEWER

Do you look at all twelve drafts?

MAMET

If I have to. Theoretically, one should be able to keep the whole play in one's mind. The main thing is, I want to know that they're there. The idea of taking everything and cramming it into this little electronic box designed by some nineteen-year-old in Silicon Valley . . . I can't imagine it.

INTERVIEWER

In looking back at your work, are there plays that you feel were more successful than others?

MAMET

The most challenging dramatic form, for me, is the tragedy. I think I'm proudest of the craft in the tragedies I've written — *The Cryptogram*, *Oleanna*, *American Buffalo* and *The Woods*. They are classically structured tragedies.

INTERVIEWER

How do you distinguish tragedy from drama?

Circumstance. Drama has to do with circumstance, tragedy has to do with individual choice. The precipitating element of a drama can be a person's sexuality, their wealth, their disease . . . A tragedy can't be about any of those things. That's why we identify with a tragic hero more than with a dramatic hero: we understand the tragic hero to be ourselves. That's why it's easier for the audiences initially to form an affection for the drama rather than the tragedy. Although it seems that they're exercising a capacity for identification— "Oh, yes, I understand. So-and-so is in a shitload of difficulty and I identify with them, and I see where the going's bad and I see where the hero is good"—in effect they're distancing themselves, because they'll say, "Well, shit, I couldn't get into that situation because I'm not gay, or because I am gay, because I'm not crippled or because I am crippled . . ." They're distanced. Because I can go on with drama. That's the difference between drama and tragedy. *Glengarry*, on the other hand, falls into a very specific American genre: the gang drama or the gang comedy. The prime proponent of it, the genius proponent of it—and maybe one of its coinventors—is Sidney Kingsley. Plays like *Detective Story*, *Men in White*, *Truckline Cafe*, to some extent *Waiting for Lefty*. These are slice-of-life plays investigating a milieu of society. A good example is *Lower Depths*, where the protagonist is elaborated into many parts. In a comedy of manners like *Don Quixote*, for example, we understand that the sidekick is just another aspect of the protagonist, just like everybody in our dreams is an aspect of us. A tragedy has to be the attempt of one specific person to obtain one specific goal, and when he either gets it or doesn't get it, then we know the play is over, and we can go home and put out the baby-sitter.

INTERVIEWER

I'm interested to hear you say that you thought of *Oleanna*, which is more polemical than the other plays, as a tragedy.

MAMET

Classically it's structured as a tragedy. The professor is the main character. He undergoes absolute reversal of situation, absolute recognition at the last moment of the play. He realizes that perhaps he is the cause of the plague on Thebes.

INTERVIEWER

Did it surprise you, the way the play took off?

MAMET

It stunned them.

INTERVIEWER

You were aiming for a nerve, and you hit it.

MAMET

No, I wasn't aiming for a nerve, I was just trying to write the play. After it was finished I thought, Jesus Christ, I can't put this play on! Especially at Harvard—people were going to throw rocks through the theater windows. I was frightened. And my wife was playing the part—the part was written for her—and I was always frightened that someone was going to attack her, come over the footlights and attack her. One day we were doing some notes before the performance, and I was just looking out at the empty theater, and William Macy, who played the professor, came over and said, "Don't worry, Dave, they'll have to get through me first." I always felt they were going to put me in jail some day.

INTERVIEWER

Why?

MAMET

Well, for many reasons, not the least of which is, as a kid, I became so judgmental about the House Un-American Activities Committee. This person talked to the committee, that person talked to the committee—"How could you do that?

How could you not do that? How could. . . . " Later on I realized that everybody has their own reasons, and that unless we've walked a mile in that man or woman's moccasins it's not for us to say, "Well, okay, here's what you're going to get for criticizing others' bravery as a writer or as a creative artist."

INTERVIEWER

I suppose all your plays, in one way or another, come very close to saying something unacceptable about society, something that's very hard for people to hear.

MAMET

Well, you know, we did *American Buffalo* here on Broadway, right around the corner, and I remember some businessmen—night after night one or two of them would come storming out, muttering to themselves furiously, "What the *fuck* does this play have to do with me?" and words to that effect.

INTERVIEWER

Where did the idea for *American Buffalo* come from?

MAMET

Macy and I were in Chicago one time, and he was living in this wretched hovel—we'd both become screamingly poor—and I came over to talk to him about something, some play equipment. I opened the refrigerator, and there was this big piece of cheese. I hadn't had anything to eat in a long time, so I picked it up, cut off a big chunk and started eating. And Macy said, "Hey, *help yourself*." I was really hurt. I went away and fumed about that for several days. Then I just started writing, and out of that came this scene, which was the start of the play: Ruthie comes in furious because someone had just said to him, "Help yourself."

INTERVIEWER

What about when you were working on *The Village*? Did that change your routine?

MAMET

With a novel it's different. It's kind of exhilarating not to have to cut to the bone constantly. "Oh, well I can go over here for a moment." I can say what I think the guy was thinking, or what the day looked like, or what the bird was doing. If you do that as a playwright, you're dead.

INTERVIEWER

Have you considered putting stage directions in your screenplays?

MAMET

No, because if you're writing a drama, to get involved in it is kind of nonsense. It's like, you read a screenplay and it says, "BRENDA comes into the room. She's beautiful, she's sassy, she's smart, she's twenty-five, she's built like a brick shithouse: this is the kind of girl that you'll leave your wife for. When you see those deep blue eyes . . ." I mean, you're going to cast an actress, and she's going to look like something, right? Some idiot script-reader from Yale is going to get a kick out of what you've thrown in, but it has nothing to do with making the movie, because you're going to cast an actress who will have qualities that are going to have nothing to do with what you made up. When you write stage directions: unless they're absolutely essential for the understanding of the action of the play ("He leaves." "She shoots him.") something else is going to happen when the actors and directors get them on the stage.

INTERVIEWER

What led you to the movies? It seems to me that the demands of the truth that can be told in the theater are so much deeper and more intense than on the screen. If you could tell stories, in my view, the way you tell stories, why bother with the cinema?

MAMET

I like it. I think it's a fascinating medium. It's so similar to the theater in many ways, and yet so very different. It's great: it takes place with a huge number of people, which is fine; it's very technical in ways that the theater isn't; it calls for a lot of different ways of thinking, purely mechanical ways of thinking, that I find fascinating. A lot of it, directing especially, is how many boxes are hidden in this drawing? That kind of thing. It's a fascinating medium to me.

INTERVIEWER

But I feel that if you have a gift that's so enormous in a certain area, it would be very hard not to give yourself to that entirely. Is it simply a desire to make your life interesting, or to change pace, or . . . ?

MAMET

I think that's a large part of it.

INTERVIEWER

Where do you feel you have to work the hardest?

MAMET

That's a good question. I don't know the answer to it. I just feel like I have to work hard at all of it; it's not something that comes naturally to me. So maybe that's why I like it: I get a great sense of accomplishment from being able to complete a project with a certain level of technical efficiency. Frankly, I don't feel I have a lot of talent for it, but I love doing it and have a certain amount of hard-won technical ability.

INTERVIEWER

Do you have a lot of unfinished work?

MAMET

I've got a lot of stuff I just shelved. Some of it I come back to and some I don't.

INTERVIEWER

It tempts you.

MAMET

It challenges me, a lot of it, and it angers me.

INTERVIEWER

But are you prepared just to write and write and write, like pissing into a well or something?

MAMET

Sometimes.

INTERVIEWER

Not knowing where you're going, trying to see what the story is.

MAMET

I think it would be a lot easier to write to a formula, but it's just not fun to me. It's not challenging.

INTERVIEWER

I find it hard to understand how you can live with the tension of knowing something is unresolved, not knowing where it's going.

MAMET

But that's great. It's like Hemingway said: give yourself something to do tomorrow.

INTERVIEWER

So you let go and wait till later for a resolution. That's very hard, isn't it, to live with that?

MAMET

Well, I think that's the difference between the Christian and the Jewish ethic. Judaism is not a religion or a culture

built on faith. You don't have to have faith. You don't have
to believe anything; you just have to do it.

INTERVIEWER

But what happens when you follow a character or a situation
and it doesn't pan out?

MAMET

You do it again. Or, in some instances, stick it on the shelf
and either do or don't come back to it sometime.

INTERVIEWER

Do you try to put in five or six hours a day writing?

MAMET

I try to do as little writing as possible, as I look back on it.
I like to talk on the telephone and, you know, read magazines.

INTERVIEWER

And sit in your office and forestall writing?

MAMET

Yes, and sometimes I like to do the opposite.

INTERVIEWER

Whatever happens, you get a lot out for somebody who
doesn't write a lot, or doesn't like to write.

MAMET

I never saw the point in not.

INTERVIEWER

But you just said you spend a lot of time trying not to write.

MAMET

That's true. But the actual point of being a writer, and
doing something every once in a while mechanically, I just

don't see the point in it, and it wouldn't be good for me. I've got to do it anyway. Like beavers, you know. They chop, they eat wood, because if they don't, their teeth grow too long and they die. And they hate the sound of running water. Drives them crazy. So, if you put those two ideas together, *they are going to build dams.*

—John Lahr

The Cripple of Inishmaan

Martin McDonagh

BILLY	17/18. Crippled.
EILEEN	Mid 60s.
KATE	Mid 60s.
JOHNNY	Mid 60s.
BARTLEY	16/17.
HELEN	17/18. Pretty.
BOBBY	Early 30s. Handsome, muscular.
DOCTOR	Early 40s.
MAMMY	Early 90s.

SCENE ONE

A small country shop on the island of Inishmaan circa 1934. Door in right wall. Counter along back, behind which hang shelves of canned goods, mostly peas. An old dusty cloth sack hangs to the right of these, and to the left a doorway leads off to an unseen back room. A mirror hangs on the left wall and a table and chair are situated a few yards away from it. As the play begins, Eileen Osbourne, late sixties, is placing some more cans onto the shelves. Her sister Kate enters from the back room.

KATE: Is Billy not yet home?

EILEEN: Not yet is Billy home.

KATE: I do worry awful about Billy when he's late returning home.

EILEEN: I banged me arm on a can of peas worrying about Cripple Billy.

KATE: Was it your bad arm?

EILEEN: No, it was me other arm.

KATE: It would have been worse if you'd banged your bad arm.

EILEEN: It would have been worse, although it still hurt.

KATE: Now you have two bad arms.

EILEEN: Well, I have one bad arm and one arm with a knock.

KATE: The knock will go away.

EILEEN: The knock will go away.

KATE: And you'll be left with the one bad arm.

EILEEN: The one bad arm will never go away.

KATE: Until the day you die.

EILEEN: I should think about poor Billy, who has not only bad arms but bad legs too.

KATE: Billy has a host of troubles.

EILEEN: Billy has a hundred troubles.

KATE: What time was this his appointment with McSharry was and his chest?

EILEEN: I don't know what time.

KATE: I do worry awful about Billy when he's late in returning, d'you know?

EILEEN: Already once you've said that sentence.

KATE: Am I not allowed to repeat me sentences so when I'm worried.

EILEEN: You *are* allowed.

KATE: (*Pause*) Billy may've fell down a hole with them feet of his.

EILEEN: Billy has sense enough not to fall down holes, sure.

That's more like something Bartley McCormick'd do is fall down holes.

KATE: Do you remember the time Bartley McCormick fell down the hole?

EILEEN: Bartley McCormick's an awful thick.

KATE: He's either a thick or he doesn't look where he's going proper. (*Pause*) Has the egg-man been?

EILEEN: He has but he had no eggs.

KATE: A waste of time him coming, so.

EILEEN: Well it was nice of him to come and not have us waiting for eggs that would never arrive.

KATE: If only Billy would pay us the same courtesy. Not with eggs but to come home quick and not have us worrying.

EILEEN: Maybe Billy stopped to look at a cow like the other time.

KATE: A fool waste of time that is, looking at cows.

EILEEN: If it makes him happy, sure, what harm? There are a hundred worse things to occupy a lad's time than cow-watching. Things would land him up in hell. Not just late for his tea.

KATE: Kissing lasses.

EILEEN: Kissing lasses.

KATE: (*Pause*) Ah, no chance of that with poor Billy.

EILEEN: Poor Billy'll never be getting kissed. Unless it was be a blind girl.

KATE: A blind girl or a backward girl.

EILEEN: Or Jim Finnegan's daughter.

KATE: She'd kiss anything.

EILEEN: She'd kiss a bald donkey.

KATE: She'd kiss a bald donkey. And she'd still probably draw the line at Billy. Poor Billy.

EILEEN: A shame too.

KATE: A shame too, because Billy does have a sweet face if you ignore the rest of him.

EILEEN: Well he doesn't really.

KATE: He has a bit of a sweet face.

EILEEN: Well he doesn't really, Kate.

KATE: Or his *eyes*, I'm saying. They're nice enough.

EILEEN: Not being cruel to Billy but you'd see nicer eyes on a goat. If he had a nice personality you'd say all well and good, but all Billy has is he goes around staring at cows.

KATE: I'd like to ask him one day what good he gets, staring at cows.

EILEEN: Staring at cows and reading books then.

KATE: No one'll ever marry him. We'll be stuck with him till the day we die.

EILEEN: We will. (*Pause*) I don't mind being stuck with him.

KATE: *I* don't mind being stuck with him. Billy's a good gosawer, despiting the cows.

EILEEN: I hope that the news from McSharry was nothing to worry o'er.

KATE: I hope he gets home soon and not have us worrying. I do worry awful when Billy's late in returning.

The shop door opens and Johnnypateenmike, an old man of about the same age as them, enters.

EILEEN: Johnnypateenmike.

KATE: Johnnypateen.

JOHNNY: How is all? Johnnypateenmike does have three pieces of news to be telling ye this day . . .

KATE: You didn't see Cripple Billy on your travels now, Johnnypateen?

JOHNNY: (*Pause. Put out.*) You have interrupted me pieces of news now, Mrs. Osbourne, and the third piece of news was a great piece of news, but if you want to interrupt me with fool questions so be it. Aye, I saw Cripple Billy on me travels. I saw him sitting on the hedgebank, the bottom of Darcy's fields.

KATE: What was he doing sitting on the hedgebank?

JOHNNY: Well what does he usually be doing? He was looking at a cow. Do ye have any more interruptions?

KATE: (*Sadly*) We don't.

JOHNNY: I will get on with me three pieces of news so. I will leave me best piece of news 'til the end so's you will be waiting for it. Me first piece of news, a fella o'er in Lettermore stole a book out of another fella's house and pegged it in the sea then.

EILEEN: Sure that's no news at all, sure.

JOHNNY: I suppose it's not, now, only that the fella was the other fella's brother and the book he pegged was the *Holy Bible*! Eh?!

KATE: Lord save us!

JOHNNY: Now is that no news at all?!

EILEEN: That *is* news, Johnnypateen, and big news.

JOHNNY: I know well it's big news, and if I have any more doubting of how big me news is I'll be off on the road for meself to somewhere me news is more appreciated.

EILEEN: Your news *is* appreciated, Jahnnypateenmike.

KATE: We never once doubted how big your news was, Johnnypateen.

JOHNNY: Me second piece of news, Jack Ellery's goose bit Patty Brennan's cat on the tail and hurt that tail and Jack Ellery didn't even apologise for that goose's biting, and now Patty Brennan doesn't like Jack Ellery at all and Patty and Jack used to be great friends. Oh aye.

EILEEN: (*Pause*) Is that the end of that piece of news?

JOHNNY: That *is* the end of that piece of news.

EILEEN: (*Pause*) Oh that's an awful big piece of news that is. Oh aye.

Eileen rolls her eyes to the ceiling.

JOHNNY: That *is* an awful big piece of news. That goose might start a feud. I *hope* that goose does start a feud. I like a feud.

KATE: I hope Patty and Jack do put it behind them and make up. Didn't they used walk hand-in-hand to school as ladeens?

JOHNNY: *There's* a woman speaking if ever I heard one. What news is there in putting things behind ya? No news. You want a good feud, or at least a bible pegged about, or a thing like me third piece of news, which is about the biggest piece of news Johnnypateenmike has ever had . . .

Billy, seventeen, one arm and one leg crippled, enters, shuffling.

BILLY: I'm sorry I'm late, Aunty Kate and Aunty Eileen.

JOHNNY: You've interrupted me news-telling, Cripple Billy.

KATE: What did the doctor say to you, Billy?

BILLY: He said there was nothing on me chest at all but a bit of a wheeze and nothing but a bit of a wheeze.

JOHNNY: I didn't hear the lad had a wheeze. Why wasn't Johnnypateen informed?

KATE: Why are you so late home so, Billy? We was worried.

BILLY: Oh I just had a sit-down for meself in the sun there at Darcy's fields.

KATE: A sit-down and did what?

BILLY: A sit-down and did nothing.

KATE: Did nothing at all?

BILLY: Did nothing at all.

KATE: (*To Johnny*) Now!

BILLY: Nothing at all but look at a couple of cows came over to me.

Kate turns away from him.

JOHNNY: (*To Kate*) Now who's nowing?! Eh?!

EILEEN: Can't you just leave cows alone, Billy?

BILLY: I was just looking at them cows.

KATE: There's nothing to see in cows! You're a grown man!

BILLY: Well I *like* looking at a nice cow, and I won't let anybody tell me the differ.

JOHNNY: (*Screaming*) If ye don't want to hear me news I'll take it and go!! Talking about cows with a fecking eej!

BILLY: A fecking eej, is it?

EILEEN: Tell us your news, now, Johnnypateenmike.

JOHNNY: If ye've finished with the cow-talk I'll tell you me news, although I'm sure I'd get a better audience for it from fried winkles.

KATE: We're a good audience for it . . .

EILEEN: We're a good audience for it . . .

BILLY: Don't pander to him.

JOHNNY: Pander, is it, Cripple Billy?

BILLY: And don't call me Cripple Billy, you.

JOHNNY: For why? Isn't your name Billy and aren't you a cripple?

BILLY: Well do I go calling you "Johnnypateenmike with the news that's so boring it'd bore the head off a dead bee"?

JOHNNY: Boring is it? How is this for boring news so . . .

BILLY: At least you do agree it's boring news anyways. That's one thing.

JOHNNY: (*Pause*) From Hollywood, California, in America they're coming, led be a Yank be the name of Robert Flaherty, one of the most famous and richest Yanks there is. Coming there to Inishmore they're coming and why are they coming? I'll tell you why they're coming. To go making a moving picture film will cost o'er a million dollars, will be shown throughout the world, will show life how it's lived on the islands, will make film stars of whosoever should be chose to take part in it and will take them back to Hollywood then and be giving them a life free of work, or anyways only acting work which couldn't be called work at all, it's only talking. Colman King I know already they've chosen for a role, and a hundred dollars a week he's on, and if Colman King can play a role in a film anybody can play a role in a film, for Colman King is as ugly as a brick of baked shite and everybody agrees, and excuse me language but I'm only being descriptive. A little exodus Johnnypateenmike foresees to the big island so, of any lasses or lads in these parts with the looks of a film star about them, wants to make their mark in America. That rules out all in this household, I know, it goes without saying, unless of course it's cripples and ingrates they're looking for. Me in me younger days they'd've been sure to've took, what with me blue eyes and me fine head of hair, and probably still today they'd be after taking me, what with me fine oratory skills could outdo any beggar the Dublin stage, only, as ye know, I have me drunkard mammy to look after. *The Man of Aran* they're

going calling the film, and Ireland mustn't be such a bad place
so if the Yanks want to come to Ireland to do their filming.

Billy sits on the side-table, deep in thought.

JOHNNY: That was Johnnypateenmike's third piece of news,
and I'll ask you now, bad-leg boy, if that was a boring piece
of news?
BILLY: That wasn't nearly a boring piece of news. That was
the biggest piece of news I did ever hear.
JOHNNY: Well if we've agreed on the bigness of me news . . .
bigness isn't a word, I know, but I can't be bothered to think
of a better one for the likes of ye . . . I will take me payment
in kind for that piece of big news, and me payment today
will be a small boxeen of eggs for I do fancy an omelette, I
do.
EILEEN: Oh.
JOHNNY: What "oh"!
EILEEN: The egg-man came and he had no eggs.
JOHNNY: No eggs?! I've gave you me big piece of news on
top of me two smaller but almost as good pieces of news and
ye've no eggs?!
EILEEN: He said the hens weren't laying and Slippy Helen
dropped the only eggs he had.
JOHNNY: What do ye have for me tea so?
EILEEN: We've peas.
JOHNNY: Peas! Sure peas won't go far for a grown man's tea.
Give me that bit of bacon there, so. That one there.
EILEEN: Which one? The lean one?
JOHNNY: The lean one, aye.
EILEEN: Jeez, your news wasn't that bloody big, Johnnypateen.

Johnny stares at them hatefully, then exits, fuming.

That fella.
KATE: We oughtn't be getting on his wrong side, now, Eileen.
How else will we know what's going on in the outside world
but for Johnny?

EILEEN: But isn't that the first decent bit of news that fella's had in twenty years?

KATE: Aye, and we might miss out on the next bit, now.

EILEEN: Coming with his egg extortions every week.

BILLY: That was an interesting bit of news, aye.

KATE: (*Approaching him*) You're not usually at all interested in Johnnypats biteens of news, Billy.

BILLY: Not when they're about frogs falling over, no. When they're about films and getting away from Inishmaan I am, aye.

KATE: You're not thinking about your poor mammy and daddy again, are ya?

BILLY: No, now. I'm just thinking about general things for meself, now.

EILEEN: Is he off again?

KATE: (*Sighing*) He is.

EILEEN: Off thinking?

KATE: That lad'll never be told.

EILEEN: The doctor didn't look at your head when he looked at your chest did he, Billy?

BILLY: (*Blankly*) No.

EILEEN: I think that's the next thing to go checking out is his head.

KATE: I think that's the next item on the agenda, aye.

The shop door bangs open. Johnny sticks his head in.

JOHNNY: (*Angrily*) If ye aren't chasing after me I'll take your bloody peas, so!

Eileen hands Johnny a can of peas. Johnny slams the door on his exit, Billy not noticing him at all, the women bemused. Blackout.

SCENE TWO

Bartley, sixteen, at the counter, looking over the penny sweets in the two rectangular boxes Eileen is tilting up for him. Billy is sitting on the chair, reading.

BARTLEY: (*Pause*) Do ya have any Mintios?

EILEEN: We have only what you see, Bartley McCormick.

BARTLEY: In America they do have Mintios.

EILEEN: Go to America so.

BARTLEY: Me Aunty Mary did send me seven Mintios in a package.

EILEEN: Good on your Aunty Mary.

BARTLEY: From Boston Massachusetts.

EILEEN: From Boston Massachusetts, uh-huh.

BARTLEY: But you have none?

EILEEN: We have only what you see.

BARTLEY: You should get some Mintios really, because Mintios are nice sweeties. You should order some in. You should get somebody from America to go sending you some. In a package. Now I'll have to be taking another look for meself.

EILEEN: Take another look for yourself, aye.

Bartley looks over the boxes again. Billy smiles at Eileen, who rolls her eyes to the ceiling and smiles back.

BARTLEY: (*Pause*) Do ya have any Yalla-mallows?

EILEEN: (*Pause*) We have only what you see.

BARTLEY: They do have Yalla-mallows in America.

EILEEN: Oh aye, I suppose your Aunty Mary did send you some in a package.

BARTLEY: No. She sent me a photograph of some in a package. The only proper sweeties she sent me were the seven Mintios. (*Pause*) Really it would've been better if she'd only sent me *four* Mintios and then put in three Yalla-mallows with them, so then I could've had like a selection. Or three Mintios and four Yalla-mallows. Aye. But, ah, I was happy enough with the seven Mintios if truth be told. Mintios are nice sweeties. Although the photograph of the Yalla-mallows did raise me curiosity about them. (*Pause*) But you have none?

EILEEN: Yalla-mallows?

BARTLEY: Aye.

EILEEN: No.

BARTLEY: Oh.

EILEEN: We have only what you see.

BARTLEY: I'll have to be taking another look for meself so. I want something to go sucking on. For the trip, y'know?

BILLY: For what trip, Bartley?

The shop door bangs open and Helen, a pretty girl of about seventeen, enters, shouting at Bartley.

HELEN: Are you fecking coming, you, fecker?!

BARTLEY: I'm picking me sweeties.

HELEN: Oh you and your fecking sweeties!

EILEEN: Lasses swearing, now!

HELEN: Lasses swearing, aye, and why shouldn't lasses be swearing when it's an hour for their eejit fecking brother it is they're kept waiting. Hello, Cripple Billy.

BILLY: Hello there, Helen.

HELEN: Is it another oul book you're going reading?

BILLY: It is.

HELEN: You never stop, do ya?

BILLY: I don't. Or I do *sometimes* stop . . .

EILEEN: I heard you did drop all the eggs on the egg-man the other day, Helen, broke the lot of them.

HELEN: I didn't drop them eggs at all. I went pegging them at Father Barratt, got him bang in the gob with fecking four of them.

EILEEN: You went pegging them at Father Barratt?

HELEN: I did. Are you repeating me now, Mrs?

EILEEN: Sure, pegging eggs at a priest, isn't it pure against God?

HELEN: Oh, maybe it is, but if God went touching me arse in choir practice I'd peg eggs at that fecker too.

EILEEN: Father Barratt went touching your . . . behind in choir pr . . .

HELEN: Not me behind, no. Me *arse*, Mrs. Me *arse*.

EILEEN: I don't believe you at all, Helen McCormick.

HELEN: And what the feck d'you think I care what you believe?

BILLY: Helen, now . . .

BARTLEY: The worst part of the entire affair, it was a sheer waste of eggs, because I do like a nice egg, I do, oh aye.

HELEN: Are you entering the egg-debate or are you buying your fecking sweeties, you?

BARTLEY: (*To Eileen*) Do you have any Chocky-top Drops, Mrs?

EILEEN: (*Pause*) You know what me answer's going to be, don't you, Bartley?

BARTLEY: Your answer's going to be ye have only what I see.

EILEEN: We're getting somewhere now.

BARTLEY: I'll take another look for meself, so.

Helen sighs, idles over to Billy, takes his book from him, looks at its cover, grimaces and gives it back.

BILLY: Are ye going on a trip, did Bartley say?

HELEN: We're sailing o'er to Inishmore to be in this film they're filming.

BARTLEY: Ireland mustn't be such a bad place, so, if the Yanks want to come here to do their filming.

HELEN: From the entire of the world they chose Ireland, sure.

BARTLEY: There's a French fella living in Rosmuck nowadays, d'you know?

EILEEN: Is there?

BARTLEY: What's this, now, that the French fella does do, Helen? Wasn't it some funny thing?

HELEN: Dentist.

BARTLEY: Dentist. He goes around speaking French at people too, and everybody just laughs at him. Behind his back, like, y'know?

HELEN: Ireland mustn't be such a bad place if French fellas want to live in Ireland.

BILLY: When is it you're going, so, Helen, to the filming?

HELEN: The morning-tide tomorrow we're going.

BARTLEY: I can't wait to go acting in the film.

HELEN: You, are you picking or are you talking?

BARTLEY: I'm picking *and* talking.

HELEN: You'll be picking, talking and having your bollocks kicked for ya if ya back-talk me again, ya feck.

BARTLEY: Oh aye.

BILLY: Sure, why would you think they'd let ye be in the filming at all, Helen?

HELEN: Sure, look at as pretty as I am. If I'm pretty enough to get clergymen groping me arse, it won't be too hard to wrap film fellas round me fingers.

BARTLEY: Sure, getting clergymen groping your arse doesn't take much skill. It isn't being pretty they go for. It's more being on your own and small.

HELEN: If it's being on your own and small, why so has Cripple Billy never had his arse groped be priests?

BARTLEY: You don't know at all Cripple Billy's never had his arse groped be priests.

HELEN: Have you ever had your arse groped be priests, Cripple Billy?

BILLY: No.

HELEN: *Now.*

BARTLEY: I suppose they have to draw the line somewhere.

HELEN: And you, you're small and often on your own. Have you ever had your arse groped be priests?

BARTLEY: (*Quietly*) Not me arse, no.

HELEN: D'ya see?

BARTLEY: (*To Eileen*) Do ya have any Fripple-Frapples, Mrs?

Eileen stares at him, puts the boxes down on the counter and exits into the back room.

Where are you going, Mrs? What about me sweeties, Mrs?

HELEN: You've done it now, haven't ya?

BARTLEY: Your oul aunty's a mad woman, Cripple Billy.

HELEN: Mrs. Osbourne isn't Cripple Billy's aunty at all, anyways. She's only his pretend aunty, same as the other one. Isn't that right, Billy?

BILLY: It is.

HELEN: They only took him in when Billy's mam and dad went and drowned themselves, when they found out Billy was born a cripple-boy.

BILLY: They didn't go and drowned themselves.

HELEN: Oh aye, aye . . .

BILLY: They only fell o'erboard in rough seas.

HELEN: Uh-huh. What were they doing sailing in rough seas, so, and wasn't it at night-time too?

BILLY: Trying to get to America be the mainland they were.

HELEN: No, trying to get away from you they were, be distance or be death, it made no differ to them.

BILLY: Well how the hell would you know when you were just a babby at the time, the same as me?

HELEN: I gave Johnnypateen a cheesy praitie one time and he told me. Wasn't it him was left there holding ya, down be the waterside?

BILLY: Well what did he know was in their heads that night? He wasn't in that boat.

HELEN: Sure didn't they have a sackful of stones tied between themselves?

BILLY: That's only pure gossip that they had a sackful of stones tied between themselves, and even Johnnypateen agrees on that one . . .

BARTLEY: Maybe he had a telescope.

HELEN: Maybe who had a telescope?

BARTLEY: Maybe Johnnypateenmike had a telescope.

HELEN: What differ would having a telescope have?

Bartley thinks, then shrugs.

You and your fecking telescopes. You're always throwing telescopes into the fecking conversation.

BARTLEY: They do have a great array of telescopes in America now, d'know? You can see a worm a mile away.

HELEN: Why would you want to see a worm a mile away?

BARTLEY: To see what he was up to.

HELEN: What do worms usually be up to?

BARTLEY: Wriggling.

HELEN: Wriggling. And how much do telescopes cost?

BARTLEY: Twelve dollars for a good one.

HELEN: So you'd pay twelve dollars to find out worms go wriggling?

BARTLEY: (*Pause*) *Aye*. I would.

HELEN: You don't have twelve hairs on your bollocks, let alone twelve dollars.

BARTLEY: I don't have twelve dollars on me bollocks, no, you're right there. I saw no sense.

Helen approaches him.

Don't, Helen . . .

Helen punches him hard in the stomach.

(*Winded*) Hurt me ribs that punch did.

HELEN: Feck your ribs. Using that kind of fecking language to me, eh? (*Pause*) What was we talking about, Cripple Billy? Oh aye, your dead mammy and daddy.

BILLY: They didn't go drowning themselves because of me. They loved me.

HELEN: They loved you? Would *you* love you if you weren't you? You barely love you and you *are* you.

BARTLEY: (*Winded*) At least Cripple Billy doesn't punch poor lads' ribs for them.

HELEN: No, and why? Because he's too fecking feeble to. It'd feel like a punch from a wet goose.

BARTLEY: (*Excited*) Did ye hear Jack Ellery's goose bit Patty Brennan's cat on the tail and hurt that tail . . .

HELEN: We *did* hear.

BARTLEY: Oh. (*Pause*) And Jack didn't even apologise for that goose's biting and now Patty Brennan . . .

HELEN: Didn't I just say we fecking heard, sure?

BARTLEY: I thought Billy mightn't have heard.

HELEN: Sure Billy's busy thinking about his drowned mammy

and daddy, Bartley. He doesn't need any of your days-old
goose-news. Aren't you thinking about your drowned mammy
and daddy, Billy.

BILLY: I am.

HELEN: You've never been on the sea since the day they died,
have you, Billy? Aren't you too scared?

BILLY: I *am* too scared.

HELEN: What a big sissy-arse, eh, Bartley?

BARTLEY: Sure anybody with a brain is at least a biteen afraid
of the sea.

HELEN: *I'm* not a biteen afraid of the sea.

BARTLEY: Well there you go, now.

Billy laughs.

HELEN: Eh? Was that an insult?!

BARTLEY: How would that be an insult, saying you're not
afraid of the sea?

HELEN: Why did Cripple Billy laugh so?

BARTLEY: Cripple Billy only laughed cos he's an odd boy. Isn't
that right, Cripple Billy?

BILLY: It is, aye. Oh plain odd I am.

Helen pauses, confused.

BARTLEY: Is it true you got nigh on a hundred pounds insurance when your mammy and daddy drowned, Billy?

BILLY: It is.

BARTLEY: Jeebies. Do ya still have it?

BILLY: I have none of it. Didn't it all go on me medical bills
at the time?

BARTLEY: You don't have even a quarter of it?

BILLY: I don't. Why?

BARTLEY: No, only if you had a quarter of it you could probably buy yourself a pretty classy telescope, d'you know? Oh
you could.

HELEN: Do you have to bring telescopes into fecking everything, you?

BARTLEY: I don't, but I like to, ya bitch. Leave me!

Bartley dashes out of the shop as Helen advances on him. Pause.

HELEN: I don't know where he gets the fecking cheek of him from, I don't.

BILLY: (*Pause*) How are ye two sailing to Inishmore, so, Helen? Ye've no boat.

HELEN: We're getting Babbybobby Bennett to bring us in his boat.

BILLY: Are you paying him?

HELEN: Only in kisses and a bit of a hold of his hand, or I *hope* that it's only his hand I'll be holding. Although I've heard it's a big one. Jim Finnegan's daughter was telling me. She knows everybody's. I think she keeps a chart for herself.

BILLY: She doesn't know mine.

HELEN: And you say that like you're proud. I suppose she wasn't sure whether you had one, as mangled and fecked as you are.

BILLY: (*Sadly*) I have one.

HELEN: Congratulations, but would you keep it to yourself? In more ways than one. (*Pause*) Me, the only ones I've seen belong to priests. They keep showing them to me. I don't know why. I can't say they whetted me appetite. All brown. (*Pause*) What have you gone all mopey for?

BILLY: I don't know, now, but I suppose you intimating me mammy and daddy preferred death to being stuck with me didn't help matters.

HELEN: I wasn't intimating that at all. I was saying it outright.

BILLY: (*Quietly*) You don't know what was in their heads.

HELEN: Uh-huh? And do you?

Billy bows his head sadly. Pause. Helen flicks him hard in the cheek with her finger, then moves off.

BILLY: Helen? Would Babbybobby be letting me go sailing to Inishmore with ye?

HELEN: What have you to offer Babbybobby, sure? He wouldn't want to go holding *your* mangled hand.

BILLY: What has Bartley to offer Bobby, so, and he's still going with ye?

HELEN: Bartley said he'd help with the rowing. Could you help with the rowing?

Billy lowers his head again.

What would you want to be coming for, anyways?

BILLY: (*Shrugging*) To be in the filming.

HELEN: You?

She starts laughing, slowly, moving to the door.

I shouldn't laugh at you, Billy . . . but I will.

She exits laughing. Pause. Eileen returns from the back room and slaps Billy across the head.

BILLY: What was that fer?!

EILEEN: Over my dead body are you going to Inishmore filming, Billy Claven!

BILLY: Ah I was only thinking aloud, sure.

EILEEN: Well stop thinking aloud! Stop thinking aloud and stop thinking quiet! There's too much oul thinking done in this house with you around. Did you ever see the Virgin Mary going thinking aloud?

BILLY: I didn't.

EILEEN: Is right, you didn't. And it didn't do her any harm!

Eileen exits to the back room again. Pause. Billy gets up, shuffles to his mirror, looks himself over a moment, then sadly shuffles back to the table. Bartley opens the shop door and pops his head inside.

BARTLEY: Cripple Billy, will you tell your aunty or your pretend aunty I'll be in for me Mintios later, or, not me Mintios but me sweeties generally.

BILLY: I will, Bartley.

BARTLEY: Me sister just told me your idea of being in the filming with us and I did have an awful laugh. That was a great joke, Billy.

BILLY: Good-oh, Bartley.

BARTLEY: They may even bring you to Hollywood after. They may make a star out of ya.

BILLY: They might at that, Bartley.

BARTLEY: A little cripple star. Heh. So you'll remind your aunty I'll be in for me Mintios later, or, not me Mintios but me . . .

BILLY: Your sweeties generally.

BARTLEY: Me sweeties generally. Or if not later then tomorrow morning.

BILLY: Goodbye, Bartley.

BARTLEY: Goodbye, Cripple Billy, or are you okay there, Cripple Billy, you do look a little bit sad for yourself?

BILLY: I'm fine, Bartley.

BARTLEY: Good-oh.

Bartley exits. Billy wheezes slightly, feeling his chest.

BILLY: (*Quietly*) I'm fine, aye.

Pause. Blackout.

SCENE THREE

A shore at night. Babbybobby fixing his curragh. Johnny enters, slightly drunk, walks up to him and watches a while.

JOHNNY: I see you're getting your curragh ready, Babbybobby.

BOBBY: I am, Johnnypateen.

JOHNNY: (*Pause*) Are you getting your curragh ready so?

BOBBY: Didn't I just say I was getting me curragh ready?

JOHNNY: You did, aye. (*Pause*) So you're getting your curragh ready. (*Pause*) All spick and span you're getting it. (*Pause*) All nice and prepared like. (*Pause*) All ready for a trip or something. (*Pause*) That's a nice boat, that is. A nice boat for a tripeen. And it's even more nice now that you've got it all prepared for yourself. (*Pause*) All prepared and ready.

BOBBY: If it's a question you have to ask me, Johnnypateen, go ahead and ask me the question and don't be beating around the bush like some fool of an eejit schoolchild.

JOHNNY: I have no question to ask you. If Johnnypateenmike has a question to ask he comes right out and asks it. You don't see Johnnypateen beating around a bush. Oh no. (*Pause*) Just commenting on how nice your curragh is is all. (*Pause*) How nice and ready you're getting it. (*Pause*) Nice and ready for a trip or something. (*Pause. Angrily*) Well if you won't tell me where you're going I'll fecking be off with meself!

BOBBY: Be off with yourself, aye.

JOHNNY: I *will* be off with meself. After your treatment!

BOBBY: I gave you no treatment.

JOHNNY: You did give me treatment. You never tell me any news. Your Mrs. up and died of TB the other year, and who was the last to know? *I* was the last to know. I wasn't told until the day she died, and you knew for weeks and weeks, with not a thought for my feelings . . .

BOBBY: I should've kicked her arse down the road to tell you, Johnnypateen, and, d'you know I've regretted not doing so ever since.

JOHNNY: One more time I'll say it so. So you're getting your curragh ready. All nice and prepared for a *trip* or something, now.

BOBBY: Ask me a question outright and I'll be pleased to give you the answer, Johnnypateen.

Johnny stares at Bobby a second, fuming, then storms off right. Bobby continues with the boat.

(*Quietly*) Ya stupid fecking eej. (*Pause. Calling off left.*)
Who's that shuffling on the stones?

BILLY: (*Off*) It's Billy Claven, Babbybobby.

BOBBY: I should've guessed that. Who else shuffles?

BILLY: (*Entering*) No one, I suppose.

BOBBY: Are your aunties not worried you're out this late,
Cripple Billy?

BILLY: They'd be worried if they knew but they don't know.
I snuck out on them.

BOBBY: You shouldn't sneak out on aunties, Cripple Billy.
Even if they're funny aunties.

BILLY: Do you think they're funny aunties too, Babbybobby?

BOBBY: I saw your Aunty Kate talking to a stone one time.

BILLY: And she shouts at me for staring at cows.

BOBBY: Well I wouldn't hold staring at cows up as the height
of sanity, Billy.

BILLY: Sure, I only stare at cows to get away from me aunties
a while. It isn't for the fun of staring at cows. There *is* no fun
in staring at cows. They just stand there looking at you like
fools.

BOBBY: Do you never throw nothing at them cows?

BILLY: No.

BOBBY: That might liven them up.

BILLY: I wouldn't want to hurt them, sure.

BOBBY: You're too kind-hearted is your trouble, Cripple Billy.
Cows don't mind you throwing things at them.

BILLY: You don't know that, Babbybobby.

BOBBY: I threw a brick at a cow once and he didn't even moo,
and I got him bang on the arse.

BILLY: Sure that's no evidence. He may've been a quiet cow.

BOBBY: He may've. And, sure, I'm not telling you to go pegging bricks at cows. I was drunk when this happened. Just if
you get bored, I'm saying.

BILLY: I usually bring a book with me anyways. I've no desire
to injure livestock.

BOBBY: You could throw the book at the cow.

BILLY: I would rather to read the book, Bobby.

BOBBY: It takes all kinds, as they say.

BILLY: It does. (*Pause*) Are you getting your curragh ready there, Babbybobby?

BOBBY: Oh everybody's awful observant tonight, it does seem.

BILLY: Ready to bring Helen and Bartley o'er to the filming?

Bobby looks at Billy a moment, checks out right to make sure Johnny isn't around, then returns.

BOBBY: How did you hear tell of Helen and Bartley's travelling?

BILLY: Helen told me.

BOBBY: Helen told you. Jeez, and I told Helen she'd get a punch if she let anyone in on the news.

BILLY: I hear she's paying you in kisses for this boat-trip.

BOBBY: She is, and, sure, I didn't want paying at all. It was Helen insisted on that clause.

BILLY: Wouldn't you want to kiss Helen, so?

BOBBY: Ah, I get a bit scared of Helen, I do. She's awful fierce. (*Pause*) Why, would you like to kiss Helen, Cripple Billy?

Billy shrugs shyly, sadly.

BILLY: Ah I can't see Helen ever wanting to kiss a boy like me, anyways. Can you, Bobby?

BOBBY: No.

BILLY: (*Pause*) But so you'd've took the McCormicks without payment at all?

BOBBY: I would. I wouldn't mind having a look at this filming business meself. What harm in taking passengers along?

BILLY: Would you take me as a passenger too, so?

BOBBY: (*Pause*) No.

BILLY: Why, now?

BOBBY: I've no room.

BILLY: You've plenty of room.

BOBBY: Did I not say no, now?

BILLY: That boat could take four easy.

BOBBY: A cripple fella's bad luck in a boat, and everybody knows.

BILLY: Since when, now?

BOBBY: Since Poteen-Larry took a cripple fella in his boat and it sank.

BILLY: That's the most ridiculous thing I've ever heard, Babby-bobby.

BOBBY: Or if he wasn't a cripple fella, he had a bad leg on him anyways.

BILLY: You're just prejudiced against cripples is all you are.

BOBBY: I'm not at all prejudiced against cripples. I did kiss a cripple girl one time. Not only crippled but disfigured too. I was drunk, I didn't mind. You're not spoilt for pretty girls in Antrim.

BILLY: Don't go changing the subject on me.

BOBBY: Big green teeth. What subject?

BILLY: The subject of taking me to the filming with ye.

BOBBY: I thought we closed that subject.

BILLY: We hardly opened that subject.

BOBBY: Sure, what do you want to go to the filming for? They wouldn't want a cripple boy.

BILLY: You don't know what they'd want.

BOBBY: I don't, I suppose. No, you're right there. I did see a film there one time with a fella who not only had he no arms and no legs but he was a coloured fella too.

BILLY: A coloured fella? I've never seen a coloured fella, let alone a crippled coloured fella. I didn't know you could get them.

BOBBY: Oh they'd give you a terrible scare.

BILLY: Coloured fellas? Are they fierce?

BOBBY: They're less fierce with no arms or legs on them, because they can't do much to ya, but even so they're still fierce.

BILLY: I heard a coloured fella a year ago came to Dublin a week.

BOBBY: Ireland mustn't be such a bad place, so, if coloured fellas want to come to Ireland.

BILLY: It mustn't. (*Pause*) Ar, Babbybobby, you've only brought up coloured fellas to put me off the subject again.

BOBBY: There's no cripple fellas coming in this boat, Billy. Maybe some day, in a year or two, like. If your feet straighten out on ya.

BILLY: A year or two's no good to me, Bobby.

BOBBY: Why so?

Billy takes out a letter and hands it to Bobby, who starts reading it.

What's this?

BILLY: It's a letter from Doctor McSharry, and you've got to promise you'll not breathe a word of it to another living soul.

Halfway through the letter, Bobby's expression saddens. He glances at Billy, then continues.

BOBBY: When did you get this?

BILLY: Just a day ago I got it. (*Pause*) Now will you let me come?

BOBBY: Your aunties'll be upset at you going.

BILLY: Well is it their life or is it my life? I'll send word to them from over there. Ah, I may only be gone a day or two anyways. I get bored awful easy. (*Pause*) Will you let me come?

BOBBY: Nine o'clock tomorrow morning be here.

BILLY: Thank you, Bobby, I'll be here.

Bobby gives him back the letter and Billy folds it away. Johnny quickly enters, his hand held out.

JOHNNY: No, hang on there, now. What did the letter say?

BOBBY: Ah Johnnypateen, will you feck off home for yourself?

JOHNNY: Be showing Johnnypateen that letter now, you, cripple-boy.

BILLY: I won't be showing you me letter.

JOHNNY: What d'you mean you won't be showing me your letter? You showed *him* your letter. Be handing it over, now.

BOBBY: Did anybody ever tell you you're a biteen rude, Johnnypateenmike?

JOHNNY: *I'm* rude? *I'm* rude? With ye two standing there hogging letters, and letters from doctors is the most interesting kind of letters, and ye have the gall then to go calling *me* rude? Tell oul limpy to be handing over that letter, now, else there'll be things I heard here tonight that won't stay secret much longer.

BOBBY: Things like what, now?

JOHNNY: Oh, things like you rowing schoolies to Inishmore and you kissing green-teeth girls in Antrim is the kind of thing, now. Not that I'm threatening blackmail on ya or anything, or, alright yes I am threatening blackmail on ya but a newsman has to obtain his news be hook or be crook.

BOBBY: Be hook or be crook, is it? Well have this for hook or be crook.

Bobby grabs Johnny by the hair and wrenches his arm up behind his back.

JOHNNY: Aargh! Be letting go of me arm there you, ya thug! I'll get the constabulary on ya.

BOBBY: Be lying down on the sand there, you, for yourself.

Bobby forces Johnny face down on the ground.

JOHNNY: Be running for the polis now you, cripple-boy, or shuffling anyways.

BILLY: I won't. I'll be standing here watching.

JOHNNY: An accomplice that makes ya.

BILLY: Good-oh.

JOHNNY: I'm only an oul fella.

Bobby steps up onto Johnny's backside.

Aargh! Get off of me arse, you!

BOBBY: Billy, go pick up some stones for me.

BILLY: (*Doing so*) Big stones?

BOBBY: Middling-size stones.

JOHNNY: What do you want stones for?

BOBBY: To peg them at your head 'til you promise not to bandy me business about town.

JOHNNY: You'll never get me to make such a promise. I can withstand any torture. Like Kevin Barry I am.

Bobby throws a stone at Johnny's head.

Aargh! I promise, I promise.

BOBBY: On Christ ya promise?

JOHNNY: On Christ I promise.

BOBBY: That withstanding didn't last fecking long.

Bobby gets off Johnny, who stands back up, brushing himself off.

JOHNNY: I wouldn't get that kind of treatment in England! And now I have sand in me ears.

BOBBY: Take that sand home with ya and show it to your drunken mammy so.

JOHNNY: You leave my drunken mammy out of it.

BOBBY: And be remembering that promise.

JOHNNY: Under duress that promise was made.

BOBBY: I don't care if it was made under a dog's arsehole. You'll be remembering it.

JOHNNY: (*Pause*) Ya feckers, ya!

Johnny storms off right, shaking his fist.

BOBBY: I've wanted to peg stones at that man's head for fifteen years.

BILLY: I'd never get up the courage to peg stones at his head.

BOBBY: Ah, I suppose you shouldn't peg stones at an oul fella's head, but didn't he drive me to it? (*Pause*) You got up the courage to travel to Inishmore anyways, and you scared of the sea.

BILLY: I did. (*Pause.*) We'll meet at nine tomorrow so.

BOBBY: Better make it eight, Cripple Billy, in case Johnnypa-teen lets the cat out of the bag.

BILLY: Do you not trust him so?

BOBBY: I'd trust him as much as I'd trust you to carry a pint for me without spilling it.

BILLY: That's not a nice thing to say.

BOBBY: I'm a hard character, me.

BILLY: You're not a hard character at all, Babbybobby. You're a soft character.

BOBBY: (*Pause*) My wife Annie died of the same thing, d'you know? TB. But at least I got a year to spend with her. Three months is no time.

BILLY: I won't even see the summer in. (*Pause*) D'you remem-ber the time Annie made me the jam roly-poly when I had the chicken pox? And the smile she gave me then?

BOBBY: Was it a nice jam roly-poly?

BILLY: (*Reluctantly*) Not really, Bobby.

BOBBY: No. Poor Annie couldn't cook jam roly-polies to save the life of her. Ah, I still miss her, despite her awful puddings. (*Pause*.) I'm glad I was able to help you in some way anyways, Cripple Billy, in the time you've left.

BILLY: Would you do me a favour, Babbybobby? Would you not call me Cripple Billy any more long?

BOBBY: What do you want to be called so?

BILLY: Well, just Billy.

BOBBY: Oh. Okay so, Billy.

BILLY: And you, would you rather just be called Bobby and not Babbybobby?

BOBBY: For why?

BILLY: I don't know why.

BOBBY: I do like being called Babbybobby. What's wrong with it?

BILLY: Nothing at all, I suppose. I'll see you in the morning so, Babbybobby.

BOBBY: See you in the morning so, Cripple Billy. Em, *Billy*.

BILLY: Didn't I just say?

BOBBY: I forgot. I'm sorry, Billy.

Billy nods, then shuffles away.

Oh, and Billy?

Billy looks back. Bobby makes a gesture with his hand.

I'm sorry.

Billy bows his head, nods and exits right. Pause. Bobby notices something in the surf, picks a Bible up out of it, looks at it a moment, then tosses it back into the sea and continues working on the boat. Blackout.

SCENE FOUR

Bedroom of Mammy O'Dougal, Johnny's ninety-year-old mother. Mammy in bed, Doctor McSharry checking her with a stethoscope, Johnny hovering.

DOCTOR: Have you been laying off the drink. Mrs. O'Dougal?
JOHNNY: Did you not hear me question, Doctor?
DOCTOR: I did hear your question, but amn't I trying to examine your mammy without your fool questions?
JOHNNY: Fool questions, is it?
DOCTOR: Have you been laying off the drink, Mrs. O'Dougal, I said.
MAMMY: (*Burps*) I *have* been laying off the drink or I've sort of been laying off the drink.
JOHNNY: She has a pint of porter now and then is no harm at all.
MAMMY: Is no harm at all.
JOHNNY: Is good for you!
DOCTOR: So long as you keep it at a pint of porter is the main thing so.
MAMMY: It *is* the main thing, and a couple of whiskeys now and then.
JOHNNY: Didn't I only just say not to mention the whiskeys, ya thick?

DOCTOR: How often is now and then?

JOHNNY: Once in a blue moon.

MAMMY: Once in a blue moon, and at breakfast sometimes.

JOHNNY: "At breakfast," jeez . . .

DOCTOR: Johnnypateenmike, don't you know well not to go feeding a ninety-year-old woman whiskey for breakfast?

JOHNNY: Ah she likes it, and doesn't it shut her up?

MAMMY: I do like a drop of whiskey, me, I do.

JOHNNY: From the horse's mouth.

MAMMY: Although I do prefer poteen.

DOCTOR: But you don't get given poteen?

MAMMY: I don't get given poteen, no.

JOHNNY: *Now.*

MAMMY: Only on special occasions.

DOCTOR: And what qualifies as a special occasion?

MAMMY: A Friday, a Saturday or a Sunday.

DOCTOR: When your mammy's dead and gone, Johnnypateen, I'm going to cut out her liver and show it to you, the damage your fine care has done.

JOHNNY: You won't catch me looking at me mammy's liver. I can barely stomach the outside of her, let alone the inside.

DOCTOR: A fine thing that is for a fella to say in front of his mammy.

MAMMY: I've heard worse.

JOHNNY: Leave me mammy alone now, you, with your mangling. If she's been trying to drink herself dead for sixty-five years with no luck, I wouldn't start worrying about her now. Sixty-five years. Feck, she can't do anything right.

DOCTOR: Why do you want to drink yourself dead, Mrs. O'Dougal?

MAMMY: I do miss me husband Donal. Ate be a shark.

JOHNNY: 1871 he was ate be a shark.

DOCTOR: Oh you should be trying to get over that now, Mrs. O'Dougal.

MAMMY: I've tried to, Doctor, but I can't. A lovely man he was. And living with this goose all these years, it just brings it back to me.

JOHNNY: Who are you calling a goose, ya hairy-lipped fool?

Didn't I go out of me way to bring Doctor McSharry home
to ya?

MAMMY: Aye, but only to go nosing about Cripple Billy Claven
is all.

JOHNNY: No, not . . . not . . . Ah you always go spilling the
beans, you, ya lump.

MAMMY: I'm an honest woman, me, Johnnypateen.

JOHNNY: Honest me hairy hole.

MAMMY: And you didn't get me drunk enough.

The doctor packs up his black bag.

DOCTOR: If I'm only here under false pretences . . .

JOHNNY: You're not here under false pretences. Me mammy
did seem awful bad earlier . . . cough, Mammy . . .

Mammy coughs.

But she seems to be over the worst of it, you're right there,
although, now, while you're here, Doctor, what *is* all this
about Cripple Billy? He wouldn't be in a terrible way, would
he? Maybe something life-threatening, now? Oh I suppose it
must be something awful serious if you go writing letters to
him.

DOCTOR: (*Pause*) Did you ever hear of a thing called doctor-
patient confidentiality, Johnnypateenmike?

JOHNNY: I did, and I think it's a great thing. Now tell me
what's wrong with Cripple Billy, Doctor.

DOCTOR: I'm going to open up that head of yours one day,
Johnnypateen, and find nothing inside it at all.

JOHNNY: Don't go straying off the subject now, you. Tell me
what's wrong with . . . or was that a clue to the subject, now?
There's something on the inside of his head that's wrong? A
brain tumour! He has a brain tumour!

DOCTOR: I wasn't aware . . .

JOHNNY: Tell me he has a brain tumour, doctor. Oh that'd
be awful big news.

DOCTOR: I'm off home, I thank you for wasting me precious time, but before I go I'll just say one thing, and that's I don't know where you got your information from this time o'er Cripple Billy, for it's usually such accurate information you do get, oh aye . . .

JOHNNY: Polio, polio. He has polio.

DOCTOR: But as far as I'm aware, apart from those deformities he's had since birth, there is nothing wrong with Billy Claven at all, and it would be better if you didn't go spreading fool gossip about him.

JOHNNY: (*Pause*) TB, TB. Ah it must be TB.

The doctor walks away.

JOHNNY: Where are you off to? Don't go hogging all the decent news, you!

The doctor has exited.

Ya beggar! Is Billy in such good health that rowing to Inishmore in the freezing morning as he did this day'll do him no harm, so?

Pause. The doctor returns, thoughtful.

Didn't that get him running back quick?

MAMMY: Like a cat with a worm up his arse.

JOHNNY: That was a descriptive turn of phrase, mammy.

DOCTOR: Billy's gone to Inishmore?

JOHNNY: He has. With the McCormicks and Babbybobby rowing them. Babbybobby who'll be arrested for grievous bodily harm the minute he returns, or grievous headily harm anyways, for it was me head he grievously harmed. I don't know if grievous bodily harm applies to heads.

DOCTOR: They've gone to see the filming?

JOHNNY: To see the filming or to be in the filming, aye.

DOCTOR: But the filming finished yesterday, sure. It's only clearing the oul cameras and whatnot they are today.

JOHNNY: (*Pause*) I suppose they must've been given unreliable information somewhere along the way, so.

MAMMY: Aye, be this goose.

JOHNNY: Don't you be calling me goose, I said.

MAMMY: Get me a drink, goose.

JOHNNY: If you retract goose I'll get you a dr . . .

MAMMY: I retract goose.

Johnny pours her a large whiskey, the doctor aghast.

DOCTOR: Don't . . . don't . . . (*Angrily*) Have I been talking to meself all day?!

JOHNNY: (*Pause*) Would you like a drink too, Doctor, after I have stunned you with me Cripple Billy revelation?

DOCTOR: What do I care about that arse-faced revelation?

JOHNNY: Heh. We'll see if your tune's the same when Billy returns home dead because of your secrecy and you're drummed out of doctorhood and forced to scrape the skitter out of bent cows, is all you were ever really fit for anyways, oh we all know.

DOCTOR: Billy won't be returning home dead because there's nothing the matter with Billy but a wheeze.

JOHNNY: Are you persisting in that one, Doctor Useless?

DOCTOR: Shall I say it one more time, thicko? There is nothing wrong with Billy Claven. Okay?

The doctor exits.

JOHNNY: Cancer! Cancer! Come back you! Would it be cancer? Tell me what it begins with. Is it a 'C'? Is It a 'P'?

MAMMY: You're talking to thin air, ya fool.

JOHNNY: (*Calling*) I'll get to the bottom of it one way or the other, McSharry! Be hook or be crook! A good newsman never takes no for an answer!

MAMMY: No. You just take stones pegged at your head for an answer.

JOHNNY: Let the stone matter drop, I've told you twenty times, or I'll kick your black arse back to Antrim for you.

Johnny sits on the bed, reading a newspaper.

MAMMY: You and your shitey-arsed news.

JOHNNY: My news isn't shitey-arsed. My news is great news. Did you hear Jack Ellery's goose and Pat Brennan's cat have both been missing a week? I suspect something awful's happened to them, or I *hope* something awful's happened to them.

MAMMY: Even though you're me own son I'll say it, Johnnypateen, you're the most boring oul fecker in Ireland. And there's plenty of competition for that fecking post!

JOHNNY: There's a sheep here in Kerry with no ears, I'll have to make a note.

MAMMY: (*Pause*) Give me the bottle if you're going bringing up sheep deformities.

He gives her the whiskey bottle.

JOHNNY: Sheep deformities is interesting news. Is the best kind of news. Excluding major illnesses anyways. (*Pause*) And I want to see half that bottle gone be tea time.

MAMMY: Poor Cripple Billy. The life that child's had. With that mam and dad of his, and that sackful of stones of theirs . . .

JOHNNY: Shut up about the sackful of stones.

MAMMY: And now this. Although look at the life I've had too. First poor Donal bit in two, then you going thieving the hundred-pound floorboard money he'd worked all his life to save and only to piss it away in pubs. Then the beetroot fecking paella you go making every Tuesday on top of it.

JOHNNY: There's nothing the matter with beetroot paella, and hasn't half of that hundred pounds been poured down your dribbling gob the past sixty years, ya bollocks?

MAMMY: Poor Billy. It's too many of the coffins of gosawers I've seen laid in the ground in me time.

JOHNNY: Drink up, so. You may save yourself the trouble this time.

MAMMY: Ah, I'm holding out to see you in your coffin first, Johnnypat. Wouldn't that be a happy day?

JOHNNY: Isn't that funny, because I'd enjoy seeing *you* in *your* coffin the same as ya, if we can find a coffin big enough to squeeze your fat arse into. Course we may have to saw half the blubber off you first, oh there's not even a question.

MAMMY: Oh you've upset me with them harsh remarks, Johnnypateen, oh aye. (*Pause*) Ya fecking eejit. (*Pause*) Anything decent in the paper, read it out to me. But no sheep news.

JOHNNY: There's a fella here, riz to power in Germany, has an awful funny moustache on him.

MAMMY: Let me see his funny moustache.

He shows her the photo.

That's a funny moustache.

JOHNNY: You'd think he'd either grow a proper moustache or else shave that poor biteen of a straggle off.

MAMMY: That fella seems to be caught in two minds.

JOHNNY: Ah he seems a nice enough fella, despite his funny moustache. Good luck to him. (*Pause*) There's a German fella living out in Connemara now, d'you know? Out Leenane way.

MAMMY: Ireland mustn't be such a bad place if German fellas want to come to Ireland.

JOHNNY: They all want to come to Ireland, sure. Germans, dentists, everybody.

MAMMY: And why, I wonder?

JOHNNY: Because in Ireland the people are more friendly.

MAMMY: They are, I suppose.

JOHNNY: Of course they are, sure. Everyone knows that. Sure, isn't it what we're famed for? (*Long pause*) I'd bet money on cancer.

Johnny nods, returning to his paper. Blackout.

SCENE FIVE

The shop. A few dozen eggs stacked on counter.

KATE: Not a word. (*Pause*) Not a word, not a word, not a word, not a word, not a word, not a word, not a word. (*Pause*) Not a word.

EILEEN: Oh how many more times are you going to say "Not a word," Kate?

KATE: Am I not allowed to say "Not a word" so, and me terrified o'er Billy's travellings?

EILEEN: You *are* allowed to say "Not a word," but one or two times and not ten times.

KATE: Billy's going to go the same way as his mammy and daddy went. Dead and buried be the age of twenty.

EILEEN: Do you ever look on the optimistic side, you?

KATE: I do look on the optimistic side, but I fear I'll never see poor Billy alive again.

EILEEN: (*Pause*) Billy could've at least left a note that he was going to Inishmore, and not have us hear it from oul Johnnypateen.

KATE: Not a word. Not a word, not a word, not a word.

EILEEN: And Johnnypateen revelling in his news-telling then, along with his intimating o'er letters and doctors.

KATE: I fear Johnnypateen knows something about Billy he's not telling.

EILEEN: When has Johnnypateen ever known something and not told, sure? Johnnypateen tells if a horse farts.

KATE: Do you think?

EILEEN: I know.

KATE: I still worry o'er Cripple Billy.

EILEEN: Sure, if McSharry's right that the filming's o'er, it won't be long at all before Billy's home, and the rest of them with him.

KATE: You said that last week and they're still not home.

EILEEN: Maybe they stayed to see the sights.

KATE: On Inishmore? What sights? A fence and a hen?

EILEEN: Maybe a cow came o'er to Cripple Billy and he lost track of time.

KATE: It doesn't take much time to look at a cow, sure.

EILEEN: Well, you used to take an age in talking to stones, I remember.

KATE: Them stone days were when I had trouble with me nerves and you know well they were, Eileen! Didn't we agree on never bringing the stones business up?

EILEEN: We did, and I'm sorry for bringing the stones business up. It's only because I'm as worried as ya that I let them stones slip.

KATE: Because people who live in glass houses shouldn't throw stone-conversations at me.

EILEEN: What glass house do I live in?

KATE: We had twenty Yalla-mallows in the ha'penny box the other day and I see they're all gone. How are we ever to make a profit if you keep eating the new sweeties before anybody's had a chance to see them?

EILEEN: Ah, Kate. Sure with Yalla -mallows, when you eat one, there's no stopping ya.

KATE: It was the same excuse with the Mintios. Well if you lay one finger on the Fripple-Frapples when they come in, you'll be for the high jump, I'm telling ya.

EILEEN: I'm sorry, Kate. It's just all this worry o'er Billy didn't help matters.

KATE: I know it didn't, Eileen. I know you like to stuff your face when you're worried. Just try to keep a lid on it is all.

EILEEN: I will. (*Pause*) Ah sure that Babbybobby's a decent enough fella. He'll be looking after Billy, I'm sure.

KATE: Why did he bring poor Billy off with him anyways so if he's such a decent fella? Didn't he know his aunties would be worrying?

EILEEN: I don't know if he knew.

KATE: I'd like to hit Babbybobby in the teeth.

EILEEN: I suppose he . . .

KATE: With a brick.

EILEEN: I suppose he could've got Billy to send a note at the minimum.

KATE: Not a word. Not a word. (*Pause*) Not a word, not a word, not a wor . . .

EILEEN: Ah Kate, don't be starting with your "Not a words" again.

Kate watches Eileen stacking the eggs a while.

KATE: I see the egg-man's been.

EILEEN: He has. The egg-man has a rake more eggs when Slippy Helen doesn't be working for him.

KATE: I don't see why he keeps Helen on at all.

EILEEN: I think he's scared of Helen. That or he's in love with Helen.

KATE: (*Pause*) I think Billy's in love with Helen on top of it.

EILEEN: *I* think Billy's in love with Helen. It'll all end in tears.

KATE: Tears or death.

EILEEN: We ought look on the bright side.

KATE: Tears, death or worse.

Johnny enters, strutting.

EILEEN: Johnnypateenmike.

KATE: Johnnypateenmike.

JOHNNY: Johnnypateen does have three pieces of news to be telling ye this day.

KATE: Only tell us if it's happy news, Johnnypat, because we're a biteen depressed today, we are.

JOHNNY: I have a piece of news concerning the Inishmore trippers, but I will be saving that piece of news for me third piece of news.

KATE: Is Billy okay, Johnnypateen? Oh tell us that piece of news first.

EILEEN: Tell us that piece of news first, aye, Johnnypateen.

JOHNNY: Well if ye're going arranging what order I tell me pieces of news in, I think I will turn on me heels and be off with me!

KATE: Don't go, Johnnypat! Don't go!

JOHNNY: Hah?

EILEEN: Tell us your news in whatever order you like, Johnnypateen. Sure, aren't you the man who knows best about news-ordering?

JOHNNY: I *am* the man who knows best. I *know* I'm the man

who knows best. That's no news. I see you have plenty of eggs in.

EILEEN: We do, Johnnypateen.

JOHNNY: Uh-huh. Me first piece of news, there is a sheep out in Kerry with no ears at all on him.

EILEEN: (*Pause*) That's a great piece of news.

JOHNNY: Don't ask me how he hears because I don't know and I don't care. Me second piece of news, Patty Brennan's cat was found dead and Jack Ellery's goose was found dead and nobody in town is said to've seen anything, but we can all put two and two together, although not out loud because Jack Ellery's an awful tough.

KATE: That's a sad piece of news because now it sounds like a feud is starting.

JOHNNY: A feud is starting and won't be stopped 'til the one or the two of them finish up slaughtered. Good. I will take six eggs, Mrs., for the omelette I promised me mammy a fortnight ago.

EILEEN: What was the third piece of news, Johnnypateen?

JOHNNY: I mention me mammy and nobody even asks as to how she is. Oh it's the height of politeness in this quarter.

KATE: How is your mammy, Johnnypateen?

JOHNNY: Me mammy's fine, so she is, despite me best efforts.

EILEEN: Are you still trying to kill your mammy with the drink, Johnnypateen?

JOHNNY: I am but it's no use. A fortune in booze that bitch has cost me over the years. She'll never go. (*Pause*) Well now, I have me eggs, I've told you me two pieces of news. I suppose that's me business finished here for the day.

KATE: The . . . the third piece of news, Johnnypateen?

JOHNNY: Oh, the third piece of news. Wasn't I almost forgetting? (*Pause*) The third piece of news is Babbybobby's just pulled his boat up on the sands, at the headland there, and let the young adventurers off. Or, let *two* of the young adventurers off anyways, Helen and Bartley. There was no hide nor hair of Cripple Billy in that boat. (*Pause*) I'm off to have Babbybobby arrested for throwing stones at me head. I thank you for the eggs.

Johnny exits. Pause. Kate sadly caresses the old sack hanging on the wall, then sits at the table.

KATE: He's gone from us, Eileen. He's gone from us.

EILEEN: We don't know at all that he's gone from us.

KATE: I can feel it in me bones, Eileen. From the minute he left I knew. Cripple Billy's dead and gone.

EILEEN: But didn't the doctor assure us five times there was nothing wrong with Cripple Billy?

KATE: Only so not to hurt us that assuring was. It was Johnnypat who had the real story all along, same as about Billy's mam and dad's drowning he always had the real story.

EILEEN: Oh lord, I see Babbybobby coming up the pathway towards us.

KATE: Does he look glum, Eileen?

EILEEN: He does look glum, but Babbybobby usually looks glum.

KATE: Does he look glummer than he usually looks?

EILEEN: (*Pause*) He does.

KATE: Oh no.

EILEEN: And he's taken the hat off him now.

KATE: That's an awful bad sign, taking the hat off ya.

EILEEN: Maybe just being gentlemanly he is?

KATE: Babbybobby? Sure, Babbybobby pegs bricks at cows.

Bobby enters, cap in hand

BOBBY: Eileen, Kate.

EILEEN: Babbybobby.

BOBBY: Would you be sitting down a minute there for yourself, now, Eileen? I've news to be telling ye.

Eileen sits at the table

I've just brought the two McCormicks home, and I was supposed to bring yere Billy home, I know, but I couldn't bring yere Billy home because . . . because he's been taken to

America for a screen test for a film they're making about a cripple fella. Or . . . I don't think the *whole* film will be about the cripple fella. The cripple fella'd only be a minor role. Aye. But it'd still be a good part, d'you know? (*Pause*) Although, there's more important things in the world than good parts in Hollywood films about cripple fellas. Being around your family and your friends is more important, and I tried to tell Cripple Billy that, but he wouldn't listen to me, no matter how much I told him. Be boat this morning they left. Billy wrote a letter here he asked me to pass onto ye. (*Pause*) Two or three months at minimum, Billy said probably he'd be gone. (*Pause*) Ah, as he said to me, it's his life. I suppose it is, now. I hope he enjoys his time there anyways. (*Pause*) That's all there is. (*Pause*) I'll be seeing ye.

EILEEN: Be seeing you, Babbybobby . . .

KATE: Be seeing you, Bobbybabbybobby.

Bobby exits. Kate opens the letter.

EILEEN: What the devil's a screen test, Kate?

KATE: I don't know at all what a screen test is.

EILEEN: Maybe in his letter it says.

KATE: Oh the awful handwriting he has.

EILEEN: It's never improved.

KATE: "Dear aunties, can ye guess what?" Yes. We *can* guess what. "I am off to Hollywood to make a screen test for a film they're making, and if they like the look of me a contract they will give me and an actor then I'll be." He doesn't explain at all what a screen test is.

EILEEN: With all the thinking he does?

KATE: What's this, now? I can't make out even two words in this sentence with his writing . . . "But if it's a big success I am . . . it might only be two or three months before I am too busy with acting work to be getting in touch with ye too often at all . . . so if ye don't hear from me much from summertime on . . . don't be worrying about me. It'll only mean I'm happy and healthy and making a go of me life in

America. Making something of meself for ye and mammy and daddy to be proud of. Give my love to everyone on the island except Johnnypateen, and take care of yourselves, Kate and Eileen. You moan the world to me . . . *mean* the world to me." It looks like *moan*. (*Pause*) "Yours sincerely . . . Billy Claven." (*Pause*) Turned his back on us, he has, Eileen.

EILEEN: (*Crying*) And us worrying our heads off o'er him.

Eileen goes to the counter and quietly fishes through the sweetie box.

KATE: After all we've done for him down the years.

EILEEN: We looked after him and didn't care that he was a cripple boy at all.

KATE: After all the shame he brought on us, staring at cows, and this is how he repays us.

EILEEN: I hope the boat sinks before it ever gets him to America.

KATE: I hope he drowns like his mammy and daddy drowned before him.

EILEEN: (*Pause*) Or are we being too harsh on him?

KATE: (*Crying*) We're being too harsh on him but only because it's so upset about him we are. What are you eating?

EILEEN: Oh Yalla-mallows and don't be starting on me.

KATE: I thought you'd ate all the Yalla-mallows.

EILEEN: I'd put a couple of Yalla-mallows aside for emergencies.

KATE: Eat ahead, Eileen.

EILEEN: Do you want one, Kate?

KATE: I don't. I have no stomach for eating at all, this day. Let alone eating Yalla-mallows.

EILEEN: (*Pause*) We'll see Cripple Billy again one day, won't we, Kate?

KATE: I fear we've more chance of seeing Jim Finnegan's daughter in a nunnery before we see Cripple Billy again. (*Pause*) I'm not sure if I *want* to see Cripple Billy again.

EILEEN: I'm not sure if *I* want to see Cripple Billy again. (*Pause*) I want to see Cripple Billy again.

KATE: I want to see Cripple Billy again.

Pause. Blackout.

Interval

SCENE SIX

The shop, summer, four months later. A couple of flyers for
The Man of Aran, *being shown at the church hall, hang on
the walls. The sweetie boxes and a stone lie on the counter,
beside which Bartley stands, pursing his lips dumbly and doing
other stuff for a few moments to fill in time as he waits for
Kate to return. Helen enters carrying a few dozen eggs.*

HELEN: What are you waiting for?
BARTLEY: She's gone in the back to look for me Fripple-
frapples.
HELEN: Oh you and your fecking Fripple-frapples.
BARTLEY: Fripple-frapples are nice sweeties.

Helen arranges the eggs on the counter.

I see you've brought the eggs up.
HELEN: You, you're awful observant.
BARTLEY: I thought bringing the eggs was the egg-man's job.
HELEN: It *was* the egg-man's job, but I did kick the egg-man
in the shins this after and he didn't feel up to it.
BARTLEY: What did you kick the egg-man in the shins for?
HELEN: He insinuated it was me murdered Jack Ellery's goose
and Pat Brennan's cat for them.
BARTLEY: But it *was* you murdered Jack Ellery's goose and Pat
Brennan's cat for them.
HELEN: I know it was, but if it gets bandied around town I'll
never be getting paid.
BARTLEY: How much are you getting paid?
HELEN: Eight bob for the goose and ten bob for the cat.
BARTLEY: Why did you charge extra for the cat?

HELEN: I had to pay Ray Darcy for the borrow of his axe. See, the goose I only had to stomp on him. It takes more than a stomp to polish a cat off.

BARTLEY: A plankeen of wood you could've used on the cat, and saved shelling out for the axe at all.

HELEN: Sure I wanted the job carried out professional, Bartley. A plank is the weapon of a flat-faced child. I wouldn't use a plank on a blue-arsed fly.

BARTLEY: What *would* you use on a blue-arsed fly?

HELEN: I wouldn't use a thing on a blue-arsed fly. There's no money involved in killing blue-arsed flies.

BARTLEY: Jim Finnegan's daughter killed twelve worms one day.

HELEN: Aye, be breathing on them.

BARTLEY: No, be sticking needles in their eyes.

HELEN: Now there's the work of an amateur. (*Pause*) I didn't even know worms had eyes.

BARTLEY: They don't after Jim Finnegan's daughter gets through with them.

HELEN: What's this stone here for?

BARTLEY: I caught Mrs. Osbourne talking to that stone when first I came in.

HELEN: What was she saying to the stone?

BARTLEY: She was saying "How are you, stone," and then putting the stone to her ear like the stone was talking back to her.

HELEN: That's awful strange behaviour.

BARTLEY: And asking the stone, then, if it knew how oul Cripple Billy was doing for himself in America.

HELEN: And what did the stone say?

BARTLEY: (*Pause*) The stone didn't say anything, Helen, because stones they don't say anything.

HELEN: Oh, I thought you said Mrs. Osbourne was doing the voice for the stone.

BARTLEY: No, Mrs. Osbourne was just doing her own voice.

HELEN: Maybe we should hide the stone and see if Mrs. Osbourne has a nervous breakdown.

BARTLEY: Sure that wouldn't be a very Christian thing to do, Helen.

HELEN: It wouldn't be a very Christian thing to do, no, but it'd be awful funny.

BARTLEY: Ah let's leave Mrs. Osbourne's stone alone, Helen. Hasn't she enough on her mind worrying o'er Cripple Billy?

HELEN: Cripple Billy's aunties should be *told* that Billy's dead or dying, and not have them waiting for a letter from him that'll never come. Four months, now, isn't it they've been waiting, and not a word, and them the only two on Inishmaan not been informed what Babbybobby knows.

BARTLEY: What good would it do, sure, informing them? At least this way they've the hope he's still alive. What help would Babbybobby's news be to them? And you never know but maybe a miracle's happened and Cripple Billy hasn't died in Hollywood at all. Maybe three months wasn't a fair estimate for Cripple Billy.

HELEN: I hope Cripple Billy *has* died in Hollywood, after taking his place in Hollywood that was rightfully a pretty girl's place, when he knew full well he was about to kick the bucket.

BARTLEY: A pretty girl's place? What use would a pretty girl be in playing a cripple fella?

HELEN: I could turn me hand to anything, me, given a chance.

BARTLEY: I've heard.

HELEN: Heard what?

BARTLEY: I've heard Hollywood is chock-full of pretty girls, sure. It's cripple fellas they're crying out for.

HELEN: What are you defending Cripple Billy for? Didn't he promise to send you a package of Yalla-mallows you've never seen a lick of?

BARTLEY: Maybe Cripple Billy died before he had a chance of sending me them Yalla-mallows.

HELEN: It's any excuse for you, ya weed.

BARTLEY: But dying's an awful good excuse for not sending a fella the sweeties he promised.

HELEN: Too kind-hearted you are. I'm ashamed to admit you're related to me sometimes.

BARTLEY: It doesn't hurt to be too kind-hearted.

HELEN: Uh-huh. Does this hurt?

Helen pinches Bartleys arm.

BARTLEY: (*In pain*) No.
HELEN: (*Pause*) Does this hurt?

Helen gives him a Chinese burn on the forearm.

BARTLEY: (*In pain*) No.
HELEN: (*Pause*) Does this hurt?

Helen picks up an egg and breaks it against his forehead.

BARTLEY: (*Sighing*) I'd better say yes before any further you go.
HELEN: You should've said yes on the arm pinch, would've been using your brain.
BARTLEY: I should've said yes but you'd still've broken an egg on me.
HELEN: Now we'll never know.
BARTLEY: You're just a terror when you get around eggs.
HELEN: I do like breaking eggs on fellas.
BARTLEY: I had guessed that somehow.
HELEN: Or could you classify you as a fella? Isn't that going a biteen overboard?
BARTLEY: I notice you never broke an egg on Babbybobby Bennett when he reneged on your kissing proposals.
HELEN: We were in a row-boat a mile from land, sure. Where was I supposed to get an egg?
BARTLEY: Reneged because you're so witchy-looking.
HELEN: Reneged because he was upset o'er Cripple Billy, and watch your "witchy-looking" comments, you.
BARTLEY: Why is it runny eggs don't smell but boiled eggs do smell?
HELEN: I don't know why. And I don't care why.
BARTLEY: Reneged because you look like one of them ragged-looking widow women waiting on the rocks for a rascal who'll never return to her.

HELEN: That sentence had an awful lot of *R*s.

BARTLEY: It was insulting with it, on top of the *R*s.

HELEN: You've gotten awful cocky for a boy with egg running down his gob.

BARTLEY: Well there comes a time for every Irishman to take a stand against his oppressors.

HELEN: Was it Michael Collins said that?

BARTLEY: It was some one of the fat ones anyways.

HELEN: Do you want to play "England versus Ireland"?

BARTLEY: I don't know how to play "England versus Ireland."

HELEN: Stand here and close your eyes. You'll be Ireland.

Bartley faces her and closes his eyes.

BARTLEY: And what do you do?

HELEN: I'll be England.

Helen picks up three eggs from the counter and breaks the first against Bartley's forehead. Bartley opens his eyes as the yolk runs down him, and stares at her sadly. Helen breaks the second egg on his forehead.

BARTLEY: That wasn't a nice thing at all to . . .

HELEN: Haven't finished.

Helen breaks the third egg on Bartley.

BARTLEY: That wasn't a nice thing at all to do, Helen.

HELEN: I was giving you a lesson about Irish history, Bartley.

BARTLEY: I don't need a lesson about Irish history. (*Shouting*) Or anyways not with eggs when I've only washed me hair!

HELEN: There'll be worse casualties than eggy hair before Ireland's a nation once again, Bartley McCormick.

BARTLEY: And me best jumper, look at it!

HELEN: It has egg on it.

BARTLEY: I know it has egg on it! I know well! And I was going to go wearing it to the showing of the film tomorrow, but you've put paid to that idea now, haven't ya?

HELEN: I'm looking forward to the showing of the film to-morrow.

BARTLEY: I was looking forward to the showing of the film too until me jumper became destroyed.

HELEN: I think I might go pegging eggs at the film tomorrow. *The Man of Aran* me arsehole. *The Lass of Aran* they could've had, and the *pretty* lass of Aran. Not some oul shite about thick fellas fecking fishing.

BARTLEY: Does everything you do have to involve egg-pegging, Helen?

HELEN: I do take a pride in me egg-work, me. Is this bitch never bloody coming to pay for me eggs? (*Calling*) You, stone-woman!

BARTLEY: She's taking an age to bring me Fripple-Frapples.

HELEN: Ah I can't waste me youth waiting for that mingy hole. You collect me egg-money, Bartley, and give it to the egg-man on the way home.

BARTLEY: I will, Helen, aye.

Helen exits.

I will me fecking arse, ya shite-gobbed fecking bitch-fecker, ya . . .

Helen pops her head back in.

HELEN: And don't let her dock you for the four you went and broke on me.

BARTLEY: I won't, Helen.

She exits again.

(*Sighing*) Women.

Kate slowly enters from the back room, absent-mindedly, no-ticing Bartley after a second.

KATE: Hello there, Bartley. What can I be getting for ya?

BARTLEY: (*Pause. Bemused*) You were going in the back to look for your Fripple-Frapples, Mrs.

Kate thinks to herself a moment, then slowly returns to the back room. Bartley moans loudly in frustration, putting his head down on the counter. Slight pause, then Kate returns and picks up her stone.

KATE: I'll bring me stone.

She exits to the back room again. Pause. Bartley picks up a wooden mallet, smashes all the eggs on the counter with it and walks out, slamming the door. Blackout.

SCENE SEVEN

Sound of Billy's wheezing starts, as lights come up on him shivering alone on a chair in a squalid Hollywood hotel room. He wheezes slightly throughout.

BILLY: Mam? I fear I'm not longer for this world, Mam. Can't I hear the wail of the banshees for me, as far as I am from me barren island home? A home barren, aye, but proud and generous with it, yet turned me back on ye I did, to end up alone and dying in a one-dollar rooming-house, without a mother to wipe the cold sweat off me, nor a father to curse God o'er the death of me, nor a colleen fair to weep tears o'er the still body of me. A body still, aye, but a body noble and unbowed with it. An Irishman! (*Pause*) *Just* an Irishman. With a decent heart on him, and a decent head on him, and a decent spirit not broken by a century's hunger and a lifetime's oppression! A spirit not broken, no . . . (*Coughing*) but a body broken, and the lungs of him broken, and, if truth be told, the heart of him broken too, be a lass who never knew his true feelings, and now, sure, never will. What's this, Mammy, now, that you're saying to me?

He looks at a sheet of paper on the table.

Be writing home to her, I know, and make me feelings known. Ah, 'tis late, Mammy. Won't tomorrow be soon enough for that task?

He gets up and shuffles to the mirror left, quietly singing "The Croppy Boy."

"Farewell father and mother too, and sister Mary I have none but you. And for my brother, he's all alone. He's pointing pikes on the grinding stone."

He stumbles, ill, crawls up onto the bed, wheezing, and looks at the photo on the dresser.

What would Heaven be like, Mammy? I've heard 'tis a beautiful place, more beautiful than Ireland even, but even if it is, sure, it wouldn't be near as beautiful as you. I do wonder would they let cripple boys into Heaven at all. Sure, wouldn't we only be uglifying the place?

He puts the photo back on the dresser.

BILLY: "Twas in old Ireland this young man died, and in old Ireland his body's lain. All the good people that do pass by, may the lord have mercy on this croppy boy." Oh it's a bad way the chest of me is in tonight, Mammy. I think it's a little sleep I should have now for meself. For there's mighty work in the railyard tomorrow to be done. (*Pause*) What's that, Mammy? Me prayers? I know. Sure, would I be forgetting, as well as you taught them to me? (*Blesses himself*) And now I lay me down to sleep, I pray to God my soul to keep. But if . . . (*Pause*) But if I die before I wake . . . I pray to God . . . (*Tearfully*) I pray to God . . .

Pause, recovering himself. He smiles.

Ara, don't worry, Mammy. 'Tis only to sleep it is that I'm going. 'Tis only to sleep.

Billy lies down. His pained wheezes get worse and worse, until they suddenly stop with an anguished gasp, his eyes close, his head lolls to one side, and he lays there motionless. Fade to black.

SCENE EIGHT

A church hall in semi-darkness. Bobby, Mammy, Johnny, Helen, Bartley, Eileen and Kate sitting. All are staring up at the film Man of Aran *being projected. The film is nearing its end, and its soundtrack is either very low or not heard at all.*

MAMMY: What's this that's happening?

JOHNNY: What does it look like that's happening?

BARTLEY: Aren't they going catching a shark, Mrs., and a big shark?

MAMMY: Are they?

JOHNNY: Shut up and drink up, you.

MAMMY: I will, goosey.

BOBBY: I hope only water it is that's in that bottle, Johnnypateenmike.

JOHNNY: Of course it's only water. (*Whispered*) Don't be breathing out near Babbybobby, Mammy.

MAMMY: I won't be.

JOHNNY: And mind the "goosey."

BOBBY: Has your Johnny been thieving any more of your life savings lately, Mrs. O'Dougal?

JOHNNY: I never ever thieved me mammy's life savings. I only borrowed them, short-term.

MAMMY: Since 1914 this fecker's borrowed them, short-term.

JOHNNY: Well that's the definition of short-term.

KATE: (*Pause*) That's a big fish.

EILEEN: 'Tis a shark, Kate.

KATE: 'Tis a wha?

EILEEN: A shark, a shark!

HELEN: Have you forgot what a shark is, on top of talking to stones?

BARTLEY: It's mostly off America you do get sharks, Mrs., and a host of sharks, and so close to shore sometimes they come, sure, you wouldn't even need a telescope to spot them, oh no . . .

HELEN: Oh telescopes, Jesus . . . !

BARTLEY: It's rare that off Ireland you get sharks. This is the first shark I've ever seen off Ireland.

JOHNNY: Ireland mustn't be such a bad place so if sharks want to come to Ireland.

BARTLEY: (*Pause*) Babbybobby, you weren't in long with the polis at all when you was took down for Johnnypat's head-stoning, how comes?

BOBBY: Oh the guard just laughed when he heard about John-nypat's head-stoning. "Use a brick next time," he said. "Stop piddling around with stones."

JOHNNY: That guard wants drumming out of the polis. Or at least to have spiteful rumours spread about him.

BOBBY: And we all know who the man for that job'll be.

JOHNNY: He beats his wife with a poker, d'you know?

HELEN: Sure is that news? They don't let you in the polis *unless* you beat your wife with a poker.

BOBBY: And that's an outright lie anyways about the guard beating his wife with a poker. (*Pause*) A biteen of a rubber hose was all he used.

KATE: (*Pause*) Not a word. Not a word from him.

HELEN: Is stony off again?

EILEEN: She is.

HELEN: Hey, stony!

EILEEN: Ar leave her, Helen, will ya?

HELEN: (*Pause*) Ah they're never going to be catching this fecking shark. A fecking hour they've been at it now, it seems like.

BARTLEY: Uh-huh. Three minutes would be more accurate.

HELEN: If it was *me* had a role in this film the fecker wouldn't have lasted as long. One good clobber and we could all go home.

BARTLEY: One good clobber with Ray Darcy's axe, I suppose.

HELEN: Cut the axe-talk, you.

BARTLEY: Doesn't shark-clobbering take a sight more effort than cat-besecting?

JOHNNY: What's this that Johnnypateen hears?

Helen grabs Bartley by the hair and wrenches his head around as Johnny makes a note in a pocket book.

HELEN: Just you wait 'til I fecking get you home. Just you fecking wait . . .

BARTLEY: Ah that hurts, Helen, that hurts . . .

HELEN: Of course it hurts. It's supposed to fecking hurt.

BOBBY: Be leaving Bartley alone now, Helen.

HELEN: Up your arse you, Babbybobby Bennett, you fecking kiss-reneger. Would *you* like to step outside with me?

BOBBY: I wouldn't like to.

HELEN: Shut your hole so.

BOBBY: Not if there was to be kissing involved, anyways.

Helen releases Bartley roughly.

JOHNNY: A little noteen, now, Johnnypateen has made for himself. A side of lamb at minimum this news'll get me, off Patty Brennan or Jack Ellery anyways. Eheh.

HELEN: You'll be eating that lamb with a broken neck, so, if that news gets bandied about before Jack and Pat've paid up, ya feck.

JOHNNY: Oh aye.

BARTLEY: (*Pause*) Look at the size of that fella's nose. (*Pause*) Look at the size of that fella's nose I said.

KATE: Have you been falling down any holes since, Bartley?

BARTLEY: Oh Mrs, sure wasn't I seven when I fell down the hole I fell down? D'ya have to keep dragging that up every year?

HELEN: (*Pause*) Oh they still haven't caught this fecking shark! How hard is it?

Helen throws an egg at the screen.

BOBBY: Oh don't be pegging any more eggs at the film, Helen. Weren't the five you pegged at the poor woman in it enough?
HELEN: Not nearly enough. I never got her in the gob even once, the bitch. She keeps moving.
BOBBY: You'll ruin the egg-man's bedsheet anyways.
HELEN: Ah, the egg-man's bedsheet is used to being eggy.
BARTLEY: How do you know the egg-man's bedsheets are used to being eggy, Helen?
HELEN: Em, Jim Finnegan's daughter was telling me.
MAMMY: (*Pause*) Ah why don't they just leave the poor shark alone? He was doing no harm.
JOHNNY: Sure what manner of a story would that be, leaving a shark alone! You want a dead shark.
BOBBY: A dead shark, aye, or a shark with no ears on him.
JOHNNY: A dead shark, aye, or a shark kissed a green-teethed girl in Antrim.
BOBBY: Do you want a belt, you, mentioning green-teeth girls?
JOHNNY: Well you interrupted me and me mammy's shark debate.
MAMMY: They should give the shark a belt, then leave the poor gosawer alone.
JOHNNY: Why are you in love with sharks all of a sudden? Wasn't it a shark ate daddy?
MAMMY: It *was* a shark ate daddy, but Jaysus says you should forgive and forget.
JOHNNY: He doesn't say you should forgive and forget sharks.
BARTLEY: (*Pause*) Sharks have no ears to begin with, anyways.

Pause. They look at him.

Babbybobby was saying a shark with no ears. (*Pause*) Sharks have no ears to begin with, anyways.

JOHNNY: We've moved on from ears-talk, you, ya thick.

BARTLEY: What are we onto now?

JOHNNY: We're onto Jaysus forgiving sharks.

BARTLEY: Oh aye, that's an awful great topic for conversation.

HELEN: I always preferred Pontius Pilate to Jesus. Jesus always seemed full of himself.

BARTLEY: Jesus drove a thousand pigs into the sea one time, did you ever hear tell of that story? Drowned the lot of the poor devils. They always seem to gloss o'er that one in school.

KATE: I didn't know Jesus could drive.

HELEN: Mrs.? You' ve gone loopy, haven't you Mrs.? Haven't you gone loopy?

KATE: I haven't gone loopy.

HELEN: You have. Your stone was telling me earlier.

KATE: What did me stone say?

HELEN: Did you hear that one, Bartley? "What did me stone say?"

JOHNNY: Of course poor Kate's gone loopy, Helen, with the gosawer she raised and loved sixteen year preferring to take his TB to Hollywood for his dying than to bear be in the company of her.

Eileen stands with her hands to her head and turns to face Johnny, as does Bobby.

EILEEN: (*Stunned*) Wha? Wha?

JOHNNY: Em, whoops.

Bobby grabs Johnny roughly and drags him up.

BOBBY: Didn't I say to ya?! Didn't I say to ya?!

JOHNNY: Sure don't they have a right to know about their dying foster-babby, stabbed them in the back without a by-your-leave?

BOBBY: Can't you keep anything to yourself?

JOHNNY: Johnnypateenmike was never a man for secrets.

BOBBY: Outside with ya, so, and see if you can keep this beating a secret.

JOHNNY: You'll frighten me mammy, Babbybobby, you'll frighten me mammy . . .

MAMMY: Ah you won't, Bobby. Go on and give him a good beating for yourself.

JOHNNY: That was the last omelette you'll ever eat in my house, ya bitch!

MAMMY: Carrot omelettes don't go, anyways.

JOHNNY: You never like anything adventurous!

Johnny is dragged off right by Bobby. Sound of his yelps getting more and more distant. Eileen is standing in front of Bartley, hands still to her head.

EILEEN: What was this Johnnypateen was saying about . . .

BARTLEY: Would you mind out of me way, Mrs., I can't see.

Eileen moves over to Mammy.

HELEN: What's to fecking see anyways but more wet fellas with awful jumpers on them?

EILEEN: Mrs. O'Dougal, what now was this that your Johnny was saying?

MAMMY: (*Pause*) TB they say your Cripple Billy has, Eileen.

EILEEN: No . . . !

MAMMY: Or, they say he *had* anyways. Four months ago Billy was told, and told he had only three months left in him.

BARTLEY: That means he's probably been dead a month, Mrs. Simple subtraction that is. Three from four.

EILEEN: Ah sure, if this is only your Johnnypateen's oul gossiping I wouldn't be believing you at all . . .

MAMMY: Aye, if it was Johnnypat's gossiping you wouldn't need to care a skitter about it, but Babbybobby's news this is. Cripple Billy showed him a letter from McSharry the night before they sailed. Sure, Babbybobby would never've taken Cripple Billy, only his heart went out to him. Didn't Bobby's Annie die of the same thing?

EILEEN: She did, and in agony she died. Oh Cripple Billy.

The days and nights I've cursed him for not writing us, when how could he write us at all?

HELEN: When he was buried six feet under. Aye, that'd be an awful hard task.

EILEEN: But . . . but Doctor McSharry five or six times I've asked, and nothing at all wrong with Billy did McSharry say there was.

MAMMY: Sure, I suppose he was only trying not to hurt you Eileen, same as everyone around. (*Pause*) I'm sorry, Eileen.

Helen and Bartley stand and stretch, backs to screen, as the film ends. Eileen sits, tearfully.

HELEN: Oh thank Christ the fecker's over. A pile of fecking shite.

BARTLEY: And not a telescope in sight.

The film winds out, leaving the screen blank. A light goes on behind it, illuminating the silhouette of Cripple Billy on the screen, which only Kate sees. She stands and stares at it.

MAMMY: (*Wheeling herself away*) Did they catch the shark in the end, so, Helen?

HELEN: Ah it wasn't even a shark at all, Mrs. It was a tall fella in a grey donkey jacket.

MAMMY: How do you know, Helen?

HELEN: Didn't I give the fella a couple of kisses to promise to put me in his next film, and didn't I stamp on the bollocks of him when his promise turned out untrue?

MAMMY: All that fuss o'er a fella in a grey donkey jacket. I don't know.

HELEN: He won't be playing any more sharks for a while anyways, Mrs., the stamp I gave the feck.

Helen and Mammy exit. Bartley stands staring at Billy's silhouette, having just spotted it. Eileen, crying, still has her back to it. Kate pulls back the sheet, revealing Billy, alive and well.

(*Off. Calling out*) Are you coming, you, fecker?

BARTLEY: In a minute I'm coming.

BILLY: I didn't want to disturb ye 'til the film was o'er.

Eileen turns, sees him, stunned. Kate drops her stone and embraces Billy.

BARTLEY: Hello there, Cripple Billy.

BILLY: Hello there, Bartley.

BARTLEY: Just back from America are ya?

BILLY: I am.

BARTLEY: Uh-huh. (*Pause*) Did you get me me Yalla-mallows?

BILLY: I didn't, Bartley.

BARTLEY: Ar, ya fecking promised, Billy.

BILLY: They had only Fripple-Frapples.

Billy tosses Bartley a packet of sweets.

BARTLEY: Ah jeebies, Fripple-Frapples'll do just as fine. Thank you Cripple Billy.

KATE: You're not dead at all, are you, Billy?

BILLY: I'm not, Aunty Kate.

KATE: Well that's good.

BARTLEY: What was it so, Billy? Did you write that doctor's letter yourself and only to fool Babbybobby into rowing ya, when there wasn't a single thing the matter with you at all?

BILLY: I did, Bartley.

BARTLEY: You're awful clever for a cripple-boy, Billy. Was it out of *Biggles Goes to Borneo* you got that idea? When Biggles tells the cannonball he has the measles so the cannonball won't eat Biggles at all?

BILLY: No, I made the idea up meself, Bartley.

BARTLEY: Well now, it sounds awful similar, Billy.

BILLY: Well I made the idea up meself, Bartley.

BARTLEY: Well you're even more clever than I thought you was so, Billy. You've made a laughing stock of every beggar on Inishmaan, all thought you'd gone and croaked it, like eejits, me included. Fair play to ya.

EILEEN: Not everyone on Inishmaan. Some us of only believed you'd run off, and run off because you couldn't stomach the sight of us.

BILLY: Not for a second was that true, Aunty Eileen, and wasn't the reason I returned that I couldn't bear to be parted from ye any longer? Didn't I take me screen test not a month ago and have the Yanks say to me the part was mine? But I had to tell them it was no go, no matter how much money they offered me, because I know now it isn't Hollywood that's the place for me. It's here on Inishmaan, with the people who love me, and the people I love back.

Kate kisses him.

BARTLEY: Ireland can't be such a bad place, so, if cripple fellas turn down Hollywood to come to Ireland.

BILLY: To tell you the truth, Bartley, it wasn't an awful big thing at all to turn down Hollywood, with the arse-faced lines they had me reading for them. "Can I not hear the wail of the banshees for me, as far as I am from me barren island home."

Bartley laughs.

"An Irishman I am, begora! With a heart and a spirit on me not crushed be a hundred years of oppression. I'll be getting me shillelagh out next, wait'll you see." A rake of shite. And had me singing the fecking "Croppy Boy" then.

KATE: Sure I think he'd make a great little actoreen, don't you, Eileen?

BARTLEY: Them was funny lines, Cripple Billy. Do them again.

KATE: I'll be off home and air your room out for you, Billy.

BARTLEY: Em, you've forgot your stone there, Mrs. Mightn't you want a chat on the way, now?

KATE: Ah I'll leave me stone. I have me Billy-boy back now to talk to, don't I, Billy?

BILLY: You do, Aunty.

Kate exits.

Oh she hasn't started up with the bloody stones again, has she?

BARTLEY: She has. Talks to them day and night, and everybody laughs at her, me included.

BILLY: You shouldn't laugh at other people's misfortunes, Bartley.

BARTLEY: (*Confused*) Why?

BILLY: I don't know why. Just that you shouldn't is all.

BARTLEY: But it's awful funny.

BILLY: Even so.

BARTLEY: We-ell I disagree with you there, but you've got me me Fripple-Frapples so I won't argue the point. Will you tell me all about how great America is later, Cripple Billy?

BILLY: I will, Bartley.

BARTLEY: Did you see any telescopes while you were over there?

BILLY: I didn't.

BARTLEY: (*Disappointed*) Oh. How about me Aunty Mary in Boston Massachusetts? Did you see her? She has funny brown hair on her.

BILLY: I didn't, Bartley.

BARTLEY: Oh. (*Pause*) Well. I'm glad you're not dead anyways, Cripple Billy.

Bartley exits.

BILLY: (*Pause*) That's all Bartley wants to hear is how great America is.

EILEEN: Is it not so?

BILLY: It's just the same as Ireland really. Full of fat women with beards.

Eileen gets up, goes over to Billy and slaps him across the head.

BILLY: Aargh! What was that fer?!

EILEEN: Forget fat women with beards! Would it have killed you to write a letter all the time you were away? No it wouldn't, and not a word. Not a blessed word!

BILLY: Ah aunty, I was awful busy.

EILEEN: Uh-huh. Too busy to write your aunties, were worried sick about you, but not too busy to go buying Fripple-Frapples for an eejit gosawer and only to show off the big man you think you are.

BILLY: Ah it only takes a minute to buy Fripple-Frapples, sure. Is that a fair comparison?

EILEEN: Don't you go big-wording me when you know you're in the wrong.

BILLY: Sure, *comparison* isn't a big word.

EILEEN: Mr. Yankee-high-and-mighty now I see it is.

BILLY: And I found the American postal system awful complicated.

EILEEN: It's any excuse for you. Well don't expect me to be forgiving and forgetting as quick as that one. She's only forgiven cos she's gone half doolally because of ya. You won't be catching me out so easy!

BILLY: Ah don't be like that, Aunty.

EILEEN: (*Exiting*) I *will* be like that. I *will* be like that.

Long pause, Billy's head lowered. Eileen sticks her head back in.

And I suppose you'll be wanting praitie cakes for your tea too?!

BILLY: I would, Aunty.

EILEEN: Taahhh!

She exits again. Pause. Billy looks at the sheet/screen, pulls it back across to its original dimensions and stands there staring at it, caressing it slightly, deep in thought. Bobby quietly enters right, Billy noticing him after a moment.

BILLY: Babbybobby. I daresay I owe you an explanation.

BOBBY: There's no need to explain, Billy.

BILLY: I want to, Bobby. See, I never thought at all this day would come when I'd have to explain. I'd hoped I'd disappear forever to America. And I would've too, if they'd wanted me there. If they'd wanted me for the filming. But they didn't want me. A blond lad from Fort Lauderdale they hired instead of me. He wasn't crippled at all, but the Yank said, "Ah, better to get a normal fella who can act crippled than a crippled fella who can't fecking act at all." Except he said it ruder. (*Pause*) I thought I'd done alright for meself with me acting. Hours I practised in me hotel there. And all for nothing. (*Pause*) I gave it a go anyways. I had to give it a go. I had to get away from this place, Babbybobby, be any means, just like me mammy and daddy had to get away from this place. (*Pause*) Going drowning meself I'd often think of when I was here, just to . . . just to end the laughing at me, and the sniping at me, and the life of nothing but shuffling to the doctor's and shuffling back from the doctor's and pawing over the same oul books and finding any other way to piss another day away. Another day of sniggering, or the patting me on the head like a broken-brained gosawer. The village orphan. The village cripple, and nothing more. Well, there are plenty round here just as crippled as me, only it isn't on the outside it shows. (*Pause*) But the thing is, you're not one of them, Babbybobby, nor never were. You've a kind heart on you. I suppose that's why it was so easy to cod you with the TB letter, but that's why I was so sorry for codding you at the time and why I'm just as sorry now. Especially for codding you with the same thing your Mrs. passed from. Just I thought that would be more effective. But, in the long run, I thought, or I hoped, that if you had a choice between you being codded a while and me doing away with meself, once your anger had died down anyways, you'd choose you being codded every time. Was I wrong, Babbybobby? Was I?

Bobby slowly walks over to Billy, stops just in front of him, and lets a length of lead piping slide down his sleeve into his hand.

BOBBY: Aye.

Bobby raises the pipe . . .

BILLY: No, Bobby, no . . . !

Billy covers up as the pipe scythes down. Blackout, with the sounds of Billy's pained screams and the pipe scything down again and again.

SCENE NINE

The shop, late evening. The doctor tending to Billy's bruised and bloody face. Kate at the counter, Eileen at the door, looking out.

EILEEN: Johnnypateenmike's near enough running o'er the island with his news of Billy's return to us.
KATE: This is a big day for news.
EILEEN: He has a loaf in one hand and a leg o' mutton neath each armeen.
KATE: Billy's return and Babbybobby's arrest and Jim Finnegan's daughter joining the nunnery then. That was the biggest surprise.
EILEEN: The nuns must be after anybody if they let Jim Finnegan's daughter join them.
KATE: The nuns' standards must have dropped.
BILLY: Sure why shouldn't Jim Finnegan's daughter become a nun? It's only pure gossip that Jim Finnegan's daughter is a slut.
DOCTOR: No, Jim Finnegan's daughter *is* a slut.
BILLY: Is she?
DOCTOR: Aye.
BILLY: How do you know?
DOCTOR: Just take me word.
EILEEN: Isn't he a doctor?
BILLY: (*Pause*) Just I don't like people gossiping about people is all. Haven't I had enough of that meself to last me a lifetime?

DOCTOR: But aren't you the one who started half the gossiping about you, with your forging of letters from me you'll yet have to answer for?

BILLY: I'm sorry about the letter business, Doctor, but wasn't it the only avenue left open to me?

EILEEN: Its "Avenues" now, do ya hear?

KATE: Its always big-talk when from America they return.

EILEEN: Avenues. I don't know.

BILLY: Aunties, I think the doctor might be wanting a mug of tea, would ye's both go and get him one?

EILEEN: Is getting rid of us you're after? If it is, just say so.

BILLY: It's getting rid of ye I'm after.

Eileen stares at him a moment then moodily exits to the back room.

DOCTOR: You shouldn't talk to her like that, now, Billy.

BILLY: Ah they keep going on and on.

DOCTOR: I know they do but they're women.

BILLY: I suppose. (*Pause*) Would you tell me something, Doctor? What do you remember of me mammy and daddy, the people they were?

DOCTOR: Why do you ask?

BILLY: Oh, just when I was in America there I often thought of them, what they'd have done if they'd got there. Wasn't that where they were heading the night they drowned?

DOCTOR: They say it was. (*Pause*) As far as I can remember, they weren't the nicest of people. Your daddy was an oul drunken tough, would rarely take a break from his fighting.

BILLY: I've heard me mammy was a beautiful woman.

DOCTOR: No, no, she was awful ugly.

BILLY: Was she?

DOCTOR: Oh she'd scare a pig. But, ah, she seemed a pleasant enough woman, despite her looks, although the breath on her, well it would knock you.

BILLY: They say it was that Dad punched Mammy while she heavy with me was why I turned out the way I did.

DOCTOR: Disease caused you to turn out the way you did, Billy. Not punching at all. Don't go romanticising it.

Billy coughs/wheezes slightly.

I see you still have your wheeze.
BILLY: I still have a bit of me wheeze.
DOCTOR: That wheeze is taking a long time to go.

The doctor uses a stethoscope to check Billy's chest.

Has worse or better it got since your travelling? Breathe in.
BILLY: Maybe a biteen worse.

The doctor listens to Billy's back.

DOCTOR: But blood you haven't been coughing up, ah no.
BILLY: Ah a biteen of blood. (*Pause*) Now and again.
DOCTOR: Breathe out. How often is now and again, Billy?
BILLY: (*Pause*) Most days. (*Pause*) The TB is it?
DOCTOR: I'll have to be doing more tests.
BILLY: But the TB it looks like?
DOCTOR: The TB it looks like.
BILLY: (*Quietly*) Theres a coincidence.

Johnny enters quietly, having been listening at the door, loaf in hand, a leg of lamb under each arm, which he carries throughout.

JOHNNY: It's the TB after all?
DOCTOR: Oh Johnnypateen, will you ever stop listening at doors?
JOHNNY: Lord save us but from God I'm sure that TB was sent Cripple Billy, for claiming he had TB when he had no TB, and making Johnnypateen's news seem unreliable.
DOCTOR: God doesn't send people TB, Johnnypateen.
JOHNNY: He *does* send people TB.

DOCTOR: He doesn't, now.

JOHNNY: Well didn't he send the Egyptians boils is just as bad?

DOCTOR: Well boils is different from tuberculosis, Johnnypateen, and, *no* he *didn't* send the Egyptians boils.

JOHNNY: In Egyptian times.

DOCTOR: No, he didn't.

JOHNNY: Well he did something to the fecking Egyptians!

BILLY: He killed their first-born sons.

JOHNNY: He killed their first-born sons and dropped frogs on them, aye. There's a boy knows his scripture. Do your aunties know you have TB yet, Cripple Billy?

BILLY: No, they don't know, and you're not to tell them.

JOHNNY: Sure it's me job to tell them!

BILLY: It isn't your job at all to tell them, and don't you have enough news for one day with me return. Can't you do me a favour for once in your life?

JOHNNY: For once in me life, is it? (*Sighing*) Ah I won't tell them so.

BILLY: Thank you, Johnnypateen.

JOHNNY: Johnnypateen's a kind-hearted, Christian man.

DOCTOR: I heard you were feeding your mammy poteen at the showing of the film today, Johnnypateen.

JOHNNY: I don't know where she got hold of that poteen. She's a devil, d'you know?

DOCTOR: Where's your mammy now?

JOHNNY: At home she is. (*Pause*) Lying at the foot of me stairs.

DOCTOR: What's she doing lying at the foot of your stairs?

JOHNNY: Nothing. Just lying. Ah she seems happy enough. She has a pint with her.

DOCTOR: How did she *get* lying at the foot of your stairs?

JOHNNY: Be falling down them! How d'ya usually get lying at the foot of a fella's stairs?

DOCTOR: And you just left her there?

JOHNNY: Is it my job to go picking her up?

DOCTOR: It is!

JOHNNY: Sure, didn't I have work to do with me news-divulging? I have better things to do than picking mammies up. D'you see the two legs of lamb I got, and a loafeen too? This is a great day.

The doctor packs up his black bag, stunned, as Johnny admires his meat.

DOCTOR: I'm off now, Billy, to Johnnypateen's house, to see if his mammy's dead or alive. Will you come see me tomorrow, for those further tests?
BILLY: I will, Doctor.

The doctor exits, staring at Johnny all the way. Johnny sits down beside Billy.

JOHNNY: Me mammy isn't lying at the foot of me stairs at all. It's just I can't stand the company of that boring feck.
BILLY: That wasn't a nice thing to do, Johnnypateen.
JOHNNY: Well you're hardly the world's authority on nice things to do, now, are you, Cripple Billy?
BILLY: I'm not at that, I suppose.
JOHNNY: Ah what harm? Do what you want and feck every-body else is Johnnypateenmichael's motto.
BILLY: Did you hear McSharry talking about my mammy when you were listening at the door?
JOHNNY: A bit of it.
BILLY: Was he accurate about her?

Johnny shruggs.

Oh isn't it always on this subject your lips stay sealed, yet on every subject from feuds o'er geese to ewe-maiming be lonely fellas, your lips go flapping like a cabbage in the breeze?
JOHNNY: Now, on the subject of feuds over geese, have you heard the latest?

Billy sighs.

Well we all thought Jack Ellery and Patty Brennan were apt to go killing each other o'er the slaughter of their cat and their goose, but now d'you know what? A child seen them, just this morning there, kissing the faces off each other in a haybarn. I can't make it out for the life of me. Two fellas kissing, and two fellas who don't even like each other.

BILLY: (*Pause*) You've changed the subject, Johnnypateen.

JOHNNY: I'm great at changing subjects, me. What was the subject? Oh, your drowned mammy and daddy.

BILLY: Were they gets like McSharry says?

JOHNNY: They weren't at all gets.

BILLY: No? And yet they still left me behind when they sailed off.

Eileen returns with mug of tea.

EILEEN: I've the Doctor's tea.

BILLY: The Doctor's gone.

EILEEN: Without having his tea?

BILLY: Evidently.

EILEEN: Don't you be big-wording me again, Billy Claven.

JOHNNY: I'll have the Doctor's tea so, if it'll save a family dispute.

She gives him the tea.

Johnnypateen goes out of his way to help people out, and do you have any biscuits there, Mrs?

BILLY: You're changing the subject again, aren't ya?

JOHNNY: I'm not changing the subject. I want a biscuit.

EILEEN: We have no biscuits.

JOHNNY: I'll bet you have a rake of biscuits. What do you have on the shelf behind them peas, there?

EILEEN: We have more peas.

JOHNNY: You order too many peas. A fella can't go having peas with his tea. Unless he was an odd fella. (*Adjusting lamb*) And there's no way you could describe Johnnypateenmike as an odd fella. Oh no.

BILLY: Johnnypateen. Me mammy and daddy. Their sailing.
EILEEN: Oh that's ancient news, Billy. Just leave it alone . . .
JOHNNY: Sure if the boy wants to hear, let him hear. Isn't
he grown up and travelled enough now to be hearing?
EILEEN: You're not going telling him?

Johnny stares at her a moment.

JOHNNY: It was on the sands I met them that night, staring
off into the black, the water roaring, and I wouldn't've thought
a single thing more of it, if I hadn't seen the sack full of stones
tied to the hands of them there, as they heaved it into the
boat. A big old hemp sack like one of them there, it was.
And they handed you to me then, then started rowing, to
deep water.
BILLY: So they *did* kill themselves o'er me?
JOHNNY: They killed themsevles, aye, but not for the reasons
you think. D'you think it was to get away from ya?
BILLY: Why else, sure?
JOHNNY: Will I tell him?

Eileen nods.

A week before this it was they'd first been told you'd be dying
if they couldn't get you to the Regional Hospital and medicines
down you. But a hundred pounds or near this treatment'd
cost. They didn't have the like of a hundred pounds. I know
you know it was their death insurance paid for the treatment
saved you. I don't know if you know it was the same day I
met them on the sands there that they had taken their insurance policy out.
BILLY: (*Pause*) It was for me they killed themselves?
JOHNNY: The insurance paid up a week after, and you were
given the all-clear afore a month was out.
BILLY: So they *did* love me, in spite of everything.
EILEEN: They did love you *because* of everything, Billy.
JOHNNY: Isn't that news?

BILLY: That is news. I needed good news this day. Thank you, Johnnypateen.

They shake hands and Billy sits.

JOHNNY: You're welcome, Cripple Billy.
BILLY: *Billy.*
JOHNNY: Billy. (*Pause*) Well, I'm off home to me mammy. Hopefully she'll have dropped down dead when the Doctor barged in and we'll both have had good news this day. (*Pause*) Mrs., d'you have any payment there for Johnnypateen's good news and not peas?
EILEEN: There's Yalla-mallows.
JOHNNY: (*Looking at packet*) What are Yalla-mallows?
EILEEN: They're mallows that are yalla.
JOHNNY: (*Pause. After considering*) I'll leave them.

Johnny exits. Long pause.

BILLY: You should have told me before, Aunty.
EILEEN: I wasn't sure how you'd take the news, Billy.
BILLY: You still should've told me. The truth is always less hard than you fear it's going to be.
EILEEN: I'm sorry, Billy.

Pause. Billy lets her cuddle him slightly.

BILLY: And I'm sorry for using *evidently* on ya.
EILEEN: And so you should be.

Eileen gently slaps his face, smiling. Helen enters.

Hello, Helen. What can I get you?
HELEN: No, I've just come to look at Cripple Billy's wounds. I've heard they're deep.
BILLY: Hello, Helen.

HELEN: You look a fecking fool in all that get-up, Cripple Billy.

BILLY: I do, I suppose. Em, Aunty, is that the kettle, now, I hear boiling in the back?

EILEEN: Eh? No. Oh. (*Tuts*) Aye.

Eileen exits to back room, as Helen pulls up Billy's bandages to look under them.

BILLY: Hurts a bit that picking does, Helen.

HELEN: Ar don't be such a fecking girl, Cripple Billy. How was America?

BILLY: Fine, fine.

HELEN: Did you see any girls over there as pretty as me?

BILLY: Not a one.

HELEN: Or almost as pretty as me?

BILLY: Not a one.

HELEN: Or even a hundred times *less* pretty than me?

BILLY: Well, maybe a couple, now.

Helen pokes him hard in the face.

(*In pain*) Aargh! Not a one, I mean.

HELEN: You just watch yourself you, Cripple Billy.

BILLY: Do ya have to be so violent, Helen?

HELEN: I do have to be so violent, or if I'm not to be taken advantage of anyways I have to be so violent.

BILLY: Sure, nobody's taken advantage of you since the age of seven, Helen.

HELEN: Six is nearer the mark. I ruptured a curate at six.

BILLY: So couldn't you tone down a bit of your violence and be more of a sweet girl?

HELEN: I could, you're right there. And the day after I could shove a bent spike up me arse. (*Pause.*) I've just lost me job with the egg-man.

BILLY: Why did you lose your job with the egg-man, Helen?

HELEN: D'you know, I can't for the life of me figure out why.

Maybe it was me lack of punctuality. Or me breaking all the egg-man's eggs. Or me giving him a good kick whenever I felt like it. But you couldn't call them decent reasons.

BILLY: You couldn't at all, sure.

HELEN: Or me spitting on the egg-man's wife, but you couldn't call that a decent reason.

BILLY: What did you spit on the egg-man's wife for, Helen?

HELEN: Ah the egg-man's wife just deserves spitting on. (*Pause*) I still haven't given you a good kick for your taking your place in Hollywood that was rightfully mine. Didn't I have to kiss four of the film directors on Inishmore to book me place you took without a single kiss?

BILLY: But there was only *one* film director on Inishmore that time, Helen. The man Flaherty. And I didn't see you near him at all.

HELEN: Who was it I was kissing so?

BILLY: I think it was mostly stable-boys who could do an American accent.

HELEN: The bastards! Couldn't you've warned me?

BILLY: I was going to warn you, but you seemed to be enjoying yourself.

HELEN: You do get a decent kiss off a stable-boy, is true enough. I would probably go stepping out with a stable-boy if truth be told, if it wasn't for the smell of pig-shite you get off them.

BILLY: Are you not stepping out with anyone at the moment, so?

HELEN: I'm not.

BILLY: (*Pause*) Me, I've never been kissed.

HELEN: Of course you've never been kissed. You're a funny-looking cripple-boy.

BILLY: (*Pause*) It's funny, but when I was in America I tried to think of all the things I'd miss about home if I had to stay in America. Would I miss the scenery, I thought? The stone walls, and the lanes, and the green, and the sea? No, I wouldn't miss them. Would I miss the food? The peas, the praities, the peas, the praities and the peas? No, I wouldn't miss it. Would I miss the people?

HELEN: Is this speech going to go on for more long?

BILLY: I've nearly finished it. (*Pause*) What was me last bit? You've put me off . . .

HELEN: "Would I miss the people."

BILLY: Would I miss the people? Well, I'd miss me aunties, or, a *bit* I'd miss me aunties. I wouldn't miss Babbybobby with his lead stick or Johnnypateen with his daft news. Or all the lads used to laugh at me at school, or all the lasses used to cry if I even spoke to them. Thinking over it, if Inishmaan sank in the sea tomorrow, and everybody on it up and drowned, there isn't especially anybody I'd really miss. Anybody other than you, that is, Helen.

HELEN: (*Pause*) You'd miss the cows you go staring at.

BILLY: Oh that cow business was blown up out of all proportion. What I was trying to build up to, Helen, was . . .

HELEN: Oh, was you trying to build up to something, Cripple Billy?

BILLY: I was, but you keep interrupting me.

HELEN: Build up ahead so.

BILLY: I was trying to build up to . . . There comes a time in every fella's life when he has to take his heart in his hands and make a try for something, and even though knows it's a one in a million chance of him getting it, he has to chance it still, else why be alive at all? So, I was wondering Helen, if maybe sometime, y'know, when you're not too busy or something, if maybe . . . and I know well I'm no great shakes to look at, but I was wondering if maybe you might want go out walking with me some evening. Y'know, in a week or two or something?

HELEN: (*Pause*) Sure what would I want to go out walking with a cripple-boy for? It isn't out walking you'd be anyways, it would be out shuffling, because you can't walk. I'd have to be waiting for ya every five yards. What would you and me want to be out shuffling for?

BILLY: For the company.

HELEN: For the company?

BILLY: And . . .

HELEN: And what?

BILLY: And for the way sweethearts be.

Helen looks at him a second, then slowly and quietly starts laughing/sniggering through her nose, as she gets up and goes to the door. Once there she turns, looks at Billy again, laughs again and exits. Billy is left staring down at the floor as Kate quietly enters from the back room.

KATE: She's not a very nice girl anyways, Billy.

BILLY: Was you listening, Aunty Kate?

KATE: I wasn't listening or alright I was a biteen listening. (*Pause*) You wait for a nice girl to come along, Billy. A girl who doesn't mind at all what you look like. Just sees your heart.

BILLY: How long will I be waiting for a girl like that to come along, Aunty?

KATE: Ah not long at all, Billy. Maybe a year or two. Or at the outside five.

BILLY: Five years . . .

Billy nods, gets up, wheezes slightly and exits into the back room. Kate starts tidying and closing up the shop. Eileen enters, helping her. Sound of Billy coughing distantly in the house now and then.

EILEEN: What's Cripple Billy looking so glum for?

KATE: Billy asked Slippy Helen to go out walking with him, and Helen said she'd rather go out walking with a broken-headed ape.

EILEEN: That was a descriptive turn of phrase for Slippy Helen.

KATE: Well, I've tarted it up a bit.

EILEEN: I was thinking. (*Pause*) Cripple Billy wants to aim lower than Helen.

KATE: Cripple Billy *does* want to aim lower than Helen.

EILEEN: Billy wants to aim at ugly girls who are thick, then work his way up.

KATE: Billy should go to Antrim really. He'd be well away.

(*Pause*) But Billy probably doesn't like ugly girls who are thick.

EILEEN: Sure there's no pleasing Billy.

KATE: None.

EILEEN: (*Pause*) And you missed the story Johnnypateen spun, Kate, about Billy's mam and daddy tying a sack of stones to their hands and drowning themselves for the insurance money that saved him.

KATE: The stories Johnnypateen spins. When it was poor Billy they tied in the sack of stones, and Billy would still be at the bottom of the sea to this day, if it hadn't been for Johnnypateen swimming out to save him. And, stealing his mammy's hundred pounds then to pay for Billy's hospital treatment.

EILEEN: We should tell Billy the true story some day, Kate.

KATE: Sure, that story might only make Cripple Billy sad, or something, Eileen.

EILEEN: Do you think? Ah there's plenty of time to tell Billy that story anyways.

KATE: There is.

The two finish their closing up, Eileen locking the door, Kate turning the oil lamp low.

This'll be the first decent night's sleep in many a month I've had, Eileen.

EILEEN: I know it will, Kate. Have you finished for good with your stone shenanigans now?

KATE: I *have*. They only crop up when I've been worrying, and, you know, I know I hide it well, but I do worry awful about Billy when he's away from us.

EILEEN: I do worry awful about Billy when he's away from us too, but I try not to let stones enter into it.

KATE: Ah let's forget about stones. We have our Billy back with us now.

EILEEN: We *do* have our Billy back with us. Back for good.

KATE: Back for good.

The two smile and exit to the back room, arm-in-arm. After a pause, Billy comes in from the back, sniffling, and turns the oil lamp up, revealing his bloodshot eyes and tear-stained cheeks. He quietly takes the sack down from the wall, places inside it numerous cans of peas until it's very heavy, then ties the cords at the top of the bag tightly around one of his hands. This done, he pauses in thought a moment, then shuffles to the door. There is a knock on it. Billy dries his cheeks, hides the sack behind him and opens the door. Helen pops her head in.

HELEN: (*Forcefully*) Alright so I'll go out walking with ya, but only somewheres no fecker would see us and when it's dark and no kissing or groping, cos I don't want you ruining me fecking reputation.

BILLY: Oh. Okay, Helen.

HELEN: Or anyways not much kissing or groping.

BILLY: Would tomorrow suit?

HELEN: Tomorrow wouldn't at all suit. Isn't it Bartley's fecking birthday tomorrow?

BILLY: Is it? What have you got him?

HELEN: I got him . . . and for the life of me I don't know why I did because I know now he'll never stop fecking jabbering on about it or anyways won't stop jabbering 'til I give him a big thump in the fecking face for himself and even then he probably won't stop, but didn't I get the fecker a telescope?

BILLY: That was awful nice of ya, Helen.

HELEN: I think I must be getting soft in me old age.

BILLY: I think so too.

HELEN: Do ya?

BILLY: Aye.

HELEN: (*Coyly*) Do ya really, Billy?

BILLY: I do.

HELEN: Uh-huh. Does this feel soft?

Helen pokes Billy hard in the bandaged face. Billy yelps in pain.

BILLY: Aargh! No, it doesn't feel soft!

HELEN: Good-oh, I'll see you the day after tomorrow for our fecking walk, so.
BILLY: You will.

Helen kisses Billy briefly, winks at him, and pulls the door behind her as she exits. Billy is left standing there stunned a moment, then remembers the sack tied to his hand. Pause. He unties it, replaces the cans on the shelves and hangs the sack back up on the wall, stroking it a moment. He shuffles over towards the back room, smiling, but stops as he gets there, coughing heavily, his hand to his mouth. After the coughing stops he takes his hand away and looks down at it for a moment. Its covered in blood. Billy loses his smile, turns the oil lamp down and exits to the back room. Fade to black.

Shelley A. Berger

Archaeology of a Photo. 1939. Baranowicz.
The Ghost.

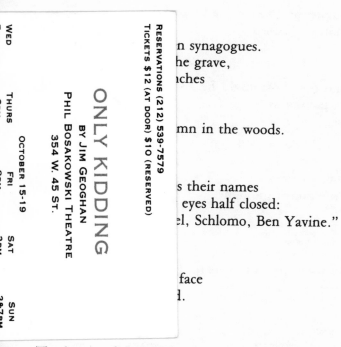

n synagogues.
he grave,
ches

mn in the woods.

s their names
eyes half closed:
l, Schlomo, Ben Yavine."

face
d.

The bones of their sadness
are like X-ray film exposed,
their garments, shrouds.

04-09-87

Over and over I listen to the echoes
in their faces, searching for clues.
The photograph stays in my nightstand drawer,
a fossil, imprinting itself on my sleep.

04-12-89

There are various explanations
for the inked-out face I came to call the ghost.
For example, perhaps a cousin married a goy.
They sat shiva, declared the cousin dead.

02-23-90

Once I thought the ghost was a beautiful girl
my grandmother disliked.

06-07-90

My sister said the ghost might be a stranger
who, out of politeness
was included in the pose.

08-05-91

In my dreams I excavate
the grave, the ghost, the light.

11-29-92

I rub my fingers over the image
of the tombstone, try to feel its roughness.

03-17-93

I learn my great,
great grandmother was blind.

07-30-94

You, Rachel, whose eyes are old,
who cannot see as far
as this new world.
You, Rachel, fall into my eyes at night,
stand quivering, smell death.

Wyatt Townley

The Afterlives of Trees

1

Trees have fallen every which
way, crossing themselves

as we pass. We break
twigs with our boots,

spider webs with brows.
We think we've come for winter

wood, saws in hand. But what
we hear is what the creek postpones,

singing along stones.

2

Our wagon full, we take
the long walk back,

glance up at a bold
checkmark of geese

revising the sunset. Gold
flings itself in our eyes,

the same gold that fills
the fireplace tonight,

warming us twice.

3

Witness the journey of the ant
as it crawls off the log,

passing from fire to snow
and back to earth. Smell

the cedar turning
into sky. No spin

is fixed. Take in
the thought like smoke,

then change into skin.

4

We bind the short
and long of it

to a *t*. Two logs cross
on a grave,

marking time,
our lives squirreled

away. Scribble
on the woods

that wrap the world.

Two Poems by Frederick Tibbetts

The Leopard Who Threatened Dante

Come, the wood is secret
And alive. Day is not yet near.
These are my paths
Through the frost. This is my lair,

Attended by whippoorwills.
This is the stiff spine of
Accidents. Hiddenness,
And the heavy moon tipping.

And the defile
Where I go to the traveller
Sightless and alone.
Where I brighten like a metal.

Behind his breast
The bird that fattens
Terrified, tied by a cord,
I instantly unpin.

Give me this, you who scent me
Singeing near your spotted page.
Before me, the god
Did not know he was stone.

I made the saplings live
Over his forehead.
I made the hungers wake up
In the stops of his ear.

Laertes

Nobody blames you for hurrying
Back to Paris, and missing
Most of what takes place onstage.
When Father sends his servant after,
To report on how you're acting,
We feel sorry for you—and your father,
And for the spy as well, perhaps:
After all it must be tedious.
The arras reverses; the seams and threads
Grow evident. Coming home,
You've been freed into hatred so pure
The whole peninsula looms
Sudden and clear. No longer
To have to listen to those who claim
They know, those who've learned
By playing, until you play fair.
Yet, when it's time, you are
Exactly as pliant as the rest
Of your drowned family, and nobody
Claims you've been overthrown.
On the contrary, useful at last,
Your engine thrums out of
The drab shallows of Act IV
(Impending war with Poland).
The poisoned accidents diminish
To a pinpoint's intention,
Which is yourself. Somehow—
We admit we didn't see it
Being done—our feelings
Are all but spent elsewhere.
And the token we have left is
A fee for passage: you hand it back,
There on the platform.

Two Poems by Tony Sanders

Montaigne

I hate bow ties. Allow me to digress.
Remember that leafy aphorisms
sometimes grow out of idle burbling
and look different when they're not in season.
What Horace calls "bumptious candor" exists
in each crop of an essayist's half-truths.
Imagine me standing in the mirror,
an airplane's idle prop around my neck.
What color should mine be? A red clip-on?
Something to divert the crowd from my eyes
might come in handy when I contradict
myself. Clothing is vocabulary,
the body is nothing more than grammar.
I would wear anything, even breeches.

Late Victorian

The early days subscribed to us,
   first warming to our blandishments,
but we, having practiced praise
   in front of mirrors facing mirrors
and knowing how to give as well as
   to take no for an answer, retreated.

It's not as if we backed out
   of the parlor like a damaged widower
looking mournfully at the baby grand
   now forever silent in the alcove,

it's not as if we took one last look
  at the sober portrait above the mantel.

Of course, we never left the premises,
  only moved to a room with less finery,
where, had we wanted, we could have sat
  and looked out of a dormer and wondered
what we had done to let the starch
  run out of the landscape.

Maybe we never had the stomach
  for the brocade world we created,
or rather, had made in the far east
  and shipped halfway round the world,
so that even on the sunniest of summer days
  we could keep out the light,

though light was what we were,
  at least on the surface, always rising
to the occasion like an infinity
  of miniature champagne bubbles in a flute,
while in our hearts what we wanted to do
  was hurl the glass into the fire.

Two Poems by John Richard Reed

Return to Sender

I've moved to be near you. My new address
is posted daily in the lost and found.
Your silences are far from obvious.

Some find your flight proof of the fickleness
they'd always feared would surface. In the end,
I'm moved to be near you. My new address

unfurls a banner with a strange device—
Dum spiro spero—hope it's deemed profound
as your silences are. Far from obvious,

you hold ten patents on the poker face.
Biding your time, you will not tip your hand.
I've moved to be near you. My new address

is permanent; it's high time to confess
your covert heart. Of course I understand,
but your silences are far from obvious.

Happenstance would have made fools of us,
but I had other plans. Enclosed please find
(I've moved to be near you) my new address.
Your silences are far from obvious.

Beata Beatrix: A Posthumous Portrait of Elizabeth Siddal

Your eyes are closed, your solemn face upraised,
features transfigured in the fading sun.
Your feathers, once so soberly appraised,
were reassessed after the bird had flown.

With no surviving photograph of you,
knowing the artist's tendency to flatter,
we might dismiss the likeness as untrue.
Did he exaggerate? It hardly matters.

Rossetti's portrait of his invalid,
painted to preserve mortal debris,
revealed mere surface, left your essence veiled.
Dante was dazzled, and he failed to see

beyond the lovely butterfly façade
so tempting to the new collector's eye.
A season brief as the ephemerid's
soon spent, you were replaced by someone new.

This crimson poppy dropped into your hands,
this descending dove with blood-red wings:
harbingers of sleep. We understand
that from this sleep there is no wakening.

"An overdose," the coroner averred,
his tone conveying weariness and tact.
"Accidental," was his parting word,
a judgment some of us have found suspect.

Had you come to that moment unprepared?
Through long tuition, you had learned to see
illness and grace as things to be endured,
but endurance is a matter of degree:

Only Rossetti's closest friends might ask
to reproduce the contours of that face.
Your pretty profile suited to the task,
your views were not required, in any case.

You sat as drowned Ophelia to Millais
for hours, uncomplaining, arms outstretched
as if in benediction while you lay
in a tub of tepid water as he sketched.

And now you pose for one exclusively
who compensates for what he lacks in skill
with patience, and he will not let us see
his work in progress, argue how we will.

                    TIMBER
She looks completely sane to me.

                    QUINCY
She's disenfranchised her femininity which will inevitably result in what
I call in Venus Raging "a good girl tragedy."

                    TIMBER
I'm just a dummy in TV News Quincy. I mostly don't understand what the
hell you print folks are talking about.

                    QUINCY
Don't worry about it. This has all been such an intense time for me. ~~I~~
~~need some advice~~ Timber. *How do you do it?* ~~I need some advice~~ *I need some advice Timber*

                    TIMBER
Yes Ma'am.

                    QUINCY
I have an offer to do commentary ~~on a variety show. Mostly women's issues~~ *commentary on a morning show*
but I'd prefer to hold out for something ~~that can't be dismissed as soft.~~ *too soft*
TIME ZONE has expressed an interestin me but the ~~scuttlebutt~~ *buzz* is before Lyssa
Hughes ~~the anchor~~ *this show* wasn't long for this world.

                    TIMBER
Don't go into television Quincy. Stay pure/ *and my agent says I should do it. help my book!*

                    QUINCY
~~Yes but~~ ~~But~~ I'm in a unique position to do both. / I'd really love to talk to you about it
some more. ~~I'm staying in Washington tonight.~~ We could probably both use some
time to unwind.

                    TIMBER
I never unwind. That's "paws up" to me. And I'm strictly a paws down kind
of guy.

                    QUINCY
I'm afraid now I don't understand what you're talking about,

                    TIMBER
I gotta be humble here, Quincy. You deserve someone much more evolved than
I am.
                    (HE walks away and signals for the cameras to be brought in
                    closer.)

A manuscript page from An American Daughter.

Wendy Wasserstein

The Art of Theater XIII

Wendy Wasserstein was born in Brooklyn, New York on October 18, 1950, the youngest of four children. Her mother, an amateur dancer, grew up in Poland, and moved to the United States when her father was suspected of being a spy. Her father was a textile manufacturer. When she was eleven, the family moved to the Upper East Side of Manhattan, where she attended a series of young women's schools before enrolling in Mount Holyoke College.

Wasserstein received her BA from Mount Holyoke in 1971 and earned her MA from New York's City University in 1973, where she studied creative writing with Israel Horovitz and Joseph Heller. The same year saw Wasserstein's first professional production: her play Any Woman Can't *was presented by Playwrights Horizons, a small off-Broadway theater that has played a large role in her career. But it was at the Yale School of Drama, in which she enrolled the next year, that Wasserstein found her metier as a playwright. She was the lone woman among a dozen men studying playwriting — a "kind of bizarre macho class," her classmate and friend Christopher Durang remembers it. "There were an awful lot of would-be Sam Shepards, and Wendy felt a little left out." At the first reading of her play* Uncommon Women and Others *a male classmate complained, "I just can't get into this." The play was later filmed as part of PBS's "Theatre in America" series.*

After receiving her MFA from Yale in 1976, Wasserstein returned to New York, where she has lived ever since. During the next several years, her plays were produced in various off-Broadway theaters. Her eighth play, The Heidi Chronicles, *was produced off Broadway by Playwrights Horizons; in 1989, within weeks of moving to Broadway, the play won both the Pulitzer Prize and the Tony Award for best play. Her next play, produced in 1992 was* The Sisters Rosensweig. *Wasserstein has also written a collection of essays,* Bachelor Girls; *a children's book,* Pamela's First Musical; *and several screenplays, although she considers these things that happen while she is "waiting for the next play."*

Soon after The Sisters Rosensweig *opened on Broadway, we met in the breakfast room of Wasserstein's apartment overlooking Central Park in New York City. "I don't use it much; I'm not good enough," she laughed. A second interview was conducted this spring, during rehearsals for her latest play,* An American Daughter.

INTERVIEWER
What do your sisters think of *The Sisters Rosensweig*?

WENDY WASSERSTEIN

I didn't show anyone in my family the play. The problem with writing plays is that everyone has an opinion. And you don't want those opinions. You want people to say I love you no matter what. I'm a forty-two-year-old woman. What would my mother say: "Oh, it's nice Wendy, and I notice the mother is dead"? I really didn't want any of them to see it until the opening, but my sister Sandy kept saying she wanted to come, so finally I said, "You can come but you can't call me tomorrow and make any comments, because if you call me and don't say anything, I'll know you think it's bad. So no comment, either way." She saw it and sent me flowers the next day. They came with a note that said, "No Commitment." I realized that either the florist had made this Freudian slip or he was the florist to some Upper West Side bachelor who regularly sends out "No Commitment" flowers.

But my mother is indefatigable. I hear her talking to my nieces and saying things like, "You want to marry young. You know, you don't want to grow old like Wendy." She's fascinating. She is not a schooled person—my grandfather wrote plays and was the head of a school district in Poland, but my mother went to high school in New Jersey and then stopped. But she is deeply funny and, for someone who has not read, verbal and witty and an original thinker. She never cooked and she took great pride in having no skills at all. She had four children and then my two cousins came to live with us. And she danced. By the time I got to high school she was going to dancing lessons. That woman is over eighty and she's still dancing. Her name is Lola, and when she walks down the street, chorus boys stop her to say hello. She wears leather! She's older now and so looks more like a grandmother, but if you had hit her when I was in college—she was a number. She's from that generation of mothers who had intelligence and creativity and no place to put that except into family. If the circumstances were different, I'm sure she would have been a dancer or set designer. She thinks she's marvelous in every way. If you said, "Wendy is so talented," she'd say, "Of course, she's my daughter." My love of the theater comes from her.

My dad doesn't talk very much. He's very gentle and sweet, and my suspicion is that he's extremely bright and reflective. He invented the process that put wires into ribbons, which I guess is a little like being a furrier. They are really a yin and yang, those two.

Did you have fun growing up?

I did because my mother was eccentric. In Brooklyn, a lot of mothers really did play mah-jongg and have their hair done. My mother looked like Bertolt Brecht when I was growing up. She had extremely short hair. She'd say to the hairdresser on Kings Highway, "You know how I like it, so it looks like you made a mistake." When I went to yeshiva, the rabbi's daughter would come to dinner and my mother would give us hamburgers and string beans with butter sauce. You're not supposed to have milk with meat, and she'd lie and say it was lemon juice.

Also, being so close to my brother was fun; we went exploring a lot. My sister Sandy got married when I was six. She was nineteen. My aunt Kiki fell through the floor at her wedding. She was dancing and fell through, which I thought was fabulous. Sandy eventually got divorced and went to live in England for eight years. She came back, and one day my mother had her pick me up from the June Taylor School of Dance. So there I was, a yeshiva girl, going to dance school on Saturdays; my mother had me lying to the rabbi about that. Between the lemon juice and the lying to the rabbi— I'm going straight to hell. Anyway, she told Sandy to take me to Howard Johnson's and Radio City. So Sandy took me to the House of Chen where we had shrimp dishes—and I knew your lips fall off from the shrimp but I was too scared to tell her I can't eat this. And then, instead of going to Radio City, she took me to see *Expresso Bongo*, which was one of those English art movies. I remember a scene where the girl was wearing kilts with suspenders and no top. And then Sandy made me lie about it all to my mother.

When I was in second grade, I made up a play that I was in; I told my mother that I was in this play and the lie got larger and larger. Finally, arbitrarily, I said my play is on tomorrow, and she got me a velvet dress and made my hair in ringlets, and off I went to school. And she came to school and there was no play. She covered for me and said, "I must be confused; it must be another one of my children." Then she came home and told me I was a fibber. She must have yelled at me because to this day I have trouble with fibbing.

INTERVIEWER

Would you call *The Sisters Rosensweig* your first well-made play?

WASSERSTEIN

Yes, in terms of structure. When I see the play, I feel I'm seeing a Broadway play in 1958, or what I wish those plays had been. I remember going to them and thinking, I really like this but where are the girls? *The Sisters Rosensweig* is like those plays—the curtain goes up and there's one set, and the play is well-made, you know, beginning, middle and end. It takes place over a weekend, the stars get applause, the stars get exit applause, they each tell their stories, it arcs in the second act, all of that. It was much harder to write than any of my other plays.

INTERVIEWER

Did your other plays prepare you for it?

WASSERSTEIN

In a way. *The Sisters Rosensweig* seems a combination of *Isn't It Romantic* and *Uncommon Women*. But those other plays are episodic, and this was a deliberate decision not to be episodic. Also, I decided not to write another play about my generation. Even though it has autobiographical materials, the focus of the play is not me. I wanted to do all those things and also evoke a fondness for plays that I love, including Chekhov. On the day I finished it I thought, This was a lot of effort just to prove to myself what a good writer Chekhov is.

INTERVIEWER

You sound as if you didn't get emotionally involved.

WASSERSTEIN

Ending *The Sisters Rosensweig* was hard, and when I finish plays I tend to get emotional and weepy. I remember the day I finished it I got weepy and then I realized it wasn't right. When we were doing the workshop in Seattle, I got weepy again and I realized it still wasn't right and I thought, How many times am I going to get weepy? Today in a taxi ride I was thinking that I would like to fix the speeches between Sara and Merv in the last scene. In the first draft, Sara sang for Merv. Then Merv sang "For Me and My Gal" in return. I was thinking, They slept together once and they're singing and running off together? What kind of play is this?

INTERVIEWER

When Sara does sing for herself—that song about Moishe Pupick, about being the only Yiddish girl in MacNamara's Band—it's an amazing moment. Jewish audiences respond to Sara's need to assimilate and her need not to. For a larger audience the moment is about identity and reconnecting with yourself after being lost for some time. When Sara first starts to sing those lyrics, the audience laughs because she's singing Yiddish words. But it's actually a deeply serious moment.

WASSERSTEIN

This play is thought of as a comedy, which is great, but to me this is a very serious play, and what you touched on in that moment is almost tonality, the heart of the play.

INTERVIEWER

One of the most moving moments in the play is when Gorgeous receives a real Chanel suit as a gift. Why is that so moving?

WASSERSTEIN

I think it comes from when I was in high school and I first realized there were people who wore real Papagallo shoes and then there were people who wore imitation Papagallo shoes from Chandlers. So I became very interested in this idea of what was real and what was imitation and what it felt like to wear the imitation and finally get the real.

INTERVIEWER

The Chanel suit touches on something that isn't seemly to speak of, which is that material things can give you almost a spiritual sense of happiness. It's almost like being loved in a way because it makes you feel safe and secure and beautiful or whatever, and that's something that very few people write about.

WASSERSTEIN

It was odd — we hired a rabbi as the religious advisor on the play, Rabbi Shnier, whom I kept calling Rabbi Schnorrer. We did this because Madeline didn't want to light the Sabbath candles unless she was doing it right. She didn't want to be offensive. A friend of mine was dating a rabbi, so I went to speak at his temple. We were talking about Jewish women and self-image, and I said that I never thought of myself as undesirable or unattractive, frankly, until I turned twelve and began watching these movies in which none of the men ever fell in love with anybody who looked remotely like me. No one was ever Jewish, no one was hardly ever brunette. I never thought of that before, but in retrospect it really makes me angry. Maybe that will change now. Just like when I was growing up and there were no smart girls in plays. Or if they were smart, were sort of these really mean career people.

You know what's interesting? *The Sisters Rosensweig* is a play that men like. Mort Zuckerman came up to me and said, "I love your play," and I looked at him and I said, "You do?"

INTERVIEWER

I notice that you use the word *girl* a lot.

WASSERSTEIN

I've been called on the table for years on that. I call myself
a Jewish girl. Maybe it's because you can't correct semantically
who in your heart you know you are. But in the last five years
feminism has opened up to humor. Women who are a bit
older can believe in something and also see it ironically. And
younger women, who once thought that to be a feminist you
had to be anti-marriage, have no sense of humor and have
hairy legs, are changing. When I saw Marilyn Quayle speak
at the convention in 1992, I thought, Everything I do is anath-
ema to this woman. She thinks I will rot and boil in hell. But
I think of her exactly what she thinks of me: poor woman.

Feminism has affected me more in my writing than in a
specifically political way. Sitting down to write a play that has
three parts for women over forty, I think, is political.

INTERVIEWER

Do you feel you are doing something important by making
images of older, complete women?

WASSERSTEIN

I do in a way. When Gorgeous returns the Chanel suit she
is in some way heroic. For a woman to be heroic she doesn't
have to save the planet. My work is often thought of as light-
weight commercial comedy, and I have always thought, No,
you don't understand: this is in fact a political act. *The Sisters
Rosensweig* had the largest advance in Broadway history, therefore nobody is going to turn down a play on Broadway because
a woman wrote it or because it's about women.

INTERVIEWER

How has the theater changed since you started out?

WASSERSTEIN

It's interesting that the two most successful straight plays
the year *Sisters Rosensweig* came out were mine and Tony
Kushner's *Angels in America* — a play about three women over

forty and an epic about a gay fantasia. Even five years before, that wouldn't have happened.

INTERVIEWER

In conversation you sometimes are angrier and more provocative than you seem in your plays.

WASSERSTEIN

My plays are my art and not just self-revelation. Creating a well-made play means you have to round the edges so they fit into the form. Also, the plays are deliberately comedic. Humor masks a lot of anger, and it's a means of breaking up others' pretenses and of not being pretentious yourself.

INTERVIEWER

You started out in the early seventies at Playwrights Horizons with Christopher Durang, Bill Finn and all those other people. What do you remember about the early days?

WASSERSTEIN

When I was at Yale, I sent a play called *Montpelier Pizz-zazz* to Playwrights Horizons, about a week after they moved to Forty-second Street. Upstairs was still the Sex Institute of Technology. Downstairs it smelled of urine, and there were pictures of the dancers on the walls. It was not a glamour spot. That's where I met André Bishop. I sent *Uncommon Women* to Playwrights Horizons, and they did a reading of it and wanted to do it. But I eventually gave it to the Phoenix Theatre instead. I thought it would get a better production and better exposure. It was because of losing that play that André decided he would turn Playwrights into the kind of theater no playwright would turn down.

INTERVIEWER

How did Playwrights attract so much raw talent when it was new?

WASSERSTEIN

It mostly had to do with André Bishop. What André managed to do was diminish the sense of competition — we all
thought this was our theater. I don't know if any other theater
has been able to accomplish that, maybe the Manhattan Theatre Club with Terrence McNally and Donald Margulies, but
it's not quite the same. I don't know whether it was because
a lot of us had gone to school together — Christopher Durang,
Alfred Uhry and Ted Tally, who writes screenplays and won
an Oscar for *Silence of the Lambs* — or because André was so
gentle and sweet. It was also cockamamy because it was on
Forty-second Street between Ninth and Tenth. When we did
the first reading of *Uncommon Women*, my dad, when he
left the theater, gave André a fifty-dollar bill and said, "Take
care of yourself, son." He could not understand why this nice
boy from Harvard was next to a massage parlor.

A set-design sketch by Thomas Lynch for The Heidi Chronicles.

INTERVIEWER

Did you have an immediate rapport with Christopher
Durang?

WASSERSTEIN

What Peter Patrone says in *The Heidi Chronicles* Christopher said to me: "You look so bored, you must be very bright." I remember in a class at Yale, E.L. Doctorow said that he was very sad because a girl at Sarah Lawrence had committed suicide. Christopher asked, "Was it for credit?" Alfred found it offensive, but I just started laughing, and I thought, This guy is great! I've never met anyone like him.

The thing about this whole group of people was that no one said, "I've got to win the Pulitzer by the time I'm thirty." That was never what it was about. It was almost like they were too eccentric, and still are, I think. They were not a slick group; they didn't go to the right parties or work a room or anything like that. But these are the people I feel aesthetically close to, as some sort of gauge of myself.

INTERVIEWER

It was André who brought you all together?

WASSERSTEIN

Well, he gave us a place where we could hear our plays read. My first play was read at Playwrights before I even went to Yale. *Any Woman Can't*.

INTERVIEWER

I've never seen it.

WASSERSTEIN

And you never will. It's an awful play. I wrote it when I took Israel Horovitz's playwriting course up at City College. My mother was walking down the street and she ran into the receptionist from the June Taylor School of Dance, where I went as a child. The receptionist asked, "How's Wendy?" My mother said, "Well, I don't know. She's not going to law school, she's not dating a lawyer; now she's writing plays. She's cuckoo." The receptionist said, "Give me Wendy's play because I work across the hall from a new theater called Play-

wrights Horizons." So my mother gave her *Any Woman Can't*.
Bob Moss was running the theater, and they did a reading.

INTERVIEWER

You're all funny and you all tend to write rather episodically.
Durang had more acts in a play than anyone had ever seen
and Bill Finn wrote musical vignettes that came together as
a whole in the end.

WASSERSTEIN

I think we were the next generation after Terrence McNally,
Lanford Wilson and John Guare, who were all breaking form
too, from Edward Albee and Arthur Miller. I guess someone
could say we were the first generation who grew up watching
television and also going to the theater.

INTERVIEWER

While the previous generation only went to the theater.

WASSERSTEIN

That's right. The next generation will go to the theater even
less. So the episodic writing was something that came to me.
I thought writing a full-length play was something I didn't
want to do and didn't know how to do. It seemed old fogyish.
But I was on a committee to evaluate the Yale School of
Drama, and there was this young woman, a directing student,
who told me that what she wanted to do was explode text. I
thought of Miss Julie exploding over the Yale School of Drama
saying, "There goes *The Sea Gull!*" I thought, Well before
you explode it you should know how to do it. I thought, I
would just like to try to do this. If in fact playwriting is like
stained glass, if it becomes more and more this obscure craft,
then it would be interesting to know how to do that craft.

INTERVIEWER

Did you learn by going?

WASSERSTEIN

Yes. When you write in an episodic mode, you know that the scene will be over. The hardest part, what's really boring, is getting people on and off the stage. You can't just bring the lights down and bring them up again. Someone has to say, "I'm leaving now."

INTERVIEWER

And there's got to be a good reason for it too. Not, "Oh, there's the phone!"

WASSERSTEIN

Exactly. That's very hard to do. I always think structurally. But for *The Sisters Rosensweig* it was very hard going. In that play there are four scenes in the first act and three in the second. I should have combined the first two scenes.

INTERVIEWER

You expressed some dissatisfaction about the end of the play. You didn't want to end with Merv and Sara singing to each other. Did that feel wrong to you?

WASSERSTEIN

I did do it originally, and it was great when Merv sang "For Me and My Gal." But suddenly this play became Mervin the Magician, this man who came into these three sisters' lives and turned the place upside down. It made the play smaller, instead of larger.

INTERVIEWER

Because it narrowed the question of whom the play was about or who got what?

WASSERSTEIN

Yes, because it was about getting a guy. For Sara, Mervin is an agent of change. But he's not the answer.

INTERVIEWER

Do you ever see actors when you write?

WASSERSTEIN

Sometimes, but they never end up doing the play. You think Julie Andrews, or people you don't even know.

INTERVIEWER

You once said that you look forward to writing because you can't wait to leave yourself.

WASSERSTEIN

Well, I was very sad when *The Sisters Rosensweig* opened the first time. People like Merv and Gorgeous are fun to write; they're nice to have in your apartment. They're really good company. So when you discover those people, *they're* talking and you're not talking anymore. I remember the day I wrote the line for Gorgeous about Benjamin Disraeli being a Jewish philanthropist: I started laughing because I thought, That's Gorgeous, there you go. The character, not my sister. If you stay with the actual people in your real life, it won't work. It's too constraining.

INTERVIEWER

What about when you are developing a character similar to yourself? Do you write what you know about yourself or do you find out things about yourself while you're writing the character?

WASSERSTEIN

It's closer to writing yourself as if you were these other people. I think the voice of the author in this play is in Geoffrey's speech to Pfeni about making the best art and the best theater. That's me, Wendy, the writer speaking, and it's interesting that I put the words into the mouth of a bisexual British man.

INTERVIEWER

Can you explain that?

WASSERSTEIN

I think because in some ways it's less inhibiting. But you're always writing different aspects of yourself into different characters. You are never writing yourself. There are aspects of me in Pfeni—the distancing aspect, the vulnerability and the need to wander. And the ability to get involved with a bisexual. Hey—when's the mixer? There are aspects of me in Sara, too. I am a Jewish girl who's been in these Waspy institutions all my life. Ed Kliban used to say that what was interesting about me was that the family moved very quickly from being middle-class Brooklyn to upper-middle-class Upper East Side and all the pretentions of it.

INTERVIEWER

Do you tend to write about what you know?

WASSERSTEIN

I think yes. I learn things from watching and listening to people. I'm not much of a reader; I'm slightly dyslexic. Take Merv—he is someone I knew when I was eight years old. I don't run into a whole lot of Mervs right now. Nor do I run into a lot of the Gorgeouses of life. But I remember these colorful people and their language. I remember going to someone's bar mitzvah in Brooklyn with my mother and young niece. And you know when they take the Torah out? My mother said to Samantha, "Quick, kiss the Torah before the Rabbi takes it out for cookies and lunch." It was such a crazy image to me.

INTERVIEWER

It sounds like a dream.

WASSERSTEIN

It was like a dream or a Philip Roth short story. But I always have this terrible memory for what people said. You always remember what someone said yesterday, so you hold them accountable—maybe that's why I tend to write about people I know.

INTERVIEWER

Where do you write?

WASSERSTEIN

I used to write in a garage out in Bridgehampton that was literally a UPS drop-off. My brother lived on fifty acres on the water, and I wrote in this place with a garage underneath, two rooms upstairs and just a little typewriter. I wrote there in the summers. I also write in this little typing room at the Society Library on Seventy-ninth Street. A friend gave me an office at Comedy Central, on Fifty-seventh and Broadway, but the problem there is that a telephone is there, and I get on the phone a lot. But when I'm alone in one of these small rooms and I'm working—if I'm in the middle of something, of a play—it's fun. That's kind of nice. I don't feel this way if I'm in the middle of something that I don't really want to be writing. That's less fun.

INTERVIEWER

You use a typewriter?

WASSERSTEIN

I've always used a typewriter or, because I go to libraries, I write longhand in a notebook. Spiral-bound, on the sides. I tend to write longhand, and then I'll start typing it on an IBM. I'll type it myself. This is why it takes me too long to write a play. Finally, I'll get it to a typist or to various young assistants, young playwrights or whomever, who type it up for me afterwards.

INTERVIEWER

Do your plays start with an image?

WASSERSTEIN

My plays start with a feeling. *The Sisters Rosensweig* started when I was living in London writing *The Heidi Chronicles*. I thought about Americans abroad, and somebody said to me,

"You're terribly Jewish, just like my brother-in-law." It was that same feeling I had at Mount Holyoke, a little bit uncomfortable with myself. Like wherever I went I was always wearing a tiara with chinchilla.

INTERVIEWER

What were you doing in London?

WASSERSTEIN

I was there on a grant from the British-American Arts Association. It was for mid-career stimulation. I loved that grant. I lived in this one room at the Nell Gwyn house. I am better in one room with a hot plate. I'm not really good at working in fancy places or in places that you're supposed to write in, like your study. I don't think I'd ever write in a room that was lined with lovely curtains.

INTERVIEWER

Why is that? Does it strike you as pretentious?

WASSERSTEIN

Or maybe too perfect. Maybe writing reminds me of school. Also, I want to shut out the other things from my life.

INTERVIEWER

So you were in London writing *Heidi*, and *The Sisters Rosensweig* was germinating?

WASSERSTEIN

The play had been germinating since the night I got this message to call my brother's secretary in New York to set up dinner with him in London that night. Here I was on a four-thousand-dollar grant from these good socialist girls. Now maybe that doesn't sound too odd, but at the time it sounded nuts. So I called Bruce—he was turning forty at the time—and we had dinner in London. It was the night of Thatcher's election: he was going to Annabel's to celebrate while my friends were having a wake somewhere. So that started me thinking about Americans in London.

INTERVIEWER

What about the genesis of *An American Daughter*?

WASSERSTEIN

I always think of new plays when I'm finishing one. I was finishing *The Sisters Rosensweig*, and was prompted by Nannygate — by what happened to Zoë Baird, what happened to Lani Guinier, what is happening to Hillary Clinton. It was also a reaction to turning forty-two — to midlife decisions, to not having children. It was both personal and political. This is a darker play than *The Sisters Rosensweig*. My plays tend to skip a generation; this one is closer to *The Heidi Chronicles,* though it is also darker than that play.

INTERVIEWER

An American Daughter seems to be your most overtly political play. Does that come partly out of your several White House invitations in the past few years?

WASSERSTEIN

It comes from going to plays, from being on panels, from being involved with arts funding. It also comes from the assumption that artists are always liberal, and that the politics of the theater are never surprising. I thought it was time to look inward. To use the theater to do that. And yes, I've been to the White House.

INTERVIEWER

Do you think that artists are unlike other people, with different needs?

WASSERSTEIN

Well, I don't know. There is something about the happiness I feel in that garage when Merv and Gorgeous are talking to me. Sitting in the garage in a nightgown with a typewriter—it might be the only time I'm calm. It's an ageless sort of happiness. It's what made me happy when I was twenty-seven and writing *Uncommon Women*, and what made me feel happy last summer. I'm a pretty nervous gal. So there is always the anxiety of writing, which is awful, but at those moments I do feel at one.

INTERVIEWER

Can you compare the feeling of writing alone in the library to the moment when the production begins and you're suddenly surrounded by people with very intense deadlines . . .

WASSERSTEIN

It's exhausting. You have to get dressed and show up. And behave yourself. You can't eat all the food on the plate because there are other people there too. But it's the best part of doing plays, if the actors are asking intelligent questions, and someone like Robert Klein is telling you how good your play is. The other difference for me is Dan Sullivan, the director, who is one of those rare creatures with a wonderful analytical and theatrical mind. That's why I go to every rehearsal. I'm not gifted visually; I can only fix my plays by hearing them. Dan will turn to me and say, "This line doesn't work," and I'll rewrite it while I'm there. So I am always on my feet.

INTERVIEWER

What stage will a play be in before you show it to someone else?

WASSERSTEIN

I always finish a draft before I show it to anybody. I'll rewrite a scene thirty-seven times before I show it to anyone. Maybe it's from insecurity. I enjoy the process of polishing until finally I set a deadline and meet it. I finished both *Heidi* and *The Rosensweigs* by my birthday. On my birthday I said to myself, "I will put this in the mail to Dan Sullivan today; I'm so sick of it."

INTERVIEWER
Where were you when you heard you won the Pulitzer Prize?

WASSERSTEIN

I was home in my nightgown writing an essay about my mother that is in *Bachelor Girls*. I had heard a rumor that David Hwang was going to win it for *M. Butterfly*. I'd never been someone who won prizes. Perhaps I wasn't pretentious enough or academic enough. I never thought of myself as an intellectual or good at school. So I just assumed I wouldn't win, which would be fine. I was home, and Mark Thibodeux, the press agent for *The Heidi Chronicles*, called up and said, "You won the Pulitzer." I said, "That's not funny." He said, "No, no, I'm serious. You won the Pulitzer Prize." I kept saying, "You're the Queen of Romania, Mark, don't do this to me." He told me to call my mother, so I did, because I thought, This woman's going to hear my name on the radio and think I died or something. I called her. She asked me, "Is that as good as a Tony?" I thought, That's my mother, undermine it, don't say congratulations, just pull the rug out from under me. I wasn't in the mood, so I said, "Why don't you just call my brother and he'll explain it to you." Then the phone started ringing off the hook, it was like the phone went up and started spinning around the room. I went out that afternoon and had champagne at the Four Seasons with my brother Bruce and sister Sandra and Walter Shapiro and André Bishop. Then I went to the theater. Edward Albee was there. He told me to go on stage and take a bow. I said I was too shy. He said that I never knew when it was going to happen again. So I did it.

INTERVIEWER

Did winning the Pulitzer mean more than winning the Tony?

WASSERSTEIN

It's hard to say, because they're different. Winning the Pulitzer was never a goal of mine but it meant a great deal to me in terms of self-esteem. Getting the Tony was quite different because I knew that for the sake of the play and its commercial life that it was very important. I remember sitting in the audience with André Bishop thinking, Should I go up with the scarf, without the scarf? When I went up, there were so many men standing behind me, I wanted to say, "So many men, so little time." I just couldn't do it because I was the first woman to win the Tony for best play alone, and I felt the need to dignify the occasion in some way. Because what's hard about being a playwright is, as Christopher Durang would say, it's all so random — getting your play done, how it's going to be reviewed . . .

INTERVIEWER

Is it any more random than other commercial art?

WASSERSTEIN

If you want to write for television, for instance, there is a supply and demand: you can make a living. Even if you're commissioned to write a play, you are not going to get paid in the same way.

INTERVIEWER

Does that make the motives of playwrights purer?

WASSERSTEIN

In a sense. It also depends on how you think, whether you think in terms of plays. I am most interested in how people talk. If I went to a movie studio and said I wanted to do a movie about three sisters over forty with a romantic lead who is fifty-four, they'd ask me to rewrite it for Geena Davis, and then they'd probably hire Beth Henley to make them all southern. In film the voice gets taken out of it unless you're the director.

INTERVIEWER

Are you saying that screenwriters are less writers than playwrights?

WASSERSTEIN

No, it's just a different craft; most screenwriters I know
would like to be directors so that they could have some sort
of control.

INTERVIEWER

Many writers detest the public life brought on by success,
the awards, the speeches. I get the feeling that you enjoy it.
Do you think of it as a reward for all the time you spend
alone?

WASSERSTEIN

There is a part of me that thinks that playwrights deserve
as much recognition as novelists or screenwriters. I also know
that if you want people to come to your plays, it helps to go
on David Letterman's show. One creates a persona. I'm actually
a shy person. Michael Kinsley is also a shy person, and there
he is on TV every night. I was talking to him about this, that
fame is not about getting a restaurant reservation. It's about
walking up Madison Avenue on the way to your therapist,
and you're thinking, My God, I'm worthless, what am I doing
with my life, I'm horrible. . . . Then some woman comes up
to you and says, "You're Wendy Wasserstein. I can't tell you
how much you mean to me." I want to say to this person,
"I'm glad I mean something to you because I mean nothing
to me. Thank you very much." Then I think, What is wrong
with me?

I like to think that those are the people who I write for—
the matinee ladies at *The Sisters Rosensweig*. I guess it is
something of a release from being alone and working. It's odd
for me to have chosen this profession because I'm not very
good at being alone and I'm not very good at sitting still. But
at the same time, I find my work very comforting.

INTERVIEWER

You are known for being nice. Can a woman afford to be
too nice?

WASSERSTEIN

I have a great interest in being ladylike, but there is also something to be said for being direct. What I hate about myself and would like to change is that I get hurt very easily. I'm too vulnerable and always have been. I don't look vulnerable. I always think vulnerable girls should have Pre-Raphaelite hair, weigh two pounds, about whom everybody says, "Oh, she's so sensitive." I admire aggressiveness in women. I try to be accommodating and entertaining, and some say that's what's wrong with my plays. But I think there are very good things about being a woman that have not been taught to men — not bullshit manners but true graciousness. I think there is real anger in life to be expressed, there is great injustice, but I also think there is dignity. That is interesting, and part of the plays I want to write.

INTERVIEWER

Did you always know you were a playwright?

WASSERSTEIN

I always loved the theater, but it would have been odd to proclaim it as my vocation. I did, however, play with my Ginny doll and imagine plays for my dolls. I thought I'd be a lawyer and get married and not practice. I find it interesting how affected one is by the time in which one comes of age. I'm sure if I had gone to Mount Holyoke in 1955 I would have gotten married my sophomore year because that's what everybody did. I think of Hillary Clinton as being of that generation as well. When I went to college there was a saying: Holyoke to wed and Smith to bed. So my mother sent me to Mount Holyoke. I grew up reading the Arts and Leisure section, thinking that I would be like Celeste Holm in *All About Eve* and that it would be the husband who was the playwright and I would be the well-educated person who loved the theater. In those four years all of that changed — a transitional generation. The fact that I am the playwright has to do with that time.

INTERVIEWER
Was there any anti-Semitism at Mount Holyoke?

WASSERSTEIN
I do remember one girl at Mount Holyoke did not want
me to come to her house over vacation because her father didn't
particularly like Jews. They lived in Newton, Massachusetts. I
came from Brooklyn, where everybody was Jewish or black or
they were parochial-school kids, but I didn't know them.
When we moved to the Upper East Side, there were people
who weren't Jewish, who went to Trinity and those fancy
schools, but I didn't know them. Mount Holyoke was the first
time I was ever in a house with a Christmas tree. So you did
have a sense that you were Jewish and everybody else wasn't —
that you were an outsider. While this could be alienating, it
affected me for the better, I think; it made me feel I did not
need to be anyone else. My close friends there were largely
Catholic. I had one Jewish friend there from New Jersey who
became a Marxist-Leninist gynecologist. How could you not
love such a person? Those are the sorts of people you're supposed to meet in college.

INTERVIEWER
Who are the playwrights you most admire?

WASSERSTEIN
Chekhov, Ibsen, Wilde, Shakespeare, Chris Durang, Lanford Wilson, August Wilson, Tina Howe. I also have admiration for the women who write musicals — Betty Comden, Car-
olyn Leigh.

INTERVIEWER
One last question: Did you ever sit through a play of yours
with your mother?

WASSERSTEIN
You mean sitting beside her? God no!

—Laurie Winer

A Remembrance of
Samuel Beckett

Israel Horovitz

Mr. Beckett is dead. So, then, is Paris, too. I'm told that he died last Friday night. So, then, all of my heroes are dead, since last Friday night.

Life clung to Samuel Beckett, irritatingly, for 83 and 3/4 years. When he told me he'd lost his teeth, I mumbled an inanity: "It could be worse."

Without pause, he struck back: "There's nothing so bad that it can't grow worse. There's no limit to how bad things can be!" And we laughed ourselves sick.

Mr. Beckett knew his way around a dirty joke. When he first met my wife, Gill, he ordered a double whiskey. "I need a stiff drink. Nothing else is stiff, these days!"

In the early 1970s, I was staying in Paris, with my friend Jean-Paul Delamotte, a *romancier manqué*. Lindon (in the magazine *Minuit*) had just brought out Beckett's newest texts, in French, called *Foirade*, *Foirade I*, *Foirade II*. As I was having a drink with Beckett later that night, I asked Jean-Paul what the word *foirade* meant, exactly.

Jean-Paul hemmed and hawed, uncharacteristically. "Foirade is actually a bit, uh, well, *disgusting*."

When I reported this to Beckett, he playacted massive outrage: "*Disgusting*?! That is just ridiculous!" The setting: we were sitting together at La Closerie des Lilas, a restaurant that had been a sort of literary hangout in the 1930s. In the days before he underwent cataract surgery, Beckett wore eyeglasses as thick as Coke bottles. He was all earthbound hawk, instantly recognizable, unmistakenly the great Samuel Beckett. As soon as we entered the restaurant, he was recognized by all. Whenever he talked, all eaters stayed their forks and listened intently. Beckett, very nearly blind, was oblivious to all eavesdropping.

He explained his reaction to Jean-Paul's "disgusting" by pointing out he had certainly ". . . chosen *foirade* carefully . . ." and that he was presently at work "searching for the perfect English equivalent" to it.

"*Foirade*: disgusting? Utter nonsense! *Une foirade* is a lamentable failure . . . something one attempts that is destined to fail, but must be attempted, nonetheless, because it is unquestionably worth the effort . . . thus, a *lamentable failure*."

At this point, it seemed that every eater in the entire restaurant was leaning in toward us, paying rapt attention to Beckett's every word. And Beckett added, with the very slightest of smiles, "Of course, *foirade* also means wet fart!"

And all around us, like the heroes of fine Keats odes, who leave the earth for extraordinary experience and return changed, the eavesdropping diners of the Closerie des Lilas returned to their dinners . . . suddenly, abruptly, absolutely *changed*.

Postscript: months later, in a New York bookshop, I came across the Grove Press edition of *Foirades*. Beckett's English-language title: *Fizzles*.

Midwinter, mid-1973. I was cold, lonely and alarmingly low on cash. I was scheduled to do a poetry reading at eight in the evening, at the Centre Culturel Americain on the rue du Dragon . . . for fifty dollars. I was having a drink with

Beckett at seven. I hadn't invited him to my reading because:

1) I thought he wouldn't approve of my doing a public reading, even for much-needed money.

2) He rarely went to public gatherings.

During our conversation, he seemed distracted. Out of nowhere, he said: "You're doing a reading of your poems, are you?" I was startled that he knew. And then he added, "Many friends expected?"

I'd obviously hurt his feelings by not inviting him. And so I did. He said, "No, thank you, I never go to those things!"

But then he asked me to recite one of my poems for him. Embarrassed, I told him that my being paid fifty dollars for the reading was definitely a fair price. He laughed but nonetheless insisted on a private recitation. (A few years later, in Hyde Park, he would insist that I run in a huge circle around him so that he could analyze my stride!) And so I recited a four-liner entitled "On Boulevard Raspail":

How easily our only smile smiles.
We will never agree or disagree.
The pretty girl is perfected in her passing.
Our love lives within the space of a quietly closing door.

He listened with closed eyes. "Very nice," he said.

"Oh, shit!" I said, suddenly. He opened his eyes, and I explained myself. "I stole that from you!"

"No, no. I've never heard that in my life . . ."

"No, no, I did! Your poem 'Dieppe' . . . you end it with 'the space of a door that opens and shuts.'"

"Oh, yes, that's true." And then, suddenly, he added: "Oh, shit!"

"What's the matter?" I asked.

"I stole it from Dante me-self!"

Samuel Beckett had strict rules for living. We'd met for a drink one night, just after Gill and I were married (her first marriage, my third).

"One wife!" he scolded. "That's all a man is meant to have! Yeats only had one, Joyce only had one—I'll only have one." Samuel Beckett had his heroes . . . and I knew that I would never be listed among them.

My most important memories of Beckett aren't memories of a superb writer, but of a superb *friend*. I was first attracted to Beckett because of his writing, but he quickly became for me one of those few men we painstakingly choose, against mother's will, to serve as father.

When I saw Sam last, some months ago, he'd grown as frail as old paper.

He was living in a room in an old people's home in the rue Remy-Dumonce, a few doors from his (holistic) doctor's house. I was stunned to realize that Beckett was now living like a character of his creation. To reach Beckett's room one had to pass through something called "the recreation room." Two dozen elderly French sat in a row like sparrows on a telephone wire, watching an obnoxious song-and-dance man via an outdated black-and-white television set. I broke into their shared reverie and asked where Beckett could be found. Nobody seemed to know him. I found the home's office. I was directed through a small courtyard to the rear of the block, where I saw a tiny ground-floor room with window blinds partly drawn. Beckett was inside, dressed in a tattered old robe, working with pen and ink at a bridge table.

I stopped and stared a while, for some reason remembering Beckett's shock, twenty-two years before, at discovering that I didn't know Yeats's "Sailing to Byzantium." Before I left the table that night, Yeats's poem had passed from Mr Beckett's memory to my memory, along with Sam's small scholarly note of caution: "I don't totally approve of that 'Soul clap its hands' part!"

Samuel Beckett's final room was seedy, small, sad: a bed, a bedside table, bridge table and a matching chair, a television set "for sporting events." It was prisonlike, pathetic. My initial impulse was to pick him up and run, carrying him out, away, to some time past. It's taken me nearly a year to let it go, to accept that this was his choice. We talked for a few hours.

He asked the usual questions about my children, about my work, about Gill's recent marathons, did I need any money, or was I okay?

My turn. I asked about the state of his health. He understood his particular illness, explaining the mechanics of it as might a scientist. His brain wasn't getting proper circulation of blood.

But when he detailed the sensation — how the problem was manifest in his particular body — he was all writer: succinct and artfully clear. "I am standing in quicksand."

When I left Sam the last time, I knew that I might never see him alive again. I organized my life so that I could return to Paris and be close by him for six weeks, starting in January. I underestimated the quicksand by nearly a month.

Say something of the man and let it go. What Beckett said of Joyce is finally what I say of Beckett: "He never wrote *about* something. He always *wrote something*."

I worry that the world will over-saint Sam and overlook the most important, most obvious truth: with his life Mr. Beckett proved that it was actually possible, even in our own inferior century, for a writer to work and to live with a great seriousness, a great caring and a great *integrity*. What Samuel Beckett was was possible. Not a saint — at times not even totally tasteful — but ever an *artist*: clear-voiced, responsible, in line with the best. Beckett was, professionally, from youth onward, an old crab. And with good cause. Around him, the quality of Life was odious, and the quality of Death an unsatisfying alternative.

Two Poems by Elizabeth Stein

Ganymede

I am a world of one,

no maiden's white horned fleece
or jealous wife to cow

myself before. From pranks of lightning
the task of cupbearer comes. An eagle

wishes itself down on me
where I am mooned, nearly always out

standing—a tilted face, an echo toward
bone-china sheen.

Like the lover in a silver pond, I am
inlaid, lazy eyed, wedged between

its hollow threats. A reflection, I put on
men's desires, raising honey to a god

in the cavity
my palms make up,

skyward of feeling.

Apocrypha of Judith

They said she chose to go to him
of her own volition. I know otherwise.
She was coerced by her own mother's remark
that she would feel better immediately
after she cinched the knot.
So Judith went.

They said she came back
the next morning, a man's head
in her burlap sack. Another lie, it wasn't
till twelve new moons chased themselves,
twenty-five times to smote their silver anniversary,
the she split his soft heel on the end of her horizon.

This made her methodical.
This made her a martyr.
This made her espouse death.

In fact

Judith thrust the sword of her weaponry
in sheaths of tears, battered quartz
of husbandry to a hymen's width. Salt put out
each speck of heat he dare lay before her
in darkness. Until, at last, he was made
to question the very name

they said was his, Holofernes,
but I call him by another. He's not
a bad guy, my father; meant her no specific ills
other than what were usual
customary
pomp of the day.

However, they did report his defeat to the letter;
a casualty, though no one speaks of it much,
or the children—she bore him three (Victoria,
William and Elizabeth)
at two year intervals. My sister was the first
to tell me the abashed truth about Judith:

the terrible love,
the *Praise of God*,
scores of the mornings

my mother woke to rain on us.

Two Poems by Susan Wood

de Kooning's Women

I've seen those paintings and I think he must hate women.
  Must hate
us. I imagine you'd say they aren't about us, our bodies,
  tongues,
or mouths, it's something else he's after. It's sex
that's scary. That terrifies. Devouring the other, the other
always devouring. And you'd probably say it doesn't matter
who we are, with whom. Whether the other is man or woman.

Still, I can't help but take it personally, the way the woman's
splayed against the canvas, dismembered. His hatred
keeps him from seeing her as a woman—she's just matter
for a painting. That's why she's all gaping mouth, her tongue
a red slash, a slit, the two breasts staring out at us like other
eyes. It's in the sculpture, too: that bronze reclining figure,
  her sex

huge, engorged. Phallic. The catalogue says it isn't sex
at all he had in mind, but a cartoon: it's images of Woman
in all of Western Art he wants to parody, the icon others
made of her. de Kooning's not a misogynist, doesn't hate
women. He meant the paintings as a joke, meant them tongue-
in-cheek. I think the joke's on us. But what does it matter

what I think? Is it self-hatred I'm projecting? What's the matter
with me? The danger's both in being seen and not, and sex
does terrify, its mess, its muck, a blur of bodies, tongues,
that obliterates the self, devours. The painting "Woman—
Red Hair, Large Mouth, Large Foot"—it's everything I hate.
I hate the way he's made her disappear, effaced her. The other-

ness of it. Of her. Of you. And here's the other
thing I haven't said: I'm trying not to say how much you matter
to me. I didn't want to feel this longing fierce as hate,
this neediness and greed, this lust. Cartoonish, it's like sex
in romance novels. You'd say my shame is a defense, a woman's
fear that I might lose my self—that's what makes me tongue-

tied in your presence. That's why I'm silent, have to bite my
    tongue
to stop my heart from speaking, to keep from saying other
things I mean, or you and I might stop being just one woman
and another, a redhead, a blonde, becoming merely matter,
not the separate selves we are. The terror lies in that, that sex
blurs the outlines like the painting does. That's what we hate

and yet desire. I should just say it, speak to you in tongues
    right now, no matter
what I fear, and there'd be no other language but the body's,
    our open sexes
like lips parting the *o* of *love*, the round vowel not found in
    hate.

Felt

In my dream of Joseph Beuys
    I'm writing a hymn for him, a hymn
of praise, and he stares out at me
    from the photograph by Lord Snowdon

in *Vanity Fair*, his skin transparent
    as a lake, some ancient burial ground,
the skull just visible beneath the surface—
    it might be a death mask

except there's so much felt life
   blazing from the cave of his eyes,
the clear gaze of a lynx,
   and his gray felt hat tips joyously

forward. *What can we face*
   without flinching? In Darmstadt the vitrines
offer up their cymbals and shells, their felt
   and skins and orange-red fat. They lie silent

as glass coffins bearing the bones
   of the saints, while altarpieces stand about
stiffly as mourners, their hats
   in their hands, gray hats muffled with snow,

but in my dream I'm walking
   through the burning wreckage of a plane
in Russia in winter in 1943, I'm dreaming
   of the Tartars who found him

and how they tended their fires
   through nights colder than we can imagine,
how tenderly they salved his wounds
   with the fat of animals and wrapped him

in blankets of felt, cloth of wool
   and fur made smooth by beating,
how it must have felt
   like a shroud to him at first.

I'm dreaming of being saved
   from history. It's you I'm dreaming of, of course.
I'm dreaming of how I walked
   through a circle of fire, some old rite

of initiation, and of my fear
   which now is like the coyote

Beuys took into the gallery,
    clever and with a story to tell,

pissing on *The Wall Street Journal*,
    the ugly made beautiful by use. I'm dreaming
your body, its fur and musk,
    its cave, the way it moves like water

under my hands. Now I'm a warrior
    and want to climb the mountain, enter the cave
and tend the fires that have burned
    all night, I want to swim the lake of your body,

my face mirrored in its depths,
    my strong arms turning the water, your heart
a drum beating its message
    on the far shore. Now I'm on that shore.

What can we face without flinching?
    I'm talking about loss, the knowledge of it
and what comes after. I'm telling you
    how it feels to me. I wanted you to know.

Two Poems by Stephen McLeod

Reflecting Pool

Stretched to fit the Mall, this pool upholds
the sky, the purple monuments, these two
just married posing at its rim. I climb
the steps to pass them as he grins, Japanese,
tuxed, and haloed by her big coiffure.
They are too dazzling for this summer day.

Behind me, stern and enormous, looms
Lincoln in his cavernous room, its gray
memorial dimness barely registered
upon the water. Soon they will be done,
off to a new and unimaginable life.
For them, I wish a monumental term:

days of cherry blossoms drifting to light
that's lifted up by water, living water.
I hum the Battle Hymn beneath our young
Republic's birthday sepulchre to steer
them from the trampled vineyards, or maybe
just to haunt this sacred place myself.

I am a pane of air and history.
I stretch, and my reflection shifts
as a small breeze charitably descends
to kiss this snapshot on the water's skin,
my loneliness and theirs. They climb
up, out, into the terror of their days.

Just by Deciding It

If you were with me, I'd be thinking
of a drive out to the white lake
even though it's raining.
We could watch the mallards' mating dance
and eat a hamburger, or listen
to Vivaldi on the radio, an oboe and guitar.

Once I tried learning to play the guitar.
You're always thinking
I know how, but I don't. If you'd listen
when I tell you these things . . . The lake
is rattled now, I imagine, by the dance
of lightning, flocks ascending. The reigning

species this fall is blue teal, but when it's raining
they disappear. Sometimes I've picked up your guitar
as if, just by deciding it, my fingers could dance
over the strings. And I wouldn't be thinking
about anything but, maybe, mist on a lake,
and I'd step out of my body and listen.

Brent, listen:
You can hardly hear it raining
from the banks that surround our tender lake
like the body of a guitar
around its vacant well. Thinking
about it, not like a death, but like a dance,

we are locked arm in arm; the dance
depends on the distance between us. We listen
for the counterpoint thinking
it's our one hope: to love rain when it's raining.
The flood hits the roof like chords on a guitar.
If we were together the lake

could be all ours. No one comes to the lake
on a day like this. No one watches ducks dance
or holds their breath to hear their quiet—*Listen*—
almost inaudible banter, like me on the guitar:
strumming but muted. It has stopped raining.
If you were here, what would we be thinking?

I lie down by the lake and listen.
Stop thinking for a minute. It isn't even raining.
That's you in the ground dancing. That's me on the guitar.

path.

　　　Nat Henkins, our clarinet player was not into the wild ~~baby~~ *baby*
It just didn't interest him ~~for some reason~~ *for some reason*
animal ~~obsession~~ *thing* like me and Mitchell. In fact, the only thing
(were) The Dorsey Brothers & *that ilk.*
that seemed to twirl Nat's ticket ~~was~~ 40's Big Band music. He
modeled himself after the young Benny Goodman, parting his hair
with Pomeade
down the middle and slicked back, wore black rimmed glasses and
shirt
kept his top button buttoned at all times. He also read sheet
music fluently which kept me and Mitchell somewhat in a state
of awe and admiration, although privately we thought he was a
dipshit. ~~dude.~~ Nat looked the most out of place pulling a wolf pup off
the railroad tracks. His body never looked fully committed to
the *task.* ~~action.~~ Neither did his clothes. He would rest too long
between pulls and spend a lot of time wiping the palms of his
hands on his pants leg and staring vacantly down the tracks
before grabbing the chain again and joining us in the struggle.
His hands were extremely white & long-fingered.
The groans he made were full of complaint rather than effort
and this started to piss me and Mitchell off. We could sense
Nat's half-heartedness and lack of urgency. Mitchell's voice
was punctuated by gasps for air as he leaned against the weight
of the baby wolf. "You understand, Nat, that the fruit train
is gonna' be blasting through here in about fifteen minutes? *You*
understand that don't you?" ~~Mitchell said.~~
　　　"It never blasts through," Nat said, "That's an exager~~ation.~~
It's a law.
ation. They're not allowed to blast through towns. Besides,
I don't see why you don't just turn him loose. Wolf's not gonna'
just stand there and let himself get smashed by a fruit train.
He's not that stupid."

　　　Mitchell stopped pulling and stood up straight, staring

A manuscript page from the story "Wild to the Wild" in Cruising Paradise.

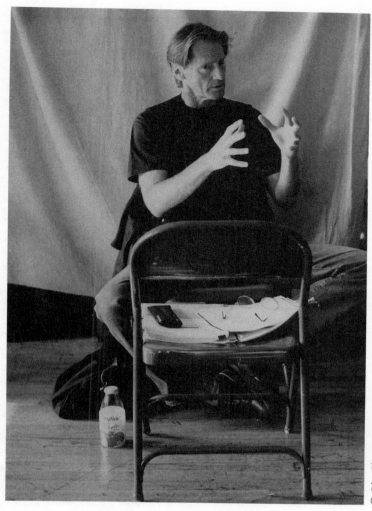

Sam Shepard

The Art of Theater XII

This interview was conducted over several days in the living room of a Manhattan apartment by the East River. For the last meeting Sam Shepard arrived at the end of a late-afternoon snowstorm, his leather jacket unbuttoned in spite of the bad weather. He immediately became distracted by an out-of-tune Steinway in the corner, then returned to the couch for a discussion of his recently completed yearlong retrospective at New York's Signature Theater. He said he had been exhausted by the theater's rehearsals, by a trip to London the previous week, and by a hectic schedule of public readings. Nevertheless, at the end of the meeting he declined to be driven back to his midtown hotel, saying he would rather walk back through Central Park instead.

Like many writers, Shepard is easy to imagine as one of the characters in his own work. In person, he is closer to the laconic and inarticulate men of his plays than to his movie roles. Self-contained, with none of the bearing of an actor, he retains a desert California accent and somehow seems smaller than one expects.

He was born on November 5, 1943, on an army base in southern Illinois where his father was stationed. He attended high schools in the Southwest, spent a year in junior college studying agricultural science, then moved to New York with designs on an acting career. In New York he quickly found an interest in writing, which brought him to the emerging world of avant-garde theater on the Lower East Side. A succession of award-winning plays followed: Chicago, Icarus's Mother, Red Cross, La Turista *and* Forensic and the Navigators *all won* Obie Awards *in the off- and off-off-Broadway categories between 1965 and 1968. During this time he was also aided by grants from the Rockefeller and Guggenheim foundations.*

In the early seventies Shepard moved to England, where he began raising a family and writing for the London theatrical scene. The period produced a number of well-received medium-length plays, including Tooth of Crime *and* Geography of a Horse Dreamer. *In 1974 he returned to California, where he had lived as a teenager, and began writing his best-known plays —* Curse of the Starving Class, Fool for Love *and the Pulitzer Prize-winning* Buried Child. *He made his feature-film debut in 1978 playing an affluent farmer in* Days of Heaven. *Though that role brought him numerous offers to continue*

acting, Shepard has deliberately limited himself to a few mov-
ies because, as he says, "the work just isn't that much fun."
Nevertheless, in 1984 he received an Academy Award nomina-
tion for his portrayal of Chuck Yeager in The Right Stuff.
That year he also received the Palm d'Or at the Cannes Film
Festival for Paris, Texas, *which he wrote and acted in.*

Shepard lives in Minnesota with the actress Jessica Lange
and their two children.

INTERVIEWER

The West figures predominantly as a mythology in many
of your plays. You grew up there, didn't you?

SAM SHEPARD

All over the Southwest, really—Cucamonga, Duarte, California, Texas, New Mexico. My dad was a pilot in the air force.
After the war he got a Fulbright fellowship, spent a little time
in Colombia, then taught high-school Spanish. He kind of
moved us from place to place.

INTERVIEWER

Do you think you'll ever live in the West again?

SHEPARD

No, I don't think so. The California I knew, old rancho
California, is gone. It just doesn't exist, except maybe in little
pockets. I lived on the edge of the Mojave Desert, an area
that used to be farm country. There were all these fresh-
produce stands with avocados and date palms. You could get
a dozen artichokes for a buck or something. Totally wiped
out now.

INTERVIEWER

True West, Buried Child, Curse of the Starving Class and
Lie of the Mind are all family dramas, albeit absurdist ones.
Have you drawn a lot from your own family?

SHEPARD

Yes, though less now than I used to. Most of it comes, I guess, from my dad's side of the family. They're a real bizarre bunch, going back to the original colonies. That side's got a real tough strain of alcoholism. It goes back generations and generations, so that you can't remember when there was a sober grandfather.

INTERVIEWER

Have you struggled with drinking?

SHEPARD

My history with booze goes back to high school. Back then there was a lot of Benzedrine around, and since we lived near the Mexican border I'd just run over, get a bag of bennies and drink ripple wine. Speed and booze together make you quite . . . omnipotent. You don't feel any pain. I was actually in several car wrecks that I don't understand how I survived.

At any rate, for a long time I didn't think I had a problem. Alcoholism is an insidious disease; until I confronted it I wasn't aware that it was creeping up on me. I finally did AA in the hardcore down on Pico Boulevard. I said, "Don't put me in with Elton John or anything, just throw me to the lions."

INTERVIEWER

Do you feel like the drinking might have aided your writing?

SHEPARD

I didn't feel like one inspired the other, or vice versa. I certainly never saw booze or drugs as a partner to writing. That was just the way my life was tending, you know, and the writing was something I did when I was relatively straight. I never wrote on drugs, or the bourbon.

INTERVIEWER

You said the men on your dad's side of the family were hard drinkers. Is this why the mothers in your plays always seem to be caught in the middle of so much havoc?

SHEPARD

Those midwestern women from the forties suffered an incredible psychological assault, mainly by men who were disappointed in a way that they didn't understand. While growing up I saw that assault over and over again, and not only in my own family. These were men who came back from the war, had to settle down, raise a family and send the kids to school — and they just couldn't handle it. There was something outrageous about it. I still don't know what it was — maybe living through those adventures in the war and then having to come back to suburbia. Anyway, the women took it on the nose, and it wasn't like they said, "Hey Jack, you know, down the road, I'm leaving." They sat there and took it. I think there was a kind of heroism in those women. They were tough and selfless in a way. What they sacrificed at the hands of those maniacs . . .

INTERVIEWER

What was your dad like?

SHEPARD

He was also a maniac, but in a very quiet way. I had a falling-out with him at a relatively young age by the standards of that era. We were always butting up against each other, never seeing eye-to-eye on anything, and as I got older it escalated into a really bad, violent situation. Eventually I just decided to get out.

INTERVIEWER

Is he alive?

SHEPARD

No, a couple of years ago he was killed coming out of a bar in New Mexico. I saw him the year before he died. Our last meeting slipped into this gear where I knew it was going to turn really nasty. I remember forcing myself, for some reason, not to flip out. I don't know why I made that decision, but I ended up leaving without coming back at him. He was boozed up, very violent and crazy. After that I didn't see him for a long time. I did try to track him down; a friend of his told me he got a haircut, a fishing license and a bottle, and then took off for the Pecos River. That was the last I heard of him before he died. He turned up a year later in New Mexico, with some woman I guess he was running with. They had a big blowout in a bar, and he went out in the street and got run over.

INTERVIEWER

Did he ever see one of your plays?

SHEPARD

Yes. There's a really bizarre story about that. He found out about a production of *Buried Child* that was going on at the Greer Garson Theater in New Mexico. He went to the show smashed, just pickled, and in the middle of the play he began to identify with some character, though I'm not sure which one, since all those characters are kind of loosely structured around his family. In the second act he stood up and started to carry on with the actors, and then yelled, "What a bunch of shit this is!" The ushers tried to throw him out. He resisted, and in the end they allowed him to stay because he was the father of the playwright.

INTERVIEWER

Were you there?

SHEPARD

No, I just heard about it. I think that's the only time he ever saw a production.

You know, all that stuff about my father and my childhood is interesting up to a certain point, but I kind of capsized with the family drama a long time ago. Now I want to get away from that. Not that I won't return to it, but a certain element has been exhausted, and it feels like: why regurgitate all this stuff?

INTERVIEWER

I read somewhere that you started writing because you wanted to be a musician.

SHEPARD

Well, I got to New York when I was eighteen. I was knocking around, trying to be an actor, writer, musician, whatever happened.

INTERVIEWER

What sort of musician were you trying to be?

SHEPARD

A drummer. I was in a band called the Holy Modal Rounders.

INTERVIEWER

How did you end up in New York?

SHEPARD

After the falling out with my father I worked on a couple of ranches—thoroughbred layup farms, actually—out toward Chino, California. That was fine for a little while, but I wanted to get out completely, and twenty miles away wasn't far enough. So I got a job delivering papers in Pasadena, and pretty soon, by reading the ad sections, I found out about an opening with a traveling ensemble called The Bishop's Company. I decided to give it a shot, thinking that this might be a way to really get out. At the audition they gave me a little Shakespeare thing to read—I was so scared I read the stage directions—and then they hired me. I think they hired everybody.

We traveled all over the country—New England, the South, the Midwest. I think the longest we stayed in one place was two days. It was actually a great little fold-up theater. We were totally self-sufficient: we put up the lights, made the costumes, performed the play and shut down. Anyway, one day we got to New York to do a production at a church in Brooklyn and I said, "I'm getting off the bus."

INTERVIEWER

Did you start right in?

SHEPARD

Not immediately. My first job was with the Burns Detective Agency. They sent me over to the East River to guard coal barges during these god-awful hours like three to six in the morning. It wasn't a very difficult job — all I had to do was make a round every fifteen minutes — but it turned out to be a great environment for writing. I was completely alone in a little outhouse with an electric heater and a little desk.

INTERVIEWER

Did you already think of yourself as a writer?

SHEPARD

I'd been messing around with it for a while, but nothing serious. That was the first time I felt writing could actually be useful.

INTERVIEWER

How did you hook up with the theaters?

SHEPARD

Well, I was staying on Avenue C and Tenth Street with a bunch of jazz musicians, one of whom happened to be Charlie Mingus's son. We knew each other from high school, and he got me a job as a busboy at the Village Gate. The headwaiter at the Gate was a guy named Ralph Cook. Ralph was just starting his theater at St. Mark's in the Bowery, and he said he'd heard that I'd been writing some stuff, and he wanted to see it. So, I showed him a few plays I'd written, and he said, "Well, let's do it." Things kind of took off from there.

New York was like that in the sixties. You could write a one-act play and start doing it the next day. You could go to one of those theaters—Genesis, La Mama, Judson Poets—and find a way to get it done. Nothing like that exists now.

INTERVIEWER

Did off-off-Broadway plays get reviewed back then?

SHEPARD

For a while the big papers wouldn't touch them, but then they started to smell something, so they came down and wrote these snide reviews. They weren't being unfair. A lot of that stuff really was shitty and deserved to get bombed. But there was one guy who was sort of on our side. His name was Michael Smith; he worked for *The Village Voice*, and he gave a glowing review to these little one-act plays, *Cowboys* and *The Rock Garden*. I remember that distinctly, not because of the praise but because it felt like somebody finally understood what we were trying to do. He was actually hooking up with us, seeing the work for what it was.

INTERVIEWER

What were the audiences like?

SHEPARD

They were incredibly different. You really felt that the community came to see the plays. They weren't people coming from New Jersey to have a dinner party. And they weren't going to sit around if they got bored. The most hostile audience I faced was up at the American Place Theatre when we were putting on *La Turista*. They invited all these Puerto Rican kids, street kids, and they were firing at the actors with peashooters.

INTERVIEWER

Did it take a long time to find your particular voice as a writer?

SHEPARD

I was amazed, actually. I've heard writers talk about "discovering a voice," but for me that wasn't a problem. There were so many voices that I didn't know where to start. It was splendid, really; I felt kind of like a weird stenographer. I don't mean to make it sound like hallucination, but there were definitely things there, and I was just putting them down. I was fascinated by how they structured themselves, and it seemed like the natural place to do it was on a stage. A lot of the time when writers talk about their voice they're talking about a narrative voice. For some reason my attempts at narrative turned out really weird. I didn't have that kind of voice, but I had a lot of other ones, so I thought, Well, I'll follow those.

INTERVIEWER

Do you feel like you're in control of those voices now?

SHEPARD

I don't feel insane, if that's what you're asking.

INTERVIEWER

What is your schedule like?

SHEPARD

I have to begin early because I take the kids to school, so usually I'm awake by six. I come back to the house afterwards and work till lunch.

INTERVIEWER

Do you have any rituals or devices to help you get started?

SHEPARD

No, not really. I mean there's the coffee and that bullshit, but as for rituals, no.

INTERVIEWER

What sort of writing situation do you have at home? Do you have an office?

SHEPARD

I've got a room out by the barn with a typewriter, a piano, some photographs and old drawings. Lots of junk and old books. I can't seem to get rid of my books.

INTERVIEWER

So, you're not a word-processor person.

SHEPARD

No, I hate green screens. The paper is important to me.

INTERVIEWER

What sort of country is it where you live?

SHEPARD

Farm country—you know, hay, horses, cattle. It's the ideal situation for me. I like the physical endeavors that go with the farm—cutting hay, cleaning out stalls or building a barn. You go do that and then come back to the writing.

INTERVIEWER

Do you write every day?

SHEPARD

When something kicks in, I devote everything to it and write constantly until it's finished. But to sit down every day and say, "I'm going to write, come hell or high water"—no, I could never do that.

INTERVIEWER

Can you write when you're acting in a film?

SHEPARD

There are certain attitudes that shut everything down. It's very easy, for example, to get a bad attitude from a movie. I mean you're trapped in a trailer, people are pounding on the door, asking if you're ready, and at the same time you're trying to write.

INTERVIEWER

Do you actually write on the set?

SHEPARD

Film locations are a great opportunity to write. I don't work on plays while I'm shooting a movie, but I've done short stories and a couple of novels.

INTERVIEWER

What was it like the first time you saw your work being performed by actors?

SHEPARD

To a certain extent it was frustrating, because the actors were in control of the material and I wasn't used to actors. I didn't know how to talk to them and I didn't want to learn, so I hid behind the director. But slowly I started to realize that they were going through an interpretive process, just like anyone else. They don't just go in there and read the script.

INTERVIEWER

Did becoming an actor help you as a writer?

SHEPARD

It did, because it helped me to understand what kinds of dilemmas an actor faces.

INTERVIEWER

Were you impressed by any particular school, like Method acting?

SHEPARD

I am not a Strasberg fanatic. In fact, I find it incredibly self-indulgent. I've seen actors come through it because they're strong people themselves, because they're able to use it and go on, but I've also seen actors absolutely destroyed by it, which is painful to see. It has to do with this voodoo that's all about the verification of behavior, so that *I become the character*. It's not true Stanislavsky. He was on a different mission, and I think Strasberg bastardized him in a way that verges on psychosis. You forget about the material, you forget that this is a play, you forget that it's for the audience. *Hey, man, I'm in my private little world. What you talkin' about? I'm over here, I'm involved with the lemons*. On film, of course, it works because of its obsessiveness; but in theater it's a complete block and a hindrance. There's no room for self-indulgence in theater; you have to be thinking about the audience. Joe Chaikin helped me understand this. He used to have this rehearsal exercise in which the actors were supposed to play a scene for some imaginary figure in the audience. He would say, "Tonight Prince Charles is in the audience. Play the scene for him," or, "Tonight a bag lady is in the audience."

INTERVIEWER

Is it true that you wrote *Simpatico* in a truck?

SHEPARD

Well, I started it in a truck. I don't like flying very much, so I tend to drive a lot, and I've always wanted to find a way to write while I'm on the open road. I wrote on the steering wheel.

INTERVIEWER

Really? What highway were you on?

SHEPARD

Forty West, the straightest one. I was going to Los Angeles. I think I wrote twenty-five pages by the time I got there, which was about five hundred miles of driving. There were these two characters I'd been thinking about for quite a while, and when I got to L.A. it seemed like I had a one-act play. Then another character popped up; suddenly there were two acts. And out of that second act, a third. It took me a year to finish it.

INTERVIEWER

How do you decide that a play is finished?

SHEPARD

The only way to test it is with actors, because that's who you're writing for. When I have a piece of writing that I think might be ready, I test it with actors, and then I see if it's what I imagined it to be. The best actors show you the flaws in the writing. They come to a certain place and there's nothing there, or they read a line and say, "Okay, now what?" That kind of questioning is more valuable than anything. They don't have to *say* anything. With the very best actors I can see it in the way they're proceeding. Sometimes I instinctively know that this little part at the end of scene two, act one is not quite there, but I say to myself, "Maybe we'll get away with it." A good actor won't let me. Not that he says, "Hey, I can't do this"; I just see that he's stumbling. And then I have to face up to the problem.

INTERVIEWER

So, as you write, your thoughts are with the actors, not the audience.

SHEPARD

Well, no. I don't think you can write a play without thinking of the audience, but it's a funny deal, because I never know who the audience is. It's like a ghost. With movies you have a better notion of who's watching; there it's the whole population.

INTERVIEWER

Do you do a lot of revisions?

Sam Shepard and Joe Chaikin at the Signature Theater.

SHEPARD

More now than I used to. I used to be just dead set against revisions because I couldn't stand rewriting. That changed when I started working with Chaikin. Joe was so persistent about finding the essence of something. He'd say, "Does this mean what we're trying to make it mean? Can it be constructed some other way?" That fascinated me, because my tendency was to jam, like it was jazz or something. Thelonius Monk style.

INTERVIEWER

How do your plays start? Do you hear the voice of a character?

SHEPARD

It's more of an attitude than a voice. With *Simpatico*, for instance, it was these two guys in completely different predicaments who began to talk to each other, one in one attitude and the other in another.

INTERVIEWER
Do your characters always tell you where to go?

SHEPARD
The characters are definitely informing you, telling you where *they* want to go. Each time you get to a crossroads you know there are possibilities. That itself can be a dilemma, though. Several times I've written a play that seemed absolutely on the money up to a certain point, and then all of a sudden it went way left field. When that happens you really have to bring it back to the point where it diverged and try something else.

INTERVIEWER
On the subject of control, Nabokov, for one, spoke of controlling his characters with a very tight rein.

SHEPARD
Yeah, but I think the whole notion of control is very nebulous. I mean, what kind of control do you have, Vladimir? Don't get me wrong, I think he's a magnificent writer. I just question the whole notion of control.

INTERVIEWER
The monologue has become something of a Shepard trademark. You are famous for your breathtaking ones, which you've referred to as arias.

SHEPARD
Originally the monologues were mixed up with the idea of an aria. But then I realized that what I'd written was extremely difficult for actors. I mean, I was writing monologues that were three or four pages long. Now it's more about elimination, but the characters still sometimes move into other states of mind, you know, without any excuses. Something lights up and the expression expands.

INTERVIEWER

What was the genesis of *Fool for Love*? Your plays don't often have a male and a female character in conflict like that.

SHEPARD

The play came out of falling in love. It's such a dumbfounding experience. In one way you wouldn't trade it for the world. In another way it's absolute hell. More than anything, falling in love causes a certain female thing in a man to manifest, oddly enough.

INTERVIEWER

Did you know when you started *Fool for Love* that the father would play such an important role?

SHEPARD

No. I was desperately looking for an ending when he came into the story. That play baffles me. I love the opening, in the sense that I couldn't get enough of this thing between Eddie and May, I just wanted that to go on and on and on. But I knew that was impossible. One way out was to bring the father in.

I had mixed feelings about it when I finished. Part of me looks at *Fool for Love* and says, "This is great," and part of me says, "This is really corny. This is a quasi-realistic melodrama." It's still not satisfying; I don't think the play really found itself.

INTERVIEWER

Do you have any idea what the end of play is going to be when you begin?

SHEPARD

I hate endings. Just detest them. Beginnings are definitely the most exciting, middles are perplexing and endings are a disaster.

INTERVIEWER

Why?

SHEPARD

The temptation towards resolution, towards wrapping up the package, seems to me a terrible trap. Why not be more honest with the moment? The most authentic endings are the ones which are already revolving towards another beginning. That's genius. Somebody told me once that *fugue* means to flee, so that Bach's melody lines are like he's running away.

INTERVIEWER

Maybe that's why jazz appeals to you, because it doesn't have any endings, the music just trails away.

SHEPARD

Possibly. It's hard, you know, because of the nature of a play.

INTERVIEWER

Have you ever tried to back up from a good ending? Start with one in mind and work backwards?

SHEPARD

Evidently that's what Raymond Chandler did, but he was a mystery writer. He said he always started out knowing who did the murder. To me there's something false about an ending. I mean, because of the nature of a play, you have to end it. People have to go home.

INTERVIEWER

The endings of *True West* and *Buried Child*, for example, seem more resolved than, say, *Angel City*.

SHEPARD

Really? I can't even remember how *Angel City* ends.

INTERVIEWER

The green slime comes through the window.

SHEPARD

Ah, yes. When in doubt, bring on the goo and slime.

INTERVIEWER

What is it you have in mind when you think of the audience?

SHEPARD

You don't want to create boredom, and it becomes an easy trap for a writer to fall into. You have to keep the audience awake in very simple terms. It's easy in the theater to create boredom—easier than it is in movies. You put something in motion and it has to have momentum. If you don't do that right away, there isn't any attention.

INTERVIEWER

Do you have a secret for doing that?

SHEPARD

You begin to learn an underlying rhythmic sense in which things are shifting all the time. These shifts create the possibility for the audience to attach their attention. That sounds like a mechanical process, but in a way it's inherent in dialogue. There's a kind of dialogue that's continually shifting and moving, and each time it moves it creates something new. There's also a kind of dialogue that puts you to sleep. One is alive and the other's deadly. It could be just the shifts of attitudes, the shifts of ideas, where one line is sent out and another one comes back. Shifts are something Joe Chaikin taught me. He had a knack for marking the spot where something shifted. An actor would be going along, full of focus and concern, and then Joe would say, "No! Shift! Different! Not the same. Sun, moon—different!" And the actors would say to themselves, "Of course it's different. Why didn't I see that before?"

INTERVIEWER

Is an ear for dialogue important?

SHEPARD

I think an ear for stage dialogue is different from an ear for language that's heard in life. You can hear things in life that don't work at all when you try to reproduce them onstage. It's not the same; something changes.

INTERVIEWER

What changes?

SHEPARD

It's being listened to in a direct way, like something overheard. It's not voyeuristic, not like I'm in the other room. I'm confronted by it, and the confrontational part of theater is the dialogue. We hear all kinds of fascinating things every day, but dialogue has to create a life. It has to be self-sustaining. Conversation is definitely not dialogue.

INTERVIEWER

Do you acknowledge the influence of playwrights like Pinter and Beckett on your work?

SHEPARD

The stuff that had the biggest influence on me was European drama in the sixties. That period brought theater into completely new territory — Beckett especially, who made American theater look like it was on crutches. I don't think Beckett gets enough credit for revolutionizing theater, for turning it upside down.

INTERVIEWER

How were you affected by winning the Pulitzer Prize?

SHEPARD

You know, in a lot of ways I feel like it was given to the wrong play. *Buried Child* is a clumsy, cumbersome play. I think *A Lie of the Mind* is a much better piece of work. It's denser, more intricate, better constructed.

INTERVIEWER

Do you have a favorite among your plays?

SHEPARD

I'll tell you, I'm not attached to any of it. I don't regret them, but for me it's much more thrilling to move on to the next thing.

—Mona Simpson, Jeanne McCulloch,
Benjamin Howe

The Man in the Back Row
Has a Question IV

Sebastian Barry	*The Steward of Christendom*
Eric Bogosian	*SubUrbia; Talk Radio*
Christopher Durang	*The Marriage of Bette and Boo; Sister Mary Ignatius Explains It All For You*
Michael Frayn	*Noises Off*
Jack Gelber	*The Connection; Chambers*
A.R. Gurney	*Sylvia; The Cocktail Hour*
David Hare	*Skylight; Plenty*
Beth Henley	*Crimes of the Heart*
Tina Howe	*Painting Churches; Birth and After Birth*
Richard Nelson	*New England; Some Americans Abroad*
Harold Pinter	*The Birthday Party; The Homecoming*
Neil Simon	*Lost in Yonkers; Brighton Beach Memoirs*
Tom Stoppard	*Rosencrantz and Guildenstern Are Dead; Arcadia*
Alfred Uhry	*The Last Night of Ballyhoo; Driving Miss Daisy*

Timberlake Werten- baker	*Our Country's Good*
Arnold Wesker	*The Friends; The Old Ones; Love* *Letters on Blue Paper*
Lanford Wilson	*5th of July; Talley's Folly*

Is the final product ever what you hoped it would be?

When a play is *written* in its final form I never know what I have, exactly, and only an ideal first production, or close, can really tell me what I was after (or remind me). I suppose I also hope that the final product might be something beyond what I wrote, the result of the sacred actors, and even the text rearranging itself a little in the drawer. Some texts disarrange themselves in the drawer. Between the peculiar stage in the head and the true stage, the text leads a funny old life. But four times out of five now, the final product, the play produced for the first time, has been beyond my hopes. Good score.

—Sebastian Barry

By the time you get to the final product you no longer have the faintest recollection what you hoped it would be.

—Michael Frayn

Is there ever anything "final" in the theater? Everything seems to be provisionally final. Most playwrights write more than one draft of a play, some many more. Rehearsal usually sets off more rewriting. The addition of an audience invariably provokes adjustments. Playwrights have been known to fiddle around with well-received, long-running plays.

—Jack Gelber

I've never written a play which was a product, so mercifully this question does not apply to me.

—David Hare

Yes. And, on rare occasions, it is more splendiferous than you ever dreamed. That is one reason I love working in a collaborative art.

— Beth Henley

It's either a great deal more or a shattering disaster.

— Tina Howe

It depends on what you hope. You *hope* it'll end up the best thing you've ever written. You *hope* people will love it and love you and cover your street with rose petals. You hope it'll make you some money. You hope it'll open up new avenues to explore, etc. You hope a lot of things writing a play. But the end is always different from what you expect — and that seems to be the point of writing, doesn't it?

— Richard Nelson

No.

— Harold Pinter

Since I've done twenty-nine plays and twenty-four films, the odds are on my side. If I said I was happy with the result half the time, it would be accurate.

— Neil Simon

Yes, and — broadly — better for the net gain of new thoughts, words, pictures (and cuts) during rehearsal. I refer to the first production of a play.

— Tom Stoppard

Not exactly. How could it be? So many other hands get into it.

— Alfred Uhry

Mostly much better than I hoped, sometimes much worse. A good actor, well-directed, multiplies the intensity of the text. A bad actor remains beneath it and the play then seems to hover over an icy void.

— Timberlake Wertenbaker

More frequently than one expects, though never frequently enough.

— Arnold Wesker

When I was writing for specific actors at Circle Rep, we got very close pretty often. *Hot L Baltimore*, *Talley's Folly*, *Angels Fall* and *5th of July* on Broadway, after Richard Thomas went into the show, were all as close to what we hoped they would be as anything in my experience. Other than that, you've got to be joking.

— Lanford Wilson

Do you write with endings and last lines in mind?

Sometimes about halfway in, during some draft or other, I hear the last line or lines of a play and put them down quickly. Very much a passing insect, have to act fast. And there is some solace in the fact of its existence there, as if an ending implies the play already in existence behind it, all the wagons to its engine. Other times all is dark as the ink itself and I'm praying for enlightenment every line of the way.

— Sebastian Barry

Like most writers today, structure is my Achilles' heel. So I don't always know where I'm going or how I'm going to get there. I write intuitively and I write a lot. Editing is my secret weapon.

— Eric Bogosian

No. I tend not to know how my plays are going to end until I get close to the end. And then sometimes, alas, I still don't know.

— Christopher Durang

Never ones that the characters would agree to perform.

— Michael Frayn

No. Or if I do, I never end up there.

— A.R. Gurney

You do need some vague sense of where you think you're going. Plainly, I had to have the ending of *Skylight* from the very first few pages, but I found my way to the ending of *The Secret Rapture* blindfolded.

— David Hare

No. I like for it to evolve and surprise me.

— Beth Henley

The final moment is what inspires the play. The agony is getting it in place. Words are the least of it. It's all about the beating of wings.

— Tina Howe

No.

— Harold Pinter

I never write with endings or last lines in mind. I don't want to know. I want to be as surprised as the audience.

— Neil Simon

No.

— Tom Stoppard

No. Sometimes you see the whole play in a flash. Of course, it always turns out completely different.

— Timberlake Wertenbaker

Mostly. Because the ending is a kind of discovery, it becomes the reason for writing in the first place — to share the discovery; and the play becomes a re-created map of the curious and arduous way the discovery was made. Sometimes a play begins with a mood—though I suspect the mood is often just a mist hiding the ending.

—Arnold Wesker

No. I sometimes come up with the last line of an act halfway through. Sometimes the end surprises me completely.

—Lanford Wilson

What was the first play you saw?

Yeats's *Cathleen ni Houlihan*, at the Abbey, when I was about nine. I didn't know what a play was really. My mother, Joan O'Hara, played the Poor Old Woman of the title. It was a great shock. My mother was beautiful and young, as well I knew, but there she was, aged and eloquent and frightening. I didn't know she was dressed up, made-up. I thought she was able to become the creature in the lights. "Did you see an old woman going down the path?—I did not, but I saw a young girl, and she had the walk of a queen." Exactly, I thought, in the astonishing dark.

—Sebastian Barry

The first plays I attended were written by fellow students at my high school. They were usually filled with violence and featured a cathartic ending.

—Eric Bogosian

Either *Damn Yankees* or *Oklahoma!* at the Paper Mill Playhouse in Millburn, New Jersey. The first Broadway show I saw was *Fiorello!* I think the second one was *How to Succeed in Business Without Really Trying* with Robert Morse; I particularly loved that, and found its cartoon, comic style very funny.

—Christopher Durang

Hay Fever, performed by the local Blackout Club, a neighborhood group got up to maintain morale during the Second

World War, when I was seven or eight. I have no conscious memory of the production, but my morale throughout the war remained consistently high.

—Michael Frayn

A one-act play about Shakespeare hiding in a trunk, probably by Bernard Shaw. I thought it was incredibly silly.

—David Hare

Jack and the Beanstalk. My mother was in it and she was painted green. I believe she must have been a bean.

—Beth Henley

The Red Mill by Henry Blossom.

—Tina Howe

Destry Rides Again on Broadway when I was, I think, eight or maybe nine. I fell asleep (it was at night) and woke up during the whip dance. I remember entering the theater, finding myself in the aisle and the stage curtain in front of me. It's just like the feeling one gets at a major-league baseball game, coming out of the tunnel and seeing the green field under the lights.

—Richard Nelson

King Lear.

—Harold Pinter

The first play I saw was Richard Wright's *Native Son* with a wonderful black actor with the interesting name of Canada Lee.

—Neil Simon

Dangerous Corner by J.B. Priestley.

—Tom Stoppard

Mister Roberts.

—Alfred Uhry

Jean Genet's *Deathwatch*. I was about eight, it was really grim, I don't think I understood very much, but I loved it. My mother had taken me to it because I was homesick for France. When she realized what it was about, she tried to take me out, but I wouldn't leave.

— Timberlake Wertenbaker

Leaving aside the dramatization of Tennyson's poem, "The Beggar Maid," in which I played the king aged eight, and leaving aside, too, the amateur plays in which I performed in my adolescence, I think the first play I saw was Sean O'Casey's *Red Roses for Me* which I was taken to see by my sister when I was fourteen or fifteen. I think we had to leave in the interval because I didn't understand what I was watching.

— Arnold Wesker

Hansel and Gretel by some touring children's theater. Ten years later, *Death of a Salesman*.

— Lanford Wilson

What do you customarily do on opening night?

Oh, times have changed. On the opening night of my first play I sat square in the middle of the audience suffering. Someone said after that it was great to see the author there, but I wasn't so sure. There are rare and secret glands in the body unknown to medicine that start to leak their poisons into the playwright's body under first-night conditions. The mind starts to keel over, and then you acquire the hearing capacity of Superman. Every whisper, cough and change of body position is a contemptuous dismissal of the play. Now I might watch the first act during a preview, and have a go at the second act on opening night. I don't like dressing up because a condemned man instinctively favors informality. But ideally I have a preference to be sitting near the stage manager backstage and watch the play through whatever gap there may be, so the space within suggests a real room. I love to see the actors creeping up for their entrances and ghosting away then to their dressing rooms. Actors are mighty creatures. I don't get drunk for some reason. Couldn't hold a glass without spilling it maybe.

—Sebastian Barry

If I'm performing, I'm so exhilarated after the show that I spend the rest of the night coming down. If it's something I've written, I eat dinner with the actors and hope it's going to be a long run.

—Eric Bogosian

Run around trying to write funny notes on cards to the cast and the 356 other people who've worked on the play. Then I try to figure out whether to read the reviews or not. Lately, I've been choosing not to read them.

—Christopher Durang

Turn up. The actors have got to stand there and perform it; the least the author can do is to sit there and watch.

—Michael Frayn

The question ought to be: what haven't you done on opening night? I have done more things on opening night than the number of positions described in the *Kama Sutra*.

—Jack Gelber

Opening nights these days are for the theater family, and they are warm and reassuring. I go to those. Preview nights, when the critics come, are hell, and I usually stay away.

—A.R. Gurney

If the play is at the National Theatre in London, I walk to Brown's Hotel in Albemarle Street at curtain-up, have two whiskey sours, walk back and at the interval I generally find I'm in time to be told how things are going.

—David Hare

In New York I sit in a nearby bar with a few dear friends. It is too scary to be in the theater where people are writing on pads.

—Beth Henley

Drink myself into a stupor at the neighborhood bar.

—Tina Howe

I watch my play. Before, I usually have a little party for a few friends—I do this to do something.

—Richard Nelson

Watch the performance.

—Harold Pinter

On opening nights, I meet with my family first for a little champagne and then off to the theater. The rest of the night depends on how the reviewers treated me.

—Neil Simon

Watch the show, have a drink with the actors, go home.

—Tom Stoppard

Have stomach problems.

—Alfred Uhry

I leaf through the Job Vacancies page.

—Timberlake Wertenbaker

Sit in the audience to share the experience with my cast—an act of solidarity. And sometimes pleasure. Then everyone is invited to a first-night party usually made by my wife.

—Arnold Wesker

Watch from the back, listen over a speaker in some dressing room, go out on the street, a bar, anywhere I can smoke.

—Lanford Wilson

What is the most difficult aspect of writing plays?

Waiting for them to begin. I spent two and a half years waiting for *The Steward of Christendom* to begin. Plenty of drafts, grand, very decent no doubt, but not the play. Then between one thing and another, I had the powerful inclination to place him in the county home in Baltinglas, and he, the Steward, began to speak. But that's the hardest part, the ignorance, the dislocation, the stupidity and even the education of the writer. Forget everything, listen and look, hope your neck doesn't snap when the train moves at last.

— Sebastian Barry

Sticking with them. Saying what I wanted to say in the first place.

— Eric Bogosian

Sometimes I find it easy, not difficult. Other times, I find it difficult how hard it is to predict how a play will live in front of a breathing audience. Sometimes how an audience pays attention or hooks in will show you how you've gone away from what is interesting them; unfortunately, once you're in performance, preview or not, it becomes more and more difficult to make substantial changes. So that part is hard.

— Christopher Durang

Persuading the characters that they have an obligation to repay your kindness in inventing them by coming to life and writing the play for you.

— Michael Frayn

The current economic restrictions (small casts, simple or unit sets) imposed on the already compressed nature of the form make playwriting as tough as writing a sonnet.

— A.R. Gurney

Coming to terms with the fact that the element in which you have to live is opinion.

—David Hare

Surrendering to the fever of the moment.

—Tina Howe

I tend to underwrite as a playwright. By that I mean I try to have a great amount happening just under the surface of the play, which I suggest by subtle detail. If you're too subtle, not only won't the audience get it, but neither will the actors and director. So knowing how little is not too little is for me the hardest part of a play.

—Richard Nelson

?

—Harold Pinter

The most difficult aspect of writing a play is knowing when you've got a good one working in your mind. It's easy to start mediocre plays, and you waste a lot of time writing them before you quit.

—Neil Simon

Structure.

—Tom Stoppard

Getting started.

—Alfred Uhry

Everything. There's only one easy aspect, and that's sitting through technical complaining about the lack of light on stage.

—Timberlake Wertenbaker

Getting them performed. Few people, even experienced theater people, know how to lift a play off the page.

—Arnold Wesker

(a) Waiting to be hit with the first idea. (b) Enduring the workshop process with a lot of well-meaning support. Tie.

—Lanford Wilson

Has the theatergoing audience changed significantly since you began in the theater?

Well, it's only ten years ago that I began. Each play seems to bring in a particular audience, the tribe of the play. I mean even across languages. The crowd coming out from a recent reading of *The Steward* in the Comédie Française was very familiar to me. I had seen them in New Zealand, London, Dublin, wherever. People in their good clothes, a little quiet, getting into their cars to drive away home together, not saying much. Sometimes theater is fashionable and sometimes the only notices around for it are obituaries. Audiences come in their new coats, but the curious souls inside must be unchanging. Uncomfortably for modern criticism, the soul is the thing being entertained in the theater.

—Sebastian Barry

Twenty years ago, when I got to New York, there was a flood of college graduates coming to New York. We had been taught by our liberal-arts professors to embrace the new and offbeat, so young playwrights like Shepard and Mamet were in vogue. Tickets were much cheaper, so people with menial jobs could afford to see all this new writing. The situation has changed and changed again. I think it's about to come full circle once more.

—Eric Bogosian

Audiences vary these days, depending on the play, the city, the theater, the price, the time of year, you name it. My sense is that once upon a time there was a solid, well-educated, theater-loving middle-class audience that went to plays all the time. Nowadays, subscribers are older and sleepy, younger audiences are choosier, and playwrights themselves tend to narrow their sights and speak to a particular tribal constituency.

—A.R. Gurney

Not as much as I would have liked.

—David Hare

They cough more.

—Harold Pinter

The theatergoing audience has changed significantly since I started writing plays. First of all, they don't go to plays. That's because they mostly produce musicals today. Also the demographics have changed. Only about 40 percent of New Yorkers see shows. The rest are from out of town or out of country.

—Neil Simon

Yes. They know "less," i.e., they know different things, being in general younger, nowadays, than I am.

—Tom Stoppard

Yes, there's a lot less of it.

—Alfred Uhry

I've not made a study or read studies of how theater audiences are made up these days, but when I attend successful plays in theaters such as the Royal Court, the National or the Almeida, it seems to me I still see the kind of faces I saw in the late fifties and early sixties when my first plays were appearing—eager, alert, intelligent, inquiring.

—Arnold Wesker

How much do critics affect you?

I've developed a finely tuned rationality that can both accept good reviews as proof of my genius and dismiss bad reviews as misguided attempts to tarnish my good name. Once in a great while a critique will mention something I'm puzzling over and I may actually take the critic's advice.

—Eric Bogosian

I get bogged down being upset with critics, so I don't want to talk about it. The brief version: there's no forum to talk back when they say wildly debatable things; and they affect whether audiences come to the play or not. They also seem unwilling to let you go in new directions as a writer. With my last play, I felt as if I had invited people to, say, a chicken dinner; and the next day all the critics said, "You remember when he used to make steak? Why doesn't he do that anymore?" So I hate being reviewed. Though one does need the publicity, so what can you do?

—Christopher Durang

Scarcely more than the lions affected the Christians.

—Michael Frayn

Critics affect me a lot psychologically, very little aesthetically.

—A.R. Gurney

In general, they depress me.

—David Hare

Very much. They can close your play in New York and elsewhere really hurt your feelings.

—Beth Henley

Totally, utterly beyond imagining. They can give you the world and then snatch it away. We try to pretend they don't affect us, but they determine whether a play lives or dies.

—Tina Howe

My first professional production (*The Birthday Party*, 1958) was massacred by all the critics with the exception of Harold

Hobson, whose review was published after the play had closed, having given eight performances. His review encouraged me to go on writing plays.

—Harold Pinter

Critics do affect me but not always for the obvious reason. A good review is wonderful, but I would hope that I'd learn something from my play in his review. A bad one is nonsense except, of course, when he or she is right and you know it yourself in your heart.

—Neil Simon

Trigorin (in *The Sea Gull*): "When they're nice about me I like it. When they're nasty I'm depressed for a day or two."

—Tom Stoppard

They terrify me.

—Alfred Uhry

They affect morale, but I hope not the writing. The danger is that they may make you want to play safe.

—Timberlake Wertenbaker

I have difficulty reading the language critics use—it rarely seems to have anything to do with what I've written, and far more to do with who they are. For my last two plays (one new, one a revival) and for my recent autobiography, I've not read their reviews. Nor do I plan to read the reviews for my new play.

If the question means: how do critics affect the plays? then the answer is that for new plays they affect them inevitably. Not even a star can save a new play that the critics don't like. Fortunately in the U.K. choice is wide and not dependent upon one newspaper, which helps.

The conflict between artist and critic is endless and eternal. My own view of them is that they are just people whose opinions have been magnified out of proportion by print. Those of us who have achieved success, however, owe it to the impact of such disproportionate praise.

It would be helpful, I think, to acknowledge the distinction between critics and reviewers. There is a great difference between Raymond Williams and Frank Rich, though I hear that even Raymond Williams was human.

—Arnold Wesker

They usually get me somewhere in the stomach, or below and behind that. They don't change how I feel about the work one way or the other. I've never bent anything to their will. A good review is encouraging, a bad one discouraging. But beyond critics, anyone leaving the theater, the slightest pointed or overheard comment, sends me into deep depression. I have a feeling it does every writer. That's why so many people give up and go home. Granted we all know we have to develop a tough hide in this circus, but even tough hides wear thin.

—Lanford Wilson

What is your favorite opening and / or closing line — either by you or another?

The first line of *Cathleen ni Houlihan* is "What is that sound I hear?" Which is almost the playwright speaking. I would favor all opening lines — you know the poor benighted playwright has got started at last. The most overwhelming closing line I have heard in the modern theater is actually a line of music and lyrics, the man singing suddenly like Gigli at the wild, civil end of Tom Murphy's *The Gigli Concert*.

—Sebastian Barry

"I have asked you here, gentlemen, to tell you some highly disagreeable news. The Inspector-General is coming . . ." (*Inspector*)

". . . The son of a bitch stole my watch." (*The Front Page*)

—Michael Frayn

My favorite opening line is from Thornton Wilder's *The Skin of Our Teeth*: "Oh, oh, oh! Six o'clock and the master not home yet. Pray God nothing has happened to him crossing the Hudson." I love the self-conscious, clunky silliness of it. My favorite closing line is from Eugene O'Neill's *Long Day's Journey into Night*: "That was in the winter of senior year. Then in the spring something happened to me. Yes, I remember. I fell in love with James Tyrone and was so happy for a time." That's how I feel too. Excuse me, I must go upstairs and . . . do something. No, please, don't get up. I'll be fine. I'll just be a . . . minute.

—Christopher Durang

Favorite last line, from O'Neill's *Long Day's Journey*: "I fell in love with James Tyrone and was so happy for a time."

—A.R. Gurney

When the man comes on in *King Lear* and says, "I thought the King had more affected the Duke of Albany than Cornwall," I always feel a unique thrill of excitement. But perhaps that's because I know what's coming. As for endings: I was very proud when *Plenty* won a competition for Best Last Line of the Century ["There will be days and days and days like this."] but, myself, I would still give the palm to Eugene O'Neill for *Long Day's Journey Into Night*.

—David Hare

I'd say my favorite closing line is James Joyce's *Ulysses*. If you are talking about drama, the last line of Eugene O'Neill's *Long Day's Journey Into Night*.

—Beth Henley

I love the last line (and stage direction) of Hecht and Fowler's play *The Great Magoo*:
As they [the lovers] exit, TANTE emerges with a douche-bag dangling from her hand. She starts after them, calling.
"TANTE: Hey, Cinderella. You forgot your pumpkin!"

—Richard Nelson

"Who's there?" (*Hamlet*)

—Harold Pinter

My favorite closing line I suppose is from *The Front Page*: "The son of a bitch stole my watch."

—Neil Simon

"The son of a bitch stole my watch." (*The Front Page*)

—Tom Stoppard

Robert Anderson, *Tea and Sympathy*. "When you talk about this . . . and you will . . . be kind."

—Alfred Uhry

The concluding line of Ariane Mnouchkine's *Mephisto*. Hendrik Hofgen has collaborated with the Nazis. He sees the shadowy figure of one of the people he betrayed in the wings of his theater. "Why are they tormenting me? I haven't done anything. What can I do? I am only an ordinary actor."

—Timberlake Wertenbaker

If I may be permitted the few opening lines from my play *The Friends*, which I presume to offer because they come, more or less, from a letter written to me by a friend: "Only children's faces are really beautiful. Little girls with bows and broderie anglaise; spontaneous, cruel, full of uninhibited love, like tigers. The rest is stupid and vulgar, brutal and pompous."

—Arnold Wesker

The mother in Craig Lucas's *Reckless* has been separated from her son. After years she becomes a psychiatrist. One day her son walks into her waiting room. He waits all day to see her. She recognizes him, he doesn't recognize her. They agree he will see her several times a week. As he leaves she says, "I'm sorry I kept you waiting."

—Lanford Wilson

Richard Shelton

Miranda of the Sorrows

do you like my pony tail
I got it off a real pony who died
but I have always been a real literal
person things would be easier for me
if I didn't tell the truth so much
like my mother said a thousand times
Miranda don't tell the truth so much
it will only get you into trouble
but I always told her to screw it
what did she know about how precious
the truth is and she never knew
nothing about all the sorrows

just because I always tell the truth
don't mean I ain't understanding
see how I wear makeup on only one
side of my face that makes me able
to understand both sides of every issue
but we suffer Lord we all suffer
some more than others and I have been
chosen to understand the sufferings
and will probably live forever
which is why I always keep one eye
closed so my eyes will last and each one
works a four-hour shift it's only fair

sometimes children throw rocks at me
but they are mostly feral and sniff
paint from spray cans they steal
otherwise life on the streets ain't
too bad if you keep your wits about you

and don't have serious bowel problems
like I often do that's the worst
if you're willing to be honest and suffer
for others as I am we all suffer
Lord some more than others
but I was always strong in the legs

I dance sometimes to cheer everybody up
a kind of belly dance and I lift up
my shirt so they can see my belly dancing
but that's all I do because if you take off
your clothes they put you in the wagon
and take you to a place where everybody
is throwing up all over the floor
I pray for all of them but it smells bad
Lord sometimes it's hard to suffer

once when I was listening to the preacher
on the corner a man stopped and asked me
if I had a personal savior and I told
him there can't be no personal savior
because suffering ain't personal it's
general and I wanted to talk to him
for a long time but he was just passing
through the neighborhood the way
everybody does since the stores have all
gone out of business or to be literal
the business has all gone out of the stores
we suffer Lord some more than others
on the streets where we live nobody is home

Edward Hirsch

The Lectures on Love

1. Charles Baudelaire

These lectures afford me a great pleasure,
so thank you for coming. My subject is love
and my proposition is a simple one: erotic love,
which is, after all, a fatal form of pleasure,
closely resembles a surgical operation, or torture.
Forgive me if I sound ironic or cynical
but, I'm sure you'll agree, cynicism
is sometimes called for in discussing torture.

Act One, Scene One: The score is "Love."
The setting of a great operatic passion.
At first the lovers have equal passion
but, it turns out, one always seems to love
the other less. He, or she, is the surgeon
applying a scalpel to the patient, the victim.
I know because I have been that victim
though I have also been the torturer, the surgeon.

Can you hear those loud spasmodic sighs?
Who hasn't uttered them in hours of love?
Who hasn't drawn them from his (or her) lover?
It's sacrilegious to call such noises "ecstasy"
when they're really a species of decomposition,
surrendering to death. We can get drunk
on each other, but don't pretend being drunk
puts us in a sudden death-defying position.

Why are people so proud of that spellbound
look in the eyes, that stiffening between the legs?
Example One: She ran her hand down my legs
until I felt as if I'd been gagged and bound.
Example Two: She no longer gave me any pleasure,
nonetheless, I rested my hand on her nude body
almost casually, I leaned over and tasted her body
until her whole being trembled with pleasure.

The erotic is an intimate form of cruelty
and every pleasure can be used to prostitute
another: I love you, so I become your prostitute
but my generosity is your voluptuous cruelty.
Sex is humiliation, a terrifying game
in which one partner loses self-control.
The subject concerns ownership or control
and that makes it an irresistible game.

I once heard the question discussed:
Wherein consists love's greatest pleasure?
I pondered the topic with great pleasure
but the whole debate filled me with disgust.
Someone declared, *We love a higher power*.
Someone said, *Giving is better than receiving*,
though someone else returned, *I prefer receiving*.
No one there ever connected love to power.

Someone actually announced, *The greatest pleasure
in love is to populate the State with children*.
But must we really be no better than children
whenever we discuss the topic of pleasure?
Pain, I say, is inseparable from pleasure
and love is but an exquisite form of torture.
You need me, but I carry the torch for her . . .
Evil comes enswathed in every pleasure.

2. Heinrich Heine

Thank you, thank you ladies and gentlemen.
I have had myself carried here today
on what we may call my mattress-grave
where I have been entombed for years
(forgive me if I don't stand up this time)
to give a lecture about erotic love.

As a cripple talking about Eros,
a subject I've been giving up for years,
I know my situation (*this time
he's gone too far!*) is comical and grave.
But don't I still appear to be a man?
Hath not a Jew eyes, etc., at least today?

I am an addict of the human comedy
and I propose that every pleasure, esp. love,
is like the marriage of the French and Germans
or the eternal quarrel between Space and Time.
We are all creeping madly toward the grave
or leaping forward across the years

(Me, I haven't been able to leap in years)
and bowing under the fiendish blows of Time.
All that can distract us—gentlemen, ladies—
is the splendid warfare between men and women.
I don't hesitate to call the struggle "love."
Look at me: my feverish body is a grave,

I've been living so long on a mattress-grave
that I scarcely even resemble a man,
but what keeps me going is the quest for love.
I may be a dog who has had his day
(admittedly a day that has lasted for years)
but I'm also a formidable intellect of our time

and I'm telling you nothing can redeem Time
or the evident oblivions of the grave
or the crippling paralysis of the years
except the usual enchantments of love.
That's why the night hungers for the day
and the gods—heaven help us—envy the human.

Ladies and gentlemen, the days pass into years
and the body is a grave filled with time.
We are drowning. All that rescues us is love.

3. Marquis de Sade

This is the first time I have given a lecture
on my favorite subject—the nature of love—
so thank you for courageously inviting me.
I hope you won't regret having invited me
when you hear what I think about erotic love.
These are provisional notes *towards* a lecture

since what I've prepared are some observations
which, forgive me, I will not attempt to prove
but which I offer as subjective testimony.
What I *will* claim for this evidentiary testimony
is its forthright honesty, which I cannot prove.
I offer you the candor of my observations,

and I trust I will not shock you too much
(or too little) by revealing the deep abyss
at the heart—the vertiginous core—of love.
We will always desecrate whatever we love.
Eroticism stands on the edge of an abyss:
Sex is not enough until it becomes too much.

Love is erotic because it is so dangerous.
I am an apostle of complete freedom who believes

other people exist to satisfy my appetites.
I am not ashamed to pursue those appetites
and I have the will to enact my cruel beliefs.
The greatest *liaisons* are always dangerous.

Exhibit Number One is an innocent specimen.
My niece has a face aureoled by grace,
a guileless soul, and a lily-white body.
I like to masturbate all over her body
and to enter behind while she says grace.
Her humiliation is a delicious specimen.

Exhibit Number Two takes place in church.
I send my valet to purchase a young whore
and he dresses her as a sweet-faced nun.
(Do I have any compunction about this? *None*.)
In a pew I sodomize the terrified whore
until she becomes a member of my church.

It takes courage to be faithful to desire —
not many have the nerve. I myself feed
from the bottom of a cesspool for pleasure
(and I have fed from her bottom with pleasure).
I say whosoever has the courage to feed
from the ass of his beloved will sate desire.

Please don't leave. My doctrine is *isolism*:
the lack of contact between human beings.
But strangle me and you shall touch me.
Spit in my face and you shall see me.
Suck my cock and you taste a human being.
Otherwise we are the subjects of isolism.

Forgive me if I speak with too much freedom.
I am nothing more than an old libertine
who believes in the sanctity of pleasure.
Suffering, too, is a noble form of pleasure
like the strange experience of a libertine.
I would release you to a terrible freedom.

4. Margaret Fuller

Thank you for attending this conversation on love.
I am going to argue in the Nineteenth Century
a woman can no longer be sacrificed for love.
The Middle Ages are over, ladies and gentlemen,

and I am going to argue in the Nineteenth Century
we are not merely wives, whores, and mothers.
The Middle Ages are over, gentlemen. And ladies,
we can now be sea captains, if you will.

We are not merely wives, whores, and mothers.
We can be lawyers, doctors, journalists,
we can now be sea captains, if you will.
What matters to us is our own fulfillment.

We can be lawyers, doctors, journalists
who write ourselves into the official scripts.
What matters to us is our own fulfillment.
It is time for Eurydice to call for Orpheus

and to sing herself into the official scripts.
She is no longer a stranger to her inheritance.
It is time for Eurydice to call for Orpheus
and to move the earth with her triumphant song.

She is no longer a stranger to her inheritance.
She, too, leaves her footprints in the sand
and moves the earth with her triumphant song.
God created us for the purpose of happiness.

She, too, leaves her footprints in the sand.
She, too, feels divinity within her body.
God created us for the purpose of happiness.
She is not the betrothed, the bride, the spouse.

She, too, feels divinity within her body.
Man and Woman are two halves of one thought.
She is not the betrothed, the bride, the spouse.
The sexes should prophesy to one another.

Man and Woman are two halves of one thought.
They are both on equal terms before the law.
The sexes should prophesy to one another.
My love is a love that cannot be crucified.

We are both on equal terms before the law.
Our holiest work is to transform the earth.
(My love is a love that cannot be crucified.)
The earth itself becomes a parcel of heaven.

Our holiest work is to transform the earth.
Thank you for attending this conversation on love.
The earth itself becomes a parcel of heaven.
A woman can no longer be sacrificed for love.

5. Giacomo Leopardi

Thank you for listening to this new poem
which Leopardi has composed for the occasion;
he regrets he cannot read it here himself
(he is, he suggests, but a remnant of himself),
especially on such an auspicious occasion.
He has asked me to present you with this poem:

Poetry Would Be a Way of Praising God if God Existed

Deep in the heart of night
I stood on a hill in wintertime
and stared up at the baleful moon.
I was terrified of finding myself
in the midst of nothing, myself
nothingness clarified, like the moon.
I was suffocating inside time,
contemplating the empty night

when a bell rang in the distance
three times, like a heart beating
in the farthest reaches of the sky.
The music was saturated with stillness.
I stood listening to that stillness
until it seemed to fill the sky.
The moon was like a heart beating
somewhere far off in the distance.

But there is no heart in a universe
of dying planets, infinite starry spaces.
Death alone is the true mother of Eros
and only love can revivify the earth.
Look at the sky canopied over earth:
it is a black sea pulsing without Eros,
a world of infinitely dead, starry spaces.
Love alone can redeem our universe.

6. Ralph Waldo Emerson

Thank you for coming to this lecture on love.
I have been told that in public discourse
my true reverence for intellectual discourse
has made me indifferent to the subject of love,
but I almost shrink at such disparaging words
since I believe love created the world.
What else, after all, perpetuates the world
except enacted love? I savor the words.

The study of love is a question of facts
and a matter of dreams, a dream that matters.
Lovers are scientists studying heavenly matters
while their bodies connect the sweetest facts.
Please don't blush when I speak of love
as the reunion of two independent souls
who have drifted since birth as lost souls
but now come together in eternal love.

There can be no love without natural sympathy.
Let's say you're a hunter who excels at business
(I'm aware this may be none of my business)
but for me it doesn't arouse much sympathy.
Let's say, however, you drink tea in the morning
and like to eat apple pie for breakfast;
we both walk through the country very fast
watching the darkness turn into early morning

and this creates a mutual bond between us
that leads to a soulful sharing of sabbaths.
The heart has its jubilees and sabbaths
when a fiery lightning strikes between us.
I do not shy away from the subject of sex
which is, after all, a principle of the universe
(it is also, alas, a principle of my verse)
since we are bound to each other through sex.

Look how the girls flirt with the boys
while the boys slowly encircle the girls.
The village shops are crowded with girls
lingering over nothing to talk with boys.
Romance is the beginning of celestial ecstasy,
an immortal hilarity, a condition of joy:
civilization itself depends on the joy
of standing beside ourselves with ecstasy.

Love is a bright foreigner, a foreign self
that must recognize me for what I truly am;
only my lover can understand me as I am
when I am struggling to create myself.
So, too, I must love you as you truly are—
but what is that? Under your cool visage
and coy exterior, your advancing age,
I sense the young passion of who you are.

The lover comes with something to declare—
such declarations affirm the nature of love.
Here is what the lover says to his love
in the heat of passion, this I declare:
My love for you is a voluptuous world
where the seasons appear as a bright feast.
We can sit together at this delicious feast.
Come lie down with me and devour the world.

7. Colette

My young friends, this is the final lecture,
though not the last word, on the subject of love,
so thank you for listening. It is my pleasure
to address a passion I know something about
(which is something, forgive me, I can't say about
all the previous lecturers)—not just pleasure,
but the unruly depths we describe as love.
Let's call our tête-à-tête, "A Modern Lecture."

My mother used to say, "Sit down, dear,
and don't cry. The worst thing for a woman
is her first man—the one who kills you.
After that, marriage becomes a long career."
Poor Sido! She never had another career
and she knew firsthand how love ruins you.
The seducer doesn't care about his woman,
even as he whispers endearments in her ear.

Never let anyone destroy your inner spirit.
Among all the forms of truly absurd courage
the recklessness of young girls is outstanding.
Otherwise there would be far fewer marriages
and even fewer affairs that overwhelm marriages.
Look at me: it's amazing I'm still standing
after what I went through with ridiculous courage.
I was made to suffer, but no one broke my spirit.

Every woman wants her adventure to be a feast
of ripening cherries and peaches, Marseilles figs,
hothouse grapes, champagne shuddering in crystal.
Happiness, we believe, is on sumptuous display.
But unhappiness writes a different kind of play.
The gypsy gazes down into a clear blue crystal
and sees rotten cherries and withered figs.
Trust me: loneliness, too, can be a feast.

Ardor is delicious, but keep your own room.
One of my husbands said: is it impossible
for you to write a book that isn't about love,
adultery, semi-incestuous relations, separation?
(Of course, this was before our own separation.)
He never understood the natural law of love,
the arc from the possible to the impossible . . .
I have extolled the tragedy of the bedroom.

We need exact descriptions of the first passion,
so pay attention to whatever happens to you.
Observe everything: love is greedy and forgetful.
By all means fling yourself wildly into life
(though sometimes you will be flung back by life)
but don't let experience make you forgetful
and be surprised by everything that happens to you.
We are creative creatures fuelled by passion.

Consider this an epilogue to the lectures on love,
a few final thoughts about the nature of love.
Freedom should be the first condition of love
and work is liberating (*a novel about love
cannot be written while you are making love*).
Never underestimate the mysteries of love,
the eminent dignity of not talking about love.
Passionate attention is prayer, prayer is love.

Savor the world. Consume the feast with love.

A manuscript page from the lyrics of "Barcelona" from Company.
A later draft appears on p. 269.

Stephen Sondheim

The Art of the Musical

Stephen Sondheim was born in New York in 1930. He has written the music and lyrics for twelve Broadway musicals and the lyrics for West Side Story, Gypsy *and* Do I Hear a Waltz? *as well as many other songs. He has composed film scores and has won an Academy Award best original song for "Sooner or Later," which was sung by Madonna in* Dick Tracy. *He won the Tony Award and the Drama Critics Circle Award for best score for* Company, Follies, A Little Night Music, Sweeney Todd, Into the Woods *and* Passion. *He received the Pulitzer Prize for* Sunday in the Park with George. *In 1983 he was elected to the American Academy of Arts and Letters. In 1990 he was appointed the first visiting professor of contemporary theater at Oxford University and, in 1993, was a recipient of the Kennedy Center Honors for Lifetime Achievement. In 1992 he refused to accept the National Endowment's Medal of Arts Award because he felt the NEA had been, in his words, "transformed into a conduit and symbol of censorship and repression rather than encouragement and support." He accepted the award in 1997.*

This interview was excerpted from a craft seminar at the New School in New York City, which appeared on the Bravo Network as an episode of Inside the Actors Studio. *The seminar ended with a classroom session in which questions were invited from the audience.*

JAMES LIPTON

When you were ten, and your parents divorced, your mother moved to Pennsylvania, and it was there at the age of eleven that you encountered Jimmy Hammerstein and were welcomed into the family of Oscar and Dorothy Hammerstein. I understand you've said that if Hammerstein had been a geologist, you would have become a geologist.

STEPHEN SONDHEIM

Yes. He was a surrogate father and a mentor to me up until his death. When I was fifteen, I wrote a show for George School, the Friends school I went to. It was called *By George* and was about the students and the faculty. I was convinced that Rodgers and Hammerstein couldn't wait to produce it, so I gave it to Oscar and asked him to read it as if he didn't know me. I went to bed dreaming of my name in lights on

Broadway, and when I was summoned to his house the next day he asked, "Do you really want me to treat this as if I didn't know you?" "Oh, yes," I said, to which he replied, "In that case, it's the worst thing I've ever read." He saw me blanch and continued, "I didn't say it was untalented, but let's look at it." He proceeded to discuss it as if it were a serious piece. He started right from the first stage direction; and I've often said, at the risk of hyperbole, that I probably learned more about writing songs that afternoon than I learned the rest of my life. He taught me how to structure a song, what a character was, what a scene was; he taught me how to tell a story, how not to tell a story, how to make stage directions practical.

Of course, when you're fifteen you're a sponge. I soaked it all up and I still practice the principles he taught me that afternoon. From then on, until the day he died, I showed him everything I wrote, and eventually had the Oedipal thrill of being able to criticize *his* lyrics, which was a generous thing for him to let me do.

LIPTON

I've read that one of the things you learned from him was the power of a single word.

SONDHEIM

Oscar dealt in very plain language. He often used simple rhymes like *day* and *May*, and a lot of identities like "Younger than springtime am I/Gayer than laughter am I." If you look at "Oh, what a beautiful mornin!/Oh, what a beautiful day!" it doesn't seem like much on paper, but he understood what happens when music is applied to words: the words explode. They have their own rainbows, their own magic. But not on the printed page. Some lyrics read well because they're conversational lyrics. Oscar's do not read very well because they're colloquial but not conversational. Without music, they sound simplistic and *written*. Yet it's precisely the hypersimplicity of the language that gives them such force. If you listen to "What's the Use of Wond'rin'" from *Carousel*, you'll see what I mean.

LIPTON

He also stressed the importance of creating character in songs.

SONDHEIM

Remember, he'd begun as a playwright, before he became a songwriter. He believed that songs should be like one-act plays, that they should have a beginning, a middle and an end. They should set up a situation, have a development and then a conclusion . . . exactly like a classically constructed play. Arthur Pinero said about playwriting, "Tell them what you're going to do, then do it, then tell them you've done it." If that's what a play is, Oscar's songs are little plays. He utilized that approach as early as *Show Boat*. That's how he revolutionized musical theater—utilizing operetta principles and pasting them onto American musical comedy.

LIPTON

That afternoon, as I recall, Hammerstein also outlined for you a curriculum, and told you he wanted you to write four things. It sounds like a wonderful fairy tale. What were they?

SONDHEIM

"First," he said, "take a play that you like, that you think is good, and musicalize it. In musicalizing it, you'll be forced to analyze it. Next, take a play that you think is good but flawed, that you think could be improved, and musicalize that, seeing if you can improve it. Then take a non-play, a narrative someone else has written—it could be a novel, a short story—but not a play, not something that has been structured dramatically for the stage, and musicalize that. Then try an original." The first one I did was a play by George S. Kaufman and Marc Connelly, *Beggar on Horseback*, which lends itself easily to musicalization because it's essentially a long fantasy. We performed that at college when I was an undergraduate at Williams. I got permission from Kaufman to do it and we had three performances. It was a valuable experience, indeed.

The second one, which I couldn't get permission for, was a play by Maxwell Anderson called *High Tor*, which I liked but thought was sort of clumsy. Then I tried to adapt *Mary Poppins*. I didn't finish that one because I couldn't figure out how to take a series of disparate short stories, even though the same characters existed throughout, and make an evening, make an arc. After that I wrote an original musical about a guy who wanted to become an actor, and became a producer. He had a sort of Sammy Glick streak in him—he was something of an opportunist. So I wrote my idea of a sophisticated, cynical musical. It was called *Climb High*. There was a motto on a flight of stone steps at Williams, "Climb high, climb far, your aim the sky, your goal the star." I thought, Gee, that's very Hammersteinish. I sent him the whole thing. The first act was ninety-nine pages long. Now, the entire script of *South Pacific*, which lasted almost three hours on the stage, was only ninety-two pages. Oscar sent my script back, circled the ninety-nine and just wrote, "Wow!"

LIPTON

That's a step up from "the worst musical I've ever read." At Williams your major was in music, and your mentor there was Robert Barrow?

SONDHEIM

Yes. I was a mathematician by nature, and still am—I just knew I didn't want to be a mathematician. So I decided not to take any mathematics courses. Williams being a liberal-arts college, the natural, neutral major is English. As an elective my first year, I took music, which was generally known as a gut course. Williams in those days had eleven hundred students, all male, and a tiny music department. Robert Barrow was the senior of two teachers. The students hated him because he was cold and Mary Poppinsish. He taught rigidly out of a little black book compiled over the years into which he had compressed a lot of texts. He had a completely anti-romantic approach to music. I had always imagined that writing music was all about sitting in your penthouse or your studio until this lady muse twitters around your head and sits on your shoulders and goes, "Da-da-da-dum, da-da-da-dum." Instead, Robert Barrow was talking about leading tones and diatonic scales, and I fell in love. He took all the mystery out of music and taught craft. Within a year I was majoring in music. He changed my life by making me aware that art is craft, not inspiration.

LIPTON

When you graduated from Williams, you received the Hutchinson Prize for music, which was a fellowship for further study. With whom did you study?

SONDHEIM

Milton Babbitt, the avant-gardist's avant-gardist. When I started studying with him, he had already gone beyond twelve-tone music and was working up at Columbia on synthesized music, which in those days was a science fiction, the idea being that (his example) he could make a bassoon play a high C. He was a rigorous intellectual but also happened to be a frustrated songwriter. When I first met him, he was writing a musical for Mary Martin. I would meet with him once a week, for about four hours, and we'd spend the first hour analyzing his favorite songs—I can still analyze "All the Things You Are" according to Babbitt, which in fact I did for my students at Oxford. Then we'd spend the rest of the time analyzing Beethoven and Mozart.

I asked him if he would teach me atonal music. He said, "There's no point until you've exhausted tonal resources for yourself. You haven't, have you?" I said, "No, and I suspect I'll never want to." So I never did study atonal music. He taught tonal as rigorously as Barrow did. It was a similar approach: analyze the music, look at what the music *is*. How do you sustain something, hold a piece together for forty-five minutes if it's a symphony, or three minutes if it's a song? How do you manage time? That's what he taught me.

LIPTON

Why did you hesitate when you were offered the chance to write the lyrics of *West Side Story*?

SONDHEIM

I wanted primarily to write music. But Oscar advised me that the job would be an extraordinary opportunity to work with men of such ability, talent and imagination as Leonard Bernstein, Jerome Robbins and Arthur Laurents. So I took it. And he was right.

LIPTON

I've heard you disparage your lyrics for *West Side Story*, but I would give a great deal to have written, "Oh, moon, grow bright and make this endless day endless night."

SONDHEIM

It's fine until you remember that it's sung by an adolescent in a gang.

LIPTON

You've said, "I've always thought of lyric-writing as a craft rather than an art, largely a matter of sweat and time. Music is more challenging, more interesting and more rewarding." Do you still feel that way?

SONDHEIM

Sure. Because music's abstract, and it's fun, and it lives in you. Language is terrific, but the English language is a difficult tool to work with. Two of the hardest words in the language to rhyme are *life* and *love*. Of all words! In Italian, easy. But not English. Making lyrics feel natural, sit on music in such a way that you don't feel the effort of the author, so that they shine and bubble and rise and fall, is very, very hard to do. Whereas you can sit at the piano and just play, and feel you're making art.

LIPTON

The *love* rhymes are *shove*, *above*, *dove*, *glove* and *of*. That's all we've got.

SONDHEIM

And they're not easy to use. *Live* isn't easy, either. You have *give* and *sieve* and then you're in a lot of trouble.

LIPTON

The English language has forty-two sounds in it, French a dozen, so everything rhymes with everything else. That's why Molière was able to write those alexandrines, couplet after couplet, without ever straining for a rhyme.

SONDHEIM

But lyrics are also about open vowel sounds. The Italians have it all over us *and* the French because everything is *ahhhh*! Try to sing *me* on a high note. And *me* is a very useful word.

LIPTON

Or *him*.

SONDHEIM

Exactly. *Short* is terrible. Singers will tell you that their throats close up.

LIPTON

A Funny Thing Happened on the Way to the Forum was the first Broadway show for which you wrote music and lyrics and, if memory serves, when the show was out of town, you were out on the streets giving tickets away to get people into the theater.

SONDHEIM

It was a disaster out of town. It was directed by George Abbott, who was famous as a play doctor. We would stand in the back of the auditorium in New Haven and feel the discomfort of the audience; all the while we thought that what we were seeing was terrific. Finally, one evening George said, "I don't know what to do, you'd better call in George Abbott."

When we got down to Washington, we asked Jerome Robbins to come in and help. He said, "It's the opening number that's killing it. It's not telling them what the show's about. You've got to write a baggy-pants number." So I wrote this song called "Comedy Tonight." Jerry insisted, though, "I don't want you to tell any jokes, let *me* tell the jokes." Very smart of him. That's why the lyric is so bland and dull—it's background for Jerry's pyrotechnics. It may be the best opening number ever put on the stage. The audience was so satisfied at the end of it that we thought, Let's not do the rest of the show.

LIPTON

You once asked Oscar Hammerstein why he never wrote a sophisticated musical.

SONDHEIM

He said, "You mean something that takes place in penthouses?" I said yes. He said, "Because it doesn't interest me." Most people probably think that Oscar was a hayseed and sat on a porch all the time watching cattle turn into statues, but in fact he was an urban product, a New York boy, and very— well, urbane. Sharp tongue. Pointed wit. Wonderful critic. It's just that was not what he wanted to write about. He wanted to write about so-called simplicities. He was a morality playwright. He wrote about Everyman. And every time he tried to write something that was particularly urban or contemporary, it wasn't very good, as in *Me and Juliet* and parts of *Allegro*. He was sharp and smart, but he didn't feel it. That's why he didn't want to write about penthouses, and he was right.

LIPTON

But you certainly did, in *Company*, a sophisticated New York penthouse story. It has been called a revolutionary musical. Was it a plotless show?

SONDHEIM

Yes, because it didn't begin as a musical. George Furth was an actor and was in therapy. His therapist suggested that it might be good for him to do some writing. So he wrote a series of one-act plays — playlets, really. A production had been set up but had fallen through, so he sent them to me and said, "I don't know what to do with these." I wrote back, "Let me send them to Hal Prince because he's very shrewd about this sort of thing. Maybe he can give you some advice." Hal said, "Why don't we make a musical out of them?" It seemed impossible because they were such disparate plays, and that made it intriguing. So George came east, we spent two or three weeks talking, and gradually the form of the show took shape. It came from the fact that in each playlet there were two people in a relationship and a third person who often acted as a catalyst. We realized that what the show should be about is the *third* person. So we invented the character of Bobby, the outsider in five different marriages. We realized that there could be no plot in the conventional sense. A man comes home on his thirty-fifth birthday and realizes that all his friends are married; he's an outsider. And he has a combination breakdown and epiphany. The show really takes place in one second. His friends are there but they're not there, and they don't know each other but they do know each other. They're all fragments of his consciousness. That's what made it an unusual show: it took place in a single moment of time. It wasn't a conventional narrative nor was it a revue, because each of the playlets concerned the same characters. Also, none of the songs grew out of scenes. Each of the songs was either a comment or the entire scene itself. And all the songs, with one exception, dealt with marriage or relationships — a word I don't much like, but I did in those days. So it became this kind of twilight-zone revue. That whole area between revue and book is something I've always been interested in. It surfaced in *Follies*, then again in *Pacific Overtures* and *Assassins*. And that's what was, to use your word, revolutionary — at least in the commercial musical theater.

                        (Pause)
Robert: Whatcha thinking?
April: Barceloma.
Robert: ...Oh...
April: ~~Don't be mad~~. *Flight eighteen.*
Robe.t: Stay a minute.
April: I would like to.
Robert: ...so?...
April: Don't be ~~mad~~. *now.*
Robert: ~~You are crazy~~. *Stay a minute.*
April: ~~No, I'm not.~~ *No, I can't.*
Robert: ~~Yes, you are.~~ *Yes, you can.*
April: ~~No, I'm not.~~ *No, I can't.*
Robert: ~~Well, in one way~~ *Not understanding*
April: Ask me back, though.
Robert: Come on back.
April: No, not now.
Robert: Bon voyage.
        Happy ~~runway~~ *landing* and good-
        Night.
April: You're angry.
Robert: No.
April: I've got to -
Robert: Right.
April: Report to -
Robert: Go.
April: That's not to
        Say
        That if I had my way...
        Oh well, I guess okay.
Robert: What?
April: I'll stay.
Robert: But -
        (as she snuggles down)
        Oh, God.

A revision of the lyrics from "Barcelona."

LIPTON

There's a remarkable song in *Company* called "Barcelona" that's actually very well-written dialogue . . .

SONDHEIM

I'll tell you something funny about "Barcelona." I finished it the night before we went into rehearsal. Hal had been pushing me to get the April-Bobby song finished because it was an entire scene. So I wrote "Barcelona" and went up to his house and played it. He looked blank throughout the whole thing and said, "Well, look, we can do it at the read-through tomorrow, anyway." I thought, Oh God. Then his wife Judy came in and asked if she could hear the new song. I said, "I'm afraid it's not quite . . . well, I'll play it anyway." I sang the opening line, "Where you going?/Barcelona," and she laughed. I thought, All right, maybe it's got a chance. The next day, at the read-through, we get to "Barcelona" and I play and sing it. I sing the first line, and the entire cast convulses with laughter. Hal looks over at me and shrugs. He has no trouble admitting he's wrong.

LIPTON

Today the concept musical is commonplace. The British seem to have inherited it from us. Some people think they invented it. *Follies* was certainly a concept musical. Could you tell us its genesis?

SONDHEIM

First of all, I would hardly call the British musicals "concept" musicals—they seem like traditional operettas to me. And in any event, *concept musical* is a meaningless term, useful only to critics who need to categorize and directors who want to consider themselves writers. As for *Follies*, I went to Jim Goldman, a friend and a playwright I admire, and asked him if he had any ideas for musicals. He'd always wanted to write a play about reunions, he said, and he'd recently picked up a newspaper clipping about the Ziegfeld Girls' annual reunion. We thought that might be the basis of a show.

It took four years to write *Follies*—not steadily. We wrote it first as a murder mystery—not a mystery, that's not quite right—but a murder piece. It was about four people—two couples—who had been emotionally involved with each other a long time ago, and who thought their lives had been damaged because of it. The notion was that one of them was going to murder one of the others, and the suspense, so to speak, was who's going to kill whom? Every time we would do a draft, the atmosphere for the first few minutes would be fine, but then, as soon as the plot came in, it would start to get a little ratchety. So we decided to delay the plot, maybe for fifteen minutes. Again it started to get ratchety, so we delayed it for twenty-five. Finally, it struck us that maybe there shouldn't be any plot at all, that it should be all atmosphere. That is, in fact, what it turned out to be. There's minimal plot. It all takes place during a party. It's about people getting drunk, and their old emotions surging to the surface and inter-connecting . . . all in the atmosphere of the Ziegfeld Follies. What it really is about is the loss of innocence—not only among the characters but in America between the wars, which the Follies, I think, represented.

I was much influenced in those days by the movies of Alain Resnais, and I think *Follies* was probably more influenced by *Last Year at Marienbad* than anything else. It had to do with time, and Hal gave it a surreal spin in the staging—Hal and Michael Bennett. That increased the *misterioso* quality of it . . . which is the best thing about it.

LIPTON

When Richard Rodgers was asked, "Which comes first, the music or the lyrics?" he usually replied, "The check." Since you're both the composer and lyricist, what do you start with?

SONDHEIM

Two basic things. Some kind of accompaniment figure and/or some sort of refrain line or central idea for a lyric. Those are the two kinds of glue for a song. The trick is to keep them going together, so you don't get boxed in.

LIPTON

You've taken us all off the hook by admitting you use a rhyming dictionary. I think you and I use the same one, Clement Wood.

SONDHEIM

That's the best one, and for a very simple reason: all the words are listed vertically. If you use one that lists them horizontally, your eyes start to skip over the entries. The problem with Clement Wood is that it was published in 1938, so there are very few contemporary words in it. But I've written a lot of words into my main copy. The book was out of print for years but luckily, I'd bought four copies so I had them all over the place. Happily, it's now in print again. If anybody wants to write lyrics, that's the one to use.

LIPTON

The other thing that's essential is a thesaurus. Not a dictionary but a thesaurus, because you want to know what your choices are. There I also have a favorite, by Norman Lewis. It's a thesaurus in dictionary form. The way Roget arranged his thesaurus mystifies me.

SONDHEIM

But what's interesting about the Roget is that it opens your mind, because in doing the cross-referencing, when you start looking up synonyms, you have to go back and forth, you come across shadings of words you hadn't thought of, which lead to other words. The problem with the Roget is that it's been in so many editions. The one that I think offers the best balance between the number of words and the number of cross-references is the 1943 edition. That may sound fussy but, as you know, you work with the same tools over a period of time and they become important.

LIPTON

I've heard you say that you don't like to work at the piano.

SONDHEIM

Well, if you work at the piano, you're limited by your own technique. I have a very good right hand, but a left hand like a ham hock. Also, muscle memory comes into it. You start playing the same chords, the same figurations. If you force yourself to write away from the piano, you come up with more inventive things. If you're too good a piano player, as some composers are, the music may become flavorless and glib. And if you're not a very good pianist, you're limited to the same patterns. I force myself to write in keys that I haven't written in for a while. I find that most composers consider sharp keys the enemy and flat keys the friends. Flat keys somehow are more welcoming. I often force myself to write in sharp keys just to get away from the pattern. I think it's very important to try to write away from the piano.

LIPTON

I've always wanted to ask you this: why on earth name *A Little Night Music* after *Eine Kleine Nachtmusik*? It had nothing to do with Mozart. And you had *Smiles of a Summer Night* sitting there looking at you.

SONDHEIM

Yes, and we also had Ingmar Bergman, who wouldn't let us use the title of the film. He gave us the rights to everything else. However, when the show was subsequently done in Vienna, we realized that in German it would revert to *Eine Kleine Nachtmusik*, which would have made people think they were going to a Mozart concert. So we wrote Bergman and asked him to let us use *Smiles of a Summer Night* in German. He gave us permission that one time.

LIPTON

Sweeney Todd was operatic, using leitmotifs, as opera does. Characters had themes, and the themes assembled, disassembled, reassembled. You've said that you were influenced by, of all people, Bernard Herrmann.

SONDHEIM

True. When I was fifteen years old I saw a movie called *Hangover Square*, another epiphany in my life. It was a moody, romantic, gothic thriller starring Laird Cregar, about a composer in London in 1900 who was ahead of his time.

And whenever he heard a high note he went crazy and ran around murdering people. It had an absolutely brilliant score by Bernard Herrmann, centered around a one-movement piano concerto. I wanted to pay homage to him with this show, because I had realized that in order to scare people, which is what *Sweeney Todd* is about, the only way you can do it, considering that the horrors out on the street are so much greater than anything you can do on the stage, is to keep music going all the time. That's the principle of suspense sequences in movies, and Bernard Herrmann was a master in that field. So *Sweeney Todd* not only has a lot of singing, it has a lot of underscoring. It's *infused* with music, to keep the audience in a state of tension, to make them forget they're in a theater and to prevent them from separating themselves from the action. I based a lot of the score on a specific chord that Herrmann uses in almost all his film work, and spun it out from that. That and the "Dies Irae," which is one of my favorite tunes, and is full of menace.

LIPTON

Sunday in the Park with George marked a new collaboration. There was the long period in which Hal Prince produced and directed your musicals, and now we enter the Sondheim-James Lapine period, which has given us a different sensibility. Lapine comes from photography and graphic design. He's experimental, a poet.

SONDHEIM

I admired Jim Lapine's work. I'd seen a play that he wrote and directed called *Twelve Dreams*. A mutual friend, a producer, got us together, and we were talking one night about theme and variations, because that's a kind of show I had always wanted to do. I showed him a French magazine I had that was devoted to variations on the *Mona Lisa*. And we started talking about paintings. He had used the Seurat painting *La Grande Jatte* in a piece he had done up at Yale. And he said, "Did you ever notice there are over fifty people in

it, and nobody's looking at anybody else?" We started to specu-
late why. Suddenly I said, "It's like a stage set, you know. It's
like a French farce, isn't it? You know, maybe those people
aren't supposed to be seen with each other." We started to
talk about how it might make a story, and then James said
the crucial thing: "Of course, the main character's missing."
I said, "Who?" He said, "The painter." As soon as he said
that, we knew we had a show. It would be more than a stunt,
it would be a play about a man and his landscape and how
he controls it. And how hard it is to make art.

LIPTON

Into the Woods was another groundbreaking musical. Once
again you worked with Lapine.

SONDHEIM

Well, another kind of piece I'd always wanted to do was a
fairy tale, so I asked James if he'd like to write one. He said,
"The trouble with fairy tales is that they're really only five
minutes long. There's one incident, maybe two, and that's
all there should be." Which is exactly the trouble with all the
attempts to expand fairy tales and make them into plays and
musicals. So the notion arose of mashing a number of fairy
tales together. James held them together by inventing his own,
the story of a baker and his wife. Some of the fairy tales got
dropped on the road. We had the Three Little Pigs in there,
we had Rumpelstiltskin, we had everybody—*everybody* was
in the woods. But eventually we had to cut it down.

LIPTON

There seems to be a philosophical war in that musical between the theories of Bruno Bettelheim and Jung.

SONDHEIM

It's interesting you say that. Everybody assumes we were
influenced by Bruno Bettelheim. But if there's any outside
influence, it's Jung. James is interested in Jung—*Twelve*

Dreams is based on a case Jung wrote about. In fact, we spoke to a Jungian analyst about fairy tales.

LIPTON

The moral of your fairy tale seems to be: beware of wishes, they may come true.

SONDHEIM

It's about moral responsibility — the responsibility you have in getting your wish not to cheat and step on other people's toes, because it rebounds. The second act is about the consequences of not only the wishes themselves, but of the methods by which the characters achieve their wishes, which are not always proper and moral.

AUDIENCE MEMBER

I'm wondering what your musical influences are. I hear Debussy . . .

SONDHEIM

It's Ravel more than Debussy. Ravel's responsible for virtually all popular music, anyway — all those chords really started with him. My period is from Brahms through 1930s Stravinsky. I like music before and I like music after, but that's where I live. Britten shows up a lot in the stuff I write. *Sunday in the Park with George* is a Britten score, I think. I'm very fond of English music. As far as American music goes, I was brought up on show tunes from the so-called Golden Era, a phrase I deplore, but there it is. You know, Kern and Gershwin. Those are influences, too. So it's Ravel, Rachmaninoff — another wonderful harmonist — Britten, Stravinsky, Kern, Gershwin, Arlen. A *lot* of Arlen.

AUDIENCE MEMBER

How long before the opening do you freeze a musical production?

SONDHEIM

Bear in mind that musicals are *presentational* plays. The whole idea of a musical is out front. Numbers go *out front*, no matter how intense, they go out front. Therefore the performer has to make a contact with the audience, and as a writer, out front, I have to see that contact before I start to change things. If a scene or a number isn't working, it may be the performer, it may be the song. And it may be the performer not being used to the song. Or the performer still worrying about a costume change. Remember that in musicals, often there's a lot of scenery changing, a lot of costume changing. If you're smart, it takes a number of performances before you change anything in a musical because during the first couple of performances, the performers are lucky if they get away with their lives, if they don't fall into the pit, if they don't get run over by some of the moving scenery. At the same time, they're performing for an audience. And because of that, freezing a show is very useful, in the sense of letting performers play the exact same thing for, let's say, three or four performances, without our changing any of their staging, without giving them new lines or new songs or new lyrics. Minimal changes so that they can solidify what they're doing. Then you can look at the play and say, "Aha, okay, that scene's too long. She's doing that song wrong." Or, "That song is wrong for her. Is it my fault? Shall I rewrite or shall I tell her to perform the song differently?" As I say, it's *presentational*. That's what makes musicals entirely different from plays. As an actor, you can just play the scene. If you're a *performer* and it's a *number*, you have to make it land, if that's what's required. And to make it land doesn't mean just to sing loudly. It means everything—from the acting to the voice to the presentation. Also the lights. Remember, when a musical number begins, the lights go down. That doesn't often happen in a scene. So everything conspires to make the moment false. And your job is to make it *true*. And at the same time please the audience.

AUDIENCE MEMBER

You mentioned that playwrights today write great characters, they have great ideas, but very few write great stories. I just wondered what you think is a great story.

SONDHEIM

I didn't use the word *great*. That's not one of my favorite words because it implies a value judgment. I said that it's very *hard* to write narratives, very hard to write stories. I happen to like strong narratives. I also happen to be a worshipper of Chekhov. His stories are going on inside the people, and the narrative pull is perhaps not very strong. But I also like Lillian Hellman's plays where the narrative sometimes teeters over into melodrama. The Ibsen school. I'm a big melodrama fan. I'm a big farce fan. I'm a big plot fan. But I don't think it's necessary to have one. I mean, *A Streetcar Named Desire* doesn't have much of a plot. But it sure has a strong story. And by story, I mean something that takes you in a state of tension from scene to scene and moment to moment, as opposed to just inundating you with colors and moods. That's all. Something that keeps your attention going for two hours and doesn't let you off the hook. And that could be a comedy. That could be Chekhov. It could be a murder mystery. But it must have something to keep you going. Anyway, inventive narrative is very hard to do, so it isn't about "great" or even "good," it's about whether you can do it at all. I'll bet if you made a list of, say, twenty plays over the last five years, there might be two that had a real plot. You might have enjoyed some of the others, but I'll bet it was the acting, I'll bet it was a scene, a character, "Wasn't that moment wonderful when . . ?" as opposed to a substantial two-hour experience.

Lot 13: The Bone Violin

Doug Wright

a fugue for five actors

THE AUCTIONEER   A no-nonsense professional.
THE MOTHER   A well-meaning woman overwhelmed by the enormity of life.
THE FATHER   Pragmatic. Earthbound. "No Frills."
THE DOCTOR   A bespectacled woman in a lab coat. Aryan.
THE PROFESSOR   Supercilious, with discontent born of thwarted ambitions.

The Setting: Downstage sits a table, about six feet in length, covered by a linen cloth. Further upstage are four stools with corresponding music stands. Stage left, a podium.
In the distance, Paganini's Violin Concerto No.1.

Lights rise on the mother, the father, the professor and the doctor. They sit behind the four music stands, solemnly, their hands folded.

The auctioneer enters and takes his place behind the podium.
He slams his gavel. The music abruptly stops. He announces
in a loud voice:

THE AUCTIONEER: LOT THIRTEEN.

The four other characters spring to life. They speak rapidly,
their words trailing in and out of another, creating a kind of
vocal symphony. Most of the time, they address the audience
directly. Occasionally, they speak among themselves. A few
times, they reenact snippets of dialogue from the past.

THE MOTHER: I never wanted to play the violin. I don't even
like classical music.
THE FATHER: The Stones. Led Zeppelin. To me, that's classic.
THE MOTHER: Psychologists say we're always thrusting our
dreams onto the shoulders of our children. Well, I wanted to
be a dog groomer.
THE DOCTOR: Nature or nurture?
THE MOTHER: No lie. A dog groomer.
THE DOCTOR: The chicken or the egg?
THE MOTHER: You dream bigger for your kids.
THE DOCTOR: The zygote? Andover?
THE MOTHER: I went to a genealogist once. He said one of my
ancestors had been a harpsichordist. In Prague.
THE FATHER: Went back eight generations, just to come up
with that.
THE DOCTOR: PhD . . .
THE MOTHER: If we were religious, we'd call it a gift from God.
THE DOCTOR: . . . or DNA?
THE MOTHER: When he was born, the first thing I noticed:
his hands.
THE DOCTOR: The ovum, or the Ivy League?
THE MOTHER: Such elegant fingers for a baby.
THE DOCTOR: Molecules, or Montessori? Tanglewood or testes?
THE FATHER: He'd wrap those little mitts around my thumb,
and I knew he wasn't going to wind up laying bricks.

THE DOCTOR: Well . . . ?

THE MOTHER: It all started in nursery school, during Music Corner. *Peter and the Wolf.*

THE FATHER: Kid hummed it in the tub.

THE MOTHER: In his sleep.

THE FATHER: With his mouth full.

THE MOTHER: By his fourth birthday, he was hounding us for a violin.

THE FATHER: I bought him a baseball bat instead.

THE MOTHER: A mother expects certain milestones. Tying shoe-laces. Scissors. But *this?*

THE FATHER: He took his pocketknife, and his brand new Louisville Slugger . . . the kid started whittling.

THE MOTHER: There were wood chips all over his dungarees.

THE FATHER: Scrape, scrape, scrape until. . .

THE MOTHER: *Voilà.* He'd carved a perfect bow.

THE FATHER: So much for Babe Ruth.

THE MOTHER: He stole his father's tennis racket. Stripped the frame and restrung it with fishing line. A homemade violin.

THE FATHER: We shoulda known then.

THE MOTHER: He had this remarkable gift for—what would you call it?

THE PROFESSOR: (*Dryly*) Transformation.

Everyone regards the professor for a beat. The mother pauses, then opts to continue.

THE MOTHER: He'd go out back, to the old Chevy.

THE FATHER: It's on cinder blocks.

THE MOTHER: He'd sit in that car for hours.

THE FATHER: Scrap mostly, but the radio works.

THE MOTHER: Listening. Tune after tune.

THE FATHER: Only had to hear 'em once.

THE MOTHER: And he could play them right back. No, really.

THE FATHER: The kid was Memorex.

THE MOTHER: Note for note.

THE FATHER: Eerie.

THE MOTHER: I read Alice Miller. Ignore a child's creativity and he'll grow up lopsided. Encourage it, and he slices off his ear, or drowns himself.

THE FATHER: It's a no-win situation.

THE MOTHER: Suppose you were in your garden, pulling weeds. Suppose for the first time you noticed a beautiful rhododendron growing up through the crabgrass. You'd water it, wouldn't you?

THE PROFESSOR: "Natural abilities are like natural plants; they need pruning by study." Sir Francis Bacon.

THE MOTHER: We found this college instructor. In town.

THE PROFESSOR: My last tutorial had ended badly. A tiny princess with a monstrous cello between her knees. Her parents made accusations so sinister and baroque I began to question their proclivities, never mind my own.

THE MOTHER: At first, he was skeptical.

THE PROFESSOR: I'd been an early bloomer myself. At twelve, you're a marvel. At thirty, you're lucky to be playing in summer bandshells. The score to *Gigi*. The best of Barry Manilow. Or, if you've a modicum of cleverness left over from your all too distinguished adolescence . . . you teach.

THE MOTHER: Still, he agreed to audition our mini concertmaster.

THE PROFESSOR: In strode a small boy, balancing a horrific instrument under his chin—all tennis string, and jagged wood. I handed him a few sheets of Strauss.

THE MOTHER: "Oh, he can't read music. He plays by ear."

THE PROFESSOR: I cringed. And then he lifted his bow. Two distinct versions of Beethoven's Sonata No. 8. I recognized them both. The first was Zukerman's, an Angel recording circa 1974. The second was Isaac Stern's, performing with the Berliner Philharmoniker, Philips, 1986. The boy duplicated them with unerring accuracy; each tremor, each trill. He would soon play a third and superior rendition. His own.

THE MOTHER: The professor was so *impressed*.

THE PROFESSOR: I know how Pope Julius felt when Michelangelo unveiled the Sistine ceiling. I know, because that's how I felt the first time I heard him play.

THE MOTHER: He offered a *very* generous scholarship.

THE PROFESSOR: My first violin was an Amati, bequeathed to me by my Italian grandfather. I, in turn, gave it to my new protégé.

THE FATHER: The kid had one thing in his favor. He wasn't Japanese.

THE PROFESSOR: At five, he'd mastered Beethoven and Bruch. At six, he could perform Sarasate's *Zingeunenweisen* blindfolded. At seven, he was taxing my abilities as a teacher. As he played velvet phrase after velvet phrase, I'd doodle nervously on his sheet music, then offer some innocuous critique. I prayed that my feeble words wouldn't impugn his natural instincts.

THE MOTHER: If driving two hours three times a week to the university is a crime . . .

THE PROFESSOR: He should've moved on.

THE MOTHER: If taking my child to his music lessons is an act of malice . . .

THE PROFESSOR: A mentor worthy of his staggering gifts.

THE MOTHER: Go ahead.

THE PROFESSOR: But I was addicted.

THE MOTHER: String me up.

THE FATHER: Prof said our kid was a regular Perlman.

THE PROFESSOR: To him, I was vestigial. To me, he was the Grail.

THE FATHER: Who the hell's Perlman?

THE PROFESSOR: I was flying to New York for a music conference. I took the child to perform for a team of colleagues. Tschaikovsky's *Mélancolique*. Every note—the plaintive sadness soaring into despair, the lilting cry of a broken heart— poured forth with volcanic force from the body of a seven-year-old boy. I stood in the wings, reduced to tears. As he left the stage, he turned to me. "My bubble gum," he said. "Give it back." I uncurled my fist, and he popped the pink wad into his mouth. I didn't know whether to embrace or throttle him.

THE FATHER: A man should support his children, not the other way around. But the carpooling, the tuxedo fittings, the concert tours . . .

THE MOTHER: I couldn't do it alone.

THE FATHER: I let the day job go.

THE MOTHER: At the supermarket, I'd hear the other mothers whispering. "Robbed of a normal childhood." People tend to say that of children with certain . . . well . . . advantages.

THE FATHER: I grew up normal. Look where it got me.

THE PROFESSOR: The artist is a willing casualty.

THE FATHER: A backbreakin' mortgage. Bifocals. Chronic gas pains.

THE PROFESSOR: His sacrifices as well as his skills catapult him beyond mere martyrdom into the realm of the divine.

THE FATHER: You can keep "normal."

THE MOTHER: When Dick hits a home run or Jane sells the most cookies, those are achievements, too. They're just not worthy of the world's attention, that's all.

THE PROFESSOR: We toured for months. Venice. Düsseldorf.

THE MOTHER: I never dreamed I'd see Salzburg.

THE FATHER: We coulda planned a vacation. Put a little back each month.

THE MOTHER: I never knew I wanted to go, until I'd already been.

THE PROFESSOR: Soon, the parasites descended.

THE FATHER: I met Ray Charles backstage at Letterman. And we got a two-page layout in *Time*.

THE MOTHER: And that high-powered doctor.

THE DOCTOR: Is talent acquired . . . or is it bred in the bone?

THE MOTHER: All those frozen test tubes.

THE DOCTOR: I first posed that question in an article entitled "Grafting the Muse," *Genetic Engineering Journal*, September 1994.

THE FATHER: All those IQ tests we had to take.

THE DOCTOR: Now I'm not one of those fanatics up in Cambridge who believe amino acids code our taste in wallpaper, and carry the names of our grandchildren. Environment plays a part. Still, the root of who we are . . . our potential . . . that's embedded.

THE FATHER: "The Institute for Genetic Predetermination."

THE DOCTOR: Highly misunderstood. "Master race, neo-Nazi." We get that all the time.

THE FATHER: Some blue-ribbon sperm bank.

THE DOCTOR: I won't pretend our selection process is democratic. It's elitist, no question. But what the public fails to recognize—what they fail to admit, in their collective egoism—is that a born biophysicist benefits us all. A born Tolstoy benefits us all. And these people *can* be born.

THE MOTHER: Imagine. Designer children.

THE DOCTOR: What we needed was proof, on a grand scale. A scientific milestone with showbiz appeal.

THE FATHER: Three Nobel prizewinners in the fridge, and they wanted our kid, too.

THE DOCTOR: Inside that boy's body swam countless incipient Mozarts. We were confident that, with him on our team, we could clone an entire orchestra.

THE FATHER: Hell, I was flattered.

THE MOTHER: He was more than a child. He was . . . my baby was . . .

THE DOCTOR: The necessary clue.

THE PROFESSOR: A pint-sized virtuoso with gargantuan coattails.

THE FATHER: A chip off some bigger, better block.

THE MOTHER: No. No. A miracle. He was a *miracle*.

THE DOCTOR: We sanitized a vial, sat back and waited for the onset of pubescence.

They wait. Seconds tick by. Finally:

The donation never occurred.

There is a brief pause. The professor tips his head toward the auctioneer.

THE PROFESSOR (to the auctioneer): Psst.

The professor tips his head toward the downstage table.

THE MOTHER: Is it time for that? Already?
THE FATHER: Must be.

*The auctioneer crosses to the table, and pulls off the linen
cloth with a flourish, revealing a small mahogany coffin, about
four feet in length. He returns to the podium. He pounds
his gavel a second time.*

THE AUCTIONEER: PAGE NUMBER SEVEN IN YOUR CATALOGUE.

Another brief rest.

THE FATHER: Kid never saw his tenth birthday.
THE DOCTOR: When we lost him, we lost funding.
THE FATHER: Had a bicycle in the garage, waiting.
THE MOTHER: His hands.
THE FATHER: Blue bicycle. With a horn.
THE MOTHER: I'll always remember his hands.
THE DOCTOR: One day, you're the darling of the Fords, the
Mellons, the MacArthurs. The next day, you're staging phone-
a-thons. Auctions. Even the occasional car wash.
THE MOTHER: I wished I'd never heard the name Georg Solti.
THE PROFESSOR: I'd met Solti only once before, at the London
Academy. We weren't formally *introduced,* but we did ex-
change words. Rub shoulders. Rumor has it he was in the
room. And now he was requesting to perform with my prize
pupil.

The mother pulls out a small concert program.

THE MOTHER: I kept the program.
THE PROFESSOR: Together, Solti and I would ruminate over
every measure of music.
THE MOTHER: Still crisp. Unopened.
THE PROFESSOR: We'd dissect each piece with the same care
and intensity a bomb technician employs when detonating
explosives.

The mother reads from the program:

THE MOTHER: "Paganini. Concerto No. 1. The Chicago Symphony."

THE PROFESSOR: "Maestro," I'd offer, "perhaps we should conclude the evening with the *Perpetuum Mobile*." "Please," he'd respond, "Call me Georg."

THE FATHER: Rehearsing the rondo. That's when the kid cracked.

THE MOTHER: Perhaps it was exhaustion.

THE FATHER: Perhaps it was nerves.

THE DOCTOR: Perhaps it was a failed synapse.

THE PROFESSOR: Perhaps it was his own angry gesture of rebellion. The bow skidded, and the violin shrieked in pain. Like some torture victim refusing to comply.

THE FATHER: Our cat caught its tail in the screen door. Made the same sound.

THE PROFESSOR: Solti suggested we begin again. But our little prodigy refused. Eyes flashing behind his tiny horn-rims. So much fury locked inside that elfin body, it shook.

THE FATHER: Concert was canceled.

THE MOTHER: We took the first flight home.

THE FATHER: Kid didn't say a word.

THE MOTHER: Three hundred miles, not a peep.

THE FATHER: As soon as I opened the front door—whoosh, bang!—he ran upstairs, then a loud slam.

THE PROFESSOR: My reputation was wounded, to say the least.

THE MOTHER: If I'd only known . . .

THE PROFESSOR: I wrote Sir Georg a long letter of apology, expressing the fervent hope we could collaborate again . . .

THE MOTHER: If I'd had any idea . . .

THE PROFESSOR: I received no reply.

THE MOTHER: . . . that was the last time I'd ever see my angel.

THE DOCTOR: Without support from the private sector—in six, seven months—the institute will be forced to close its doors.

THE PROFESSOR: When I heard of the boy's demise, in some dark, corroded corner of my mind—I felt vindicated.

THE MOTHER: That night . . . alone in his room . . . high up at the top of the stairs . . . he began to play.

(The rondo begins.)

Rondo this. Rondo that.

THE FATHER: Forwards. Backwards. At triple speed.

THE MOTHER: It rang through the house like some terrible alarm.

THE FATHER: He was hell-bent on proving something.

THE MOTHER: But to who?

THE FATHER: Paga-whosit was turning cartwheels in his grave.

THE MOTHER: His door was locked.

THE FATHER: Windows, too. Shades drawn.

THE MOTHER: By evening, the neighbors complained.

THE FATHER: What was I 'sposed to do? Tear down a wall?

THE MOTHER: We felt foolish.

THE FATHER: Call out the fire department?

THE MOTHER: I was standing on the dining-room table, pounding the ceiling with my shoe.

THE FATHER: Same damn piece, over and over and over and over and over . . .

THE MOTHER: We started slipping sheet music under the door hoping he'd play something — *anything* — new.

THE FATHER: Even tried bluegrass.

THE MOTHER: I refused to cook for him. "When he's weak from hunger," I said, "he'll have to come down."

THE FATHER: Kid wouldn't budge.

THE MOTHER: We got used to it. That's the terrible truth.

THE FATHER: I'd be out, driving. I'd miss it.

THE MOTHER: It underscored our lives. Lunatic, I know. It became as natural to us as the sound of our own breathing. Then — when was it?

THE FATHER: Four A.M. in the middle of the third week.

THE MOTHER: He stopped playing.

The music stops.

Silence.

THE FATHER: It woke us up.

THE MOTHER: "Honey."

THE FATHER: "You go."

THE MOTHER: "We'll go together."

THE FATHER: I took a flashlight.

THE MOTHER: The stairs were so tall. The climb lasted hours.

THE FATHER: Door was ajar. In we went.

THE MOTHER: The flashlight rose and fell over the furniture. His trundle bed. His little red rocker. His music stand. No sign of him. Anywhere.

THE FATHER: Then we saw it.

THE MOTHER: It was lying in the center of the room.

THE FATHER: On the rug.

THE DOCTOR: Some days later, the parents brought it to me. Our lab performed a battery of tests.

THE PROFESSOR: I had to play it. What remarkable sound! Haunting tones more reminiscent of castrati than your conventional fiddle.

THE DOCTOR: Its cellular composition matched that of the child.

THE PROFESSOR: But its appearance . . . grotesque.

THE DOCTOR: Atom for atom. It matched the child.

THE FATHER: There . . . on the rug . . . the thing was . . .

THE MOTHER: Tell them.

THE FATHER: It was still warm.

The auctioneer crosses to the coffin and opens it. A hot white light pours forth from it, like the parched sheen of highly polished bone. The auctioneer returns to his podium.

The professor approaches the casket. Gingerly, he looks inside. He describes what he sees.

THE PROFESSOR: Hollow bone. The neck and scroll twist like a femur. The pegs resemble finger joints, and the ribs of the instrument are unnervingly authentic. The string, stretched taut across its pale white body, has the unmistakable consistency of human hair. The tuners are tiny molars laid out in a grin. But the bow. The bow is truly shocking. It has an almost spinal curve; the backbone of a child.

The doctor and the father step forward to meet the professor. Finally — with great hesitancy — the mother joins them.

Solemnly, they all gaze into the coffin. The light illuminates them from beneath, casting an eerie glow across their faces.

THE FATHER: We shoulda known then.
THE PROFESSOR: Perhaps that's all he ever was. An instrument.
THE FATHER: Way back. We shoulda known.
THE PROFESSOR: Are we to blame? For anthropomorphosizing?
THE MOTHER: We never found him.
THE PROFESSOR: The violin is real. Did we imagine the child?
THE MOTHER: We never found our little boy.

Slowly, the mother, the father, the doctor and the professor return to their music stands. The lights on them fade.

Lights intensify on the auctioneer, and on the bone violin.

The auctioneer pounds his gavel a third time.

THE AUCTIONEER: WE'LL START THE BIDDING AT TEN THOUSAND . . .

Blackout.

Two Poems by Michael Burns

.38

Never had a loaded, blue-black handgun
in my house, except for 1981,

sweltering summer, to be exact, way out
in the middle of America, about

two miles west of Oklahoma City
where I lived alone in some shitty

farmhouse. Fleas bit. The broken windmill
cried all night for the good young couple

hit by a semi, who had lived there before.
Skunks speculated at the back door,

and the pool, some folk art in concrete,
was cracked and empty. I lay in moonlight

aiming my life at the stars. I hid in the barn
when cars pulled up, fired once or twice to warn

the world away. No, I didn't do that.
I went to work, and read my mail, and sat

down in a chair, next to the telephone.
I kept the gun nearby, with the safety on.

General Sickles Sits for a Portrait

*As a northern veteran once remarked to me, "General Sickles
can well afford to leave a leg on that field."*
                    —Confederate General James Longstreet, 1902

You've seen my tibia and fibula?
I used to take my friends to visit them
each year at the museum, septic and safe,
not the way they left the battlefield

in their tiny coffin—a joke leg saved
for history out of the butchered limbs.
I wish I had a picture of me smoking
my Havana, lying there on the stretcher.

Ignore me, dear, if I drone on, and paint
my likeness as the man I'd be: dapper
in my new coat, mustache waxed, eyes dry.
Tomorrow, early, I go to Gettysburg,

and morning long my mind's kept seeing clear
what fifty years have failed to wash away.
That day I lost a thousand men an hour.
Don't stop above the waist to show me whole.

Yes, pour the wine. Set mine in the window.
Given your painter's eye, you also see
the way light gathers and compresses time
so if we let ourselves our old lies pose

more guilt than we can swallow. After all
the dead, out of all, who would I have back?
I never loved another like the first,
an old fool says. First blood stains my hand.

My young Theresa used to wait for Key
to go into that house on Fifteenth Street
and start a fire; they'd meet in that same park
where I shot him, waving his handkerchief.

When I got old, people asked me to tell
what I had learned. They meant from my mistakes.
They wanted me to say *Dig in, Repent,*
Stay Calm, Be Bold. Princess, what I know

is how we ache when even our worst wounds heal.
I remember back then what I said was
This looks like a good battlefield.
I could love you. I ought to be dead by now.

Robert Thomas

Of the White Hands

1

They call me that because of how I sew,
quick as mercury still, at my age;
the threads leap through silk like dolphins,
and I remember the white sails
careening over the Irish Sea, a grass snake
flashing through a field of heather.
Whatever they say, I never loved him,
not even when he smeared the port-red blood
on my lace garments and I had to gasp
and how he knew what I wanted and how he hid it
and took my waist and led me to the table
of our intoxicated guests; not even when awakened
by the acrid smell in the air I found him
standing on the balcony staring at nothing,
not even the deranged sky, as indifferent to *seeing*
as an ash tree struck by lightning,
a silhouette against all the fields of barley
burning madder red in the northwest;
not even when he rode the Breton cliffs so hard
I thought the earth must have quenched him
if it had dared. If they think
I cared about *her* they understand nothing.
I watched him from so far that it was absolute,
the stillness of the hoofbeats and the sea's barrage,
and saw how alone he was, riding back and forth
on the violet sands as if repeating it, *Iseult*,
over and over to erase all sense in the salt air.

2

It was as though he could feel her very breath
warming his nape, but it was the hushed forays of morning
entering the chapel nave through stained glass
as he knelt and asked for nothing. He never told me;
I knew. The sky thick with clouds,
the light itself was palpable, dark
as petals of viridian and Paris blue.
It was as if he could hear her voice
but not understand when outside the king's men
lit the fagots for him—the sweet aroma of smoke
mixed with bitterroot—and he remembered the scent
of sandalwood and quince she had worn below deck.

Four Poems by Mary Jo Bang

If Wishes Were Horses

That the wound had never been
its vast geography, red terrain forming
somewhere near the level of the heart, frayed
edges folding together

like a wake that closes after the departed.
Had it never bled so, a redundant sea
dissolving the side rails
of ships crossing at right angles.

Without the wound, she might have had
the chrome skin of a girl
behind glass, red lips just out of reach.
Yes, energy conserves

itself, but a second time it's useless,
a dull warmth embracing the ceiling's vacancy.
And the between
is but once. In a 9.7 moment of pain,

we all become expert, ancient, cousin
to simple persistence. Beggars, prodding
airy nothings, making promises: hay and a bed
in the stable, if only.

& There He Kept Her Very Well

Harsh orange, dull burn
of realization.
My imperfections, once subtle,

are now inadmissible.
Still he keeps me
like a pretty need-not

in this fusty dungeon.
Someone has chosen poorly:
a pale persimmon for the walls,

the ceiling, the floor;
a single window, no door.
Hands dip into the vat,

a vicarage of strings.
He's removing the seeds,
installing them in egg cups.

Soon a tray of tender shoots
will phosphoresce
in the dark. He wants me

to brighten,
says a well-lit face will dazzle.
Outside, the dogs

have begun to howl.
Look —
it's Hecate, a torch in each hand.

No Talking

No talking in the grass, only persistent scars
where cheek lay to hear
a sound: the distilled conversation

of minute barbed legs, fiddle bow to fiddle.
No movement on the pond surface—
water slurring its beaded lining, blunted tapestry

of black and blacker, brown and tan. No talking
on the part of two dogs engaged
in chase and turn, alike under coats

wet dun and spotted damp, the heart's steady
hiccough under layers of fascia, muscle, rib.
Hands spill the pond water. Nothing can be grasped.

Why indelible hunger? Why insatiable need?

Electra Dreams

Night is when I give you new clothes.
Suits you never owned, borrowed cuff links,
rented ties, until you look nothing like
your former self.

The gods might strike me dead if they knew
you were the object of this sad ecstasy.
Sometimes I dress you as the well-dressed man
I pass each morning on the street.

I'm drawn to his brown suede hat.
Or the doctor with soft hands who told me
it's best to think of pain as a number
between one and ten.

You've been many things, all the same.
I've grown to think of you as someone
who keeps calling me back, just
as I'm about to leave. Tonight, you are infant,

easy to love. I hum you a tired bit of Brahms
until you're almost asleep, then place you
next to my breast. This is the dream
swimmer's deep, that unbridled edge

of anarchy, where everything's a pale
blue-green and the air itself is drinkable.
It's safe to speak here.
To call love by a name other than vengeance.

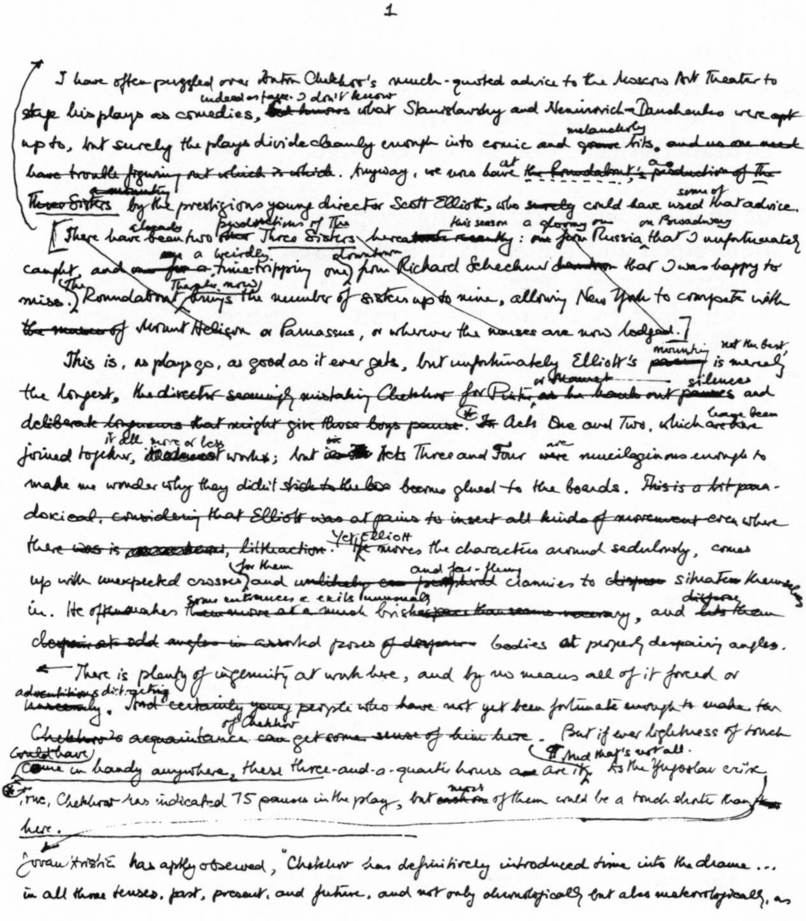

A manuscript page from a review of The Three Sisters.

John Simon
The Art of Criticism IV

John Simon lives with his wife, Patricia Hoag-Simon, in a New York city high-rise two blocks from Lincoln Center. Our interview took place mainly in his airy living room. Although the furnishings are modern, there is no evidence that modern technology supports Simon's work. He writes at a large desk in the adjoining book-lined den, and he writes in pen. He has not learned how to use a computer, nor does he want to; his wife told me that twentieth-century automation and computerization confuse him: "He didn't know that he could go to various branches of his bank to get money," she recalled.

"He thought there was a pile of money in the back of his bank labeled 'John Simon's money'."

He was dressed for something more than the occasion, wearing a light brown Zegna suit. *"He even wears a suit to bed,"* his wife joked. But his manner was informal, and when he saw I was concerned about whether my tape was picking up our voices from opposite couches, he promptly sat on the floor next to me. I joined him, and the entire interview took place on the carpet. The next day, we talked mostly in Simon's study and in a nearby restaurant where we broke for lunch.

Born in Subotica, Yugoslavia, on May 12, 1925, John Ivan Simon spoke three languages by the time he was five. His parents were fluent in German and Hungarian, and the youngster picked up Serbo-Croatian in the streets of Belgrade where they lived. *"I was language-conscious and language-intoxicated,"* he recalled. Later, he learned French and English and *"became aware of what great literatures open up if you know these languages."*

In 1941 the Simons immigrated to America. Simon went to school in Pennsylvania first, then transferred to Horace Mann in New York. He was a good student, particularly of the arts, and tried his hand at fiction. At Harvard, where he headed the Harvard Radio Workshop, he wrote plays as well as fiction and poetry. He graduated from Harvard in 1946 and completed his doctorate there in 1959. Simon has taught at Harvard, the University of Washington, the Massachusetts Institute of Technology, Bard College and the University of Pittsburgh.

He wrote his first theater criticism for the winter 1959–1960 issue of The Hudson Review. In 1962 he moved to Theater Arts, where he served as drama critic for only eight months, due to an internal struggle for ownership of the magazine. There followed the beginning of an ongoing association with The New Leader, first as film critic, today as cultural critic. He also did some reviewing for WNET-TV, but he says educational television found his criticism too strong. He reviewed film and later language for Esquire and since 1978 has been reviewing film for The National Review. He has written on the arts for other periodicals, including The New York Times Book Review, The Washington Post Book World, as well as

The New Criterion, *to which he contributes regularly, and* New York *magazine.*

Simon has published eleven collections of these reviews and one book on Ingmar Bergman. He has been honored with several awards, including the George Polk Memorial Award in film criticism, the George Jean Nathan Award for dramatic criticism, an award from the American Academy of Arts and Letters for literary criticism and a Fulbright Fellowship that took him to the University of Paris.

INTERVIEWER

When did you write your earliest criticisms?

JOHN SIMON

I guess what you might call criticism is what you do in some of your college papers, although my Horace Mann high-school history teacher said that I was the only student whose papers he could not grade while listening to the radio because my syntax was so fancy.

INTERVIEWER

Do you feel isolated from people in the arts because you're reviewing them?

SIMON

Well, yes and no. Obviously, there are a good many parties I don't get invited to, there are a good many people who, rightly or wrongly, don't have any use for me. And perhaps life would be more colorful and amusing if one didn't have that many enemies. But on the other hand, the cause is more important than mere fun, and so, rather sadly, I resign myself to being not invited to this or that thing.

INTERVIEWER

When you are invited, are you a different kind of person from the one we meet in print?

SIMON

Of course. How could one not be a different person? Conversation is not the same thing as criticism.

At the conference on criticism Robert Brustein held at Harvard, you said you write in order to educate the public, teaching in a "school without walls."

My greatest obligation is to what, correctly or incorrectly, I perceive as the truth. It is also a genuine satisfaction to express the truth as you feel it should be expressed. It's like scoring high on a test or in a sport. But after that, there also comes a certain hope that one is read by other people. The quantity is not important, but the quality is. If I could imagine that I'm being read by five hundred people in this country whom I really respect — I'm not saying there are only that few, but there are not all that many either — if they or a large segment of them were to read me, that would certainly make writing more satisfying. For example, when someone like the composer Ellen Taaffe Zwilich tells me that at one difficult point in their lives, she and her husband got a lot out of reading my reviews and going to see the movies that I recommended, that is very satisfying. On the other hand, when people tell me that they're the only ones ever to defend me in various discussions, I always say, "Look, if I had a dollar for everyone who has said this to me, I would be, perhaps not rich, but certainly comfortably off."

What do you think of other critics?

Well, that is a problem. Many people who write criticism are not that much different from the people who write me hate mail. There are several so-called critics — reviewers — who really hate my guts. There is one who slams a door in my face if he happens to pass through it ahead of me. But who cares? It's wonderful to be hated by idiots. A German writer whom I love and whom I've translated, Erich Kästner, gives advice, in one of his poems, to a would-be suicide. He tries to give this man various reasons for not blowing his brains out. The man remains unconvinced, so Kästner says, in essence, "All right, the world is full of idiots and they're in control of everything. You fool, stay alive to annoy them!" And that, in a sense, is my function in life, and my consolation. If I can't convince these imbeciles of anything, I can at least annoy them, and I think I do a reasonably good job of that.

There are always a few critics around that you feel comfortable with. It doesn't mean that you necessarily agree with them, but they're thinking human beings, and you can talk to them. There are not many of those, and most of them write for obscure publications. Sometimes, sitting at a film or drama critic's voting meeting, I feel surrounded by creatures from the black lagoon or from twenty thousand leagues beneath the sea. We don't speak the same language. A great Russian film meant nothing to them, whereas a cheap American shoot-'em-up or cowboy movie is a masterpiece. They look at me as if I were some sort of strange comic monster; I look at them and think, What do I have in common with these people? Why am I sitting here? I think press agents would be much nicer to sit with. They know much more about what we're talking about. Perhaps even cabdrivers do.

© Tony Walton

INTERVIEWER
How do you feel when artists attack you?

SIMON

Well, actually, that is a little sad, but it's so predictable.
It's like that picture of Joseph Papp, with his arm around me
after I've given him a good review, and his asking for the
picture back the next month because of a bad review. And I
thought, Screw you, I'm keeping it.

It is not important whether I suffer for a bad review or
whether the person reviewed suffers for it, because there is
something bigger than both of us—the art that is being reviewed. That is what we are all answerable to, and that is
where the truth must lie and everything else—friendships,
feuds, loves—must be forgotten.

I once dated a very beautiful girl who thought Mick Jagger
was the greatest thing in the world. So I showed her my review
of one of his movies, and she never spoke to me again. Whatever might have been, that was the end of it, and I had suspected that that was going to happen. But a critic has to get
satisfaction not from being popular or liked or invited to parties, but from having done the bloody best he could, however imperfect it may be. If somebody throws a cocktail in
your face at a party because of a bad review, you just have to
take it.

INTERVIEWER

Has that happened?

SIMON

Not often. The most famous case is Sylvia Miles throwing
some steak tartare at me, which made her into a heroine. In
fact, Andy Warhol said in one of his so-called books that
she's famous for that and not much else. This incident was
so welcomed by the Simon-hating press that the anecdote has
been much retold. She herself has retold it ten thousand times.
And this steak tartare has since metamorphosed into every
known dish, from lasagna to chop suey. It's been so many
things that you could feed the starving orphans of India or
China with it.

INTERVIEWER
Can you cover what you like in addition to the essentials?

SIMON

If you're very excited about some small thing you saw, of course, you write about that too. Those things are up to me. But the big ones *have* to be reviewed. Then, every once in a while, some press agent calls me and says, "There's a wonderful new playwright here off off off Broadway. You must review this serious work." But I'm not what Stanley Kauffmann calls a "barricade critic" who is there discovering the avant-garde, the frontline stuff. I see my function as slightly different. I'm there to review the fellow's second play and see to it that his head doesn't get too swelled, and that's a function too. And if his second play is as good as his first, I'll gladly say that as well.

INTERVIEWER
Some say you don't go downtown because you can't appreciate experimental theater.

SIMON

Well, I don't think there is such a thing as experimental theater. I think there is only theater that has something to say. The cheap way out is to say there's good theater and bad theater, but it's not quite that simple. There's theater that has something necessary to say — it may not even be good, but it has an insight it must express — and there's theater which may be very slick and accomplished but has nothing to say. That's the distinction. It is somewhat similar to good versus bad, but it's not synonymous.

So that's what I try to assess. And if it says it in an experimental way, fine. But what is experimental? Is Peter Sellars taking a boring six-hour opera by Olivier Messiaen and putting two hundred television sets on the stage experimental? Maybe it is, but it's still terrible. The Messiaen music has maybe half an hour of good stuff in it, and five and a half hours of boredom, and the television sets have nothing to say, and Peter Sellars has nothing to say. If that's experimental, I don't need it. But if somebody trying to write a new opera or play or movie says something in a different, difficult, subtle, round-about, never before seen or heard way, fine. I'm all for it, and I don't care if it's downtown or uptown or out of town, though my publications have not, on the whole, encouraged out-of-town reviewing.

INTERVIEWER

In a review of Kenneth Tynan's book *Curtains*, you wrote that the ideal critic is likable and modest. You've also said that a critic must be arrogant. Can you reconcile the two?

SIMON

Did I really say that? Well, there is a way of being arrogant in a charming way, which is more likable than charmless modesty. People who can't see that you have to ignore, charmingly.

INTERVIEWER

Some who read your reviews of gay plays say you're homophobic. What do you think?

SIMON

I don't like uniforms. I don't like people abdicating their identity to become part of some group, and then becoming obsessed with this and making capital of it. I mean, somebody like Elie Wiesel, for example, who appropriates the Holocaust and makes a cottage industry out of it. I find that distasteful. I don't care what it is, an Irishman who goes around spouting Yeats and Synge while waving his shillelagh, a professional Frenchman who puts on Gallic smoothness, the *c'est magnifique*, the bedroom eyes or whatever. Anything that is a uniform rather than an individuality I find reprehensible. As it happens, the most glaringly evident uniform in our theater at this moment is the homosexual one. I find it preposterous that these people actually think themselves more important than the rest of the world. "My cancer can beat up your cancer anytime." That's absurd.

The only true art is that which speaks to everyone without any parochialism. It can be very minor art. It doesn't have to be a grand topic treated in an epic way. It can be something very intimate, very small-scale, but it has to be ecumenical. It has to be for everybody. Blacks who go around saying, "This is black theater, and if you're not black you can't judge it, you have no right to criticize it," are talking nonsense. If it's any good, it can be as black as it wants to be, and I can feel it and understand it. And if it's lousy, it's lousy no matter what color it is. And, again, some blacks carry on as if they were all geniuses deserving preferential treatment. They want to play parts that they're not suited for, and they want privileges that they haven't earned. That's nonsense; but if they're talented, and if they can do something, by all means let them. And I'll be the first to applaud them.

INTERVIEWER

You are getting into the issue of nontraditional casting here, and I know you have strong views. What do you say then about Orson Welles playing *Othello*? Or males playing female parts?

SIMON

I do not want a black to play Romeo, if a white is playing Juliet. It upsets the true meaning of the play and sets up wholly alien reverberations. Nontraditional casting can be mere bleeding-heart liberalism, which is the source of political correctness and is one of today's chief horrors. The arrogance of a black actor who says, "I'm going to play Henry the Fifth and I'll be as black as I am and I'll sound as much like Harlem as I wish, and you will love me and write rave reviews," I do not condone. And I'm almost the only critic who dares stand his ground in this matter. Good God, I'm not for keeping anyone deprived or downtrodden. A fine actor can portray a person of any color. But when, say, Olivier played Othello, he very carefully strove to look, sound and move right, which involved a good deal of study, and a couple of hours of making up for each performance. Similarly, a black actor who makes the necessary concessions and effort to play a white part can do excellent work. But it requires accommodation to the play and the role. Nontraditional casting is okay, color-blind casting is often confusing and misleading. In *Lear*, if the good Edgar is white, and the wicked Edmund is black—or vice versa—it's very hard for the audience not to perceive it as a statement on race. But makeup can make the difference. Gender-bending, however, is never advisable: it is pointless and stupid.

I think when someone like August Wilson comes along and writes good plays and gives black actors a chance to show their stuff, it's a wonderful thing. And if a black actor is willing to make up white, which none of them seems to be anymore, by all means let him or her play whatever he or she wants to play. But if an actor is going to come on with his dreadlocks and say, "I am the Great Gatsby," and the whole liberal press cheers him on, that still won't make any sense.

INTERVIEWER

Is there a dramatic character with whom you identify?

SIMON

I don't really think so, but if I must dredge one up, I think it is Alceste in *The Misanthrope*. He is usually thought to be sneered at by Molière, but if you read that play carefully, you can see that Molière is having fun with Alceste for being too much of a purist, too much of a perfectionist, but at the same time it is clear that he prefers him to most of the men and women around him. He pokes fun at Alceste, but he is more for him than for the others. The critic should try to know better than the rest, but he should never forget to laugh at himself when he goes off the deep end. A sense of humor about oneself is one of the three or four best critical tools.

INTERVIEWER
Have you been edited for content?

SIMON
It has happened over the years that I wrote something too controversial — offensive to some group or other. I wrote a review of *Stop the World I Want to Get Off* with Sammy Davis, Jr., a revival, in which I had a funny opening paragraph that was scurrilous about Sammy Davis. If I say so myself, it was rather funny. The editors of *New York* passed it around to one another and all of them fell over in their chairs laughing, after which they said, "We can't print that." When I almost resigned over the fact that they didn't print it, they allowed me, two issues later, to print one sentence that I particularly wanted restored. However, when you print such a sentence two weeks later out of context, it no longer has much impact.

INTERVIEWER
Have you been censored since?

SIMON
In *The New Leader* I once wrote that Barbra Streisand is the sort of thing that starts pogroms. This was not considered acceptable to the editor and never saw print. A more recent excision has been a reference to Phylicia Rashad in *Jelly's Last Jam* looking like a bouncer in a lesbian bar. It is characteristic that the censorship always comes when you attack a member of a minority or putative minority. And if the person happens to belong to two minorities simultaneously, the attack is tantamount to the sin against the Holy Ghost. That is what political correctness and cowardice (assuming that they are two separate things) have reduced us to.

INTERVIEWER
Do you work hard on the opening lines of your reviews?

SIMON

No. Opening lines have to pop into your head. Opening
lines that you have to sweat and toil over are not going to be
worth the sweat. But they do pop. I once went out with a girl
many years ago, very sweet, who said, "I could write your
reviews. The only thing I don't know is how you think of those
opening lines. If I could figure that out, I could do it."

INTERVIEWER

Which of your opening quips comes first to mind?

SIMON

I try to forget my bright sayings because they're the surest
way to bore people at parties. I wouldn't be happy if a poet
at a dinner party started reciting his latest poem even if it was
good. Of course, sometimes, you can't forget them.

INTERVIEWER

Which is one you can't forget?

SIMON

An English comedian, Norman Wisdom, came to Broadway
in a play and I wrote, "If this be Norman Wisdom, give me
Saxon folly." You see, I am as good as my word. You are
asking me to remember and I can't.

INTERVIEWER

What do you use to write?

SIMON

I write in longhand. I love pens, particularly fountain pens.
I have many of them, and I'm very fond of most of them. I
like the way something handwritten looks on the page. There's
a sensuous pleasure in writing something with a pen, much
less so with a pencil, by the way. I find it very easy to correct
something on a page. I'm a two-fingered typist, and as I type,
I make changes. Not huge ones. Then, after the piece is typed,

I look at it, make a few more small changes, and that's it. I tried to use a computer that we have, and it just alienated me immediately—I can't even bring myself to learn how to use it.

INTERVIEWER

How would you describe your state of mind when the curtain is about to go up?

SIMON

One goes hoping that the theater is still alive and that this will be a good show. Nine times out of ten, one goes home with one's tail between one's legs, beaten again, and the only compensation is to sit down and write a vitriolic review. That's the only satisfaction left one.

INTERVIEWER

Purgation?

SIMON

Yes. The pleasure ought to be in seeing a play, not in knocking it down. There are pleasant surprises, however. Otherwise one really would have to quit. But they come few and far between. In all fairness, one must say that even if the play isn't very good, there could be compensations—wonderful performers, beautiful theatrical effects, and one has to learn to make do with that. I suppose there are restaurants to which one goes for the appetizers.

INTERVIEWER

Have you walked out on a play?

SIMON

Yes. Only the daily critics condemned by their editors to sit through a horror are not able to leave, but anyone remotely free should be able to leave after the first act. If a play is perfectly ghastly for one act, it's not going to be wonderful in the second. When I was a Young Turk, I sometimes left after five or ten minutes when something seemed absolutely revolting. There is an incident where I was leaving the theater when a late-coming critic was just arriving and said, "You're going in the wrong direction." I replied, "No, *you* are going in the wrong direction."

INTERVIEWER

How does your mind work during the course of a play?

SIMON

This is the crux of the matter. My first reaction is like anyone else's, a jumble of thoughts and feelings, positive or negative, but the precise diagnosis is deferred until the writing of the review. Then I empty out the contents of my mind and heart, and proceed to sort out what in that heap in front of me is most pertinent. As I sift and organize, some new insights crop up and act as cement for the mix, making the final formulation clearer, shapelier, more effective. It is the translation of impressions into expression, the making of what is merely remembered memorable.

INTERVIEWER

Have you ever been a lone voice?

SIMON

Yes, indeed. Often.

INTERVIEWER

That hasn't changed your mind at all?

SIMON

No, not at all.

INTERVIEWER

Confidence is a huge factor.

SIMON

It is. One of the problems with a lot of reviews is a lack of self-confidence on the part of the reviewer. You can read between the lines and see this man or woman didn't really like the work very much and yet it's a favorable review. That can be because the editors or publishers push for that kind of thing but, more often than not, it's because the critic wasn't sure what to think and assumes that liking is safer than disliking. You can be shown up as being just as big an idiot for having liked or disliked something if the verdict of time goes against you. There is no safety in this job. In the end, you will be judged on how this play has lasted for a quarter of a century, a century and beyond.

INTERVIEWER

What's the most difficult type of theater to judge?

SIMON

If you're a real professional, nothing should be difficult. The only problem can be if a Japanese or a Bulgarian company comes, and you're not so sure about what the language of that play is really like. Then, unless you can get hold of the translated text, you have to use your intuition. If I knew better than the playwright, I would be writing plays and he or she would be reviewing them. I am willing to assume, with a modicum of modesty, that when it comes to playwriting, the playwright knows more than I do and therefore I can state objections and explain them, but cannot rewrite the play. But rules exist essentially to be broken, and whereas journeymen playwrights probably have to play by them, geniuses can and should flout them.

INTERVIEWER

Do you alter your style at all for different magazines?

SIMON

I consider it lucky that I have a certain flexibility. I can go from a piece I will write, say, for *The New Criterion* or *The*

American Scholar to a piece I will write for *New York* or some other publication with a large circulation. Some of it is a little more egghead, and some of it is a bit more chatty, but it is not a fundamental break. I would compare it to a trained singer who can go from opera to show tunes, or a public speaker who can bring his message to different audiences. Whether there are a few more Latin quotations or a few more references to Proust doesn't matter. It all bears the stamp of my individuality; is not less well thought out or less well written; does not pull punches.

INTERVIEWER

There are nasty rumors that you've mellowed. Have you?

SIMON

Honestly, I don't know. When you live with your face and see it every day, and you've grown twenty years older, you don't fully notice the change because it's gradual. Someone else who has not seen you for several years can tell the difference. Mellowing is the kind of thing that only other people can judge. I don't think, though, that I've changed in *that* way.

I think I've changed in other ways. I have learned to say equally devastating things in a more ironic, more controlled, more polished, more understated way, so it doesn't hit the less attentive or less imaginative reader in the face quite so much, and that may look like mellowing. But it's only gaining greater control over your craft. But perhaps that is a sort of mellowing.

Actually, a Belgian-American director, André Ernotte, said something about me that my wife particularly cherishes. He said, "You know, you always take a shower before you go to the theater." And in a stupid, literal-minded way, I asked myself, "What does he mean? Of course I don't try to smell up the theater with my body odor." But then I realized that what he meant is that I'd given him a good review after giving him several bad ones, and that many critics, once they get in the habit of giving somebody bad reviews, automatically pan him. Or, *mutatis mutandis*, automatically praise. One must never close one's mind one hundred percent, and one should always give the next thing the benefit of the doubt, whatever that next thing is, even if its author was lousy ten or twenty times. You never know when lightning will strike.

INTERVIEWER

Does knowing an actor or playwright or composer personally interfere with your ability to write about him as you do about others?

SIMON

There are ways of safeguarding against that. I have never become very friendly with an artist unless I have respect for him or her as such, and that means, as far as I am concerned, that the artist is talented. And if the artist is talented, he or she is not going to produce junk. The artists I befriend — and they are not many — may come up with better things and less good ones, but even their bad things will probably not be shameful. Therefore it's safe to be friends with such a person, especially if that person is intelligent and self-assured enough to be able to take criticism.

I've lost some friends — mostly among actors, and maybe a director or two — though no writers I can think of. But if you lose them, it can't be helped. It doesn't mean that they're not very talented people and that, even if they hate and attack you, if they next do what you consider good you won't say so. But it does mean they're not strong enough, not solid enough human beings to be able to take criticism. In that case, you may need their works, but you don't need their company, their friendship.

The artists I have befriended have almost all of them been able to take criticism. What I do if I know them is two things: I bend over backward to be tougher on them, because I realize my friendship might color my reviews. But I'm also a little more careful about how I say it. I try to be still amusing, still readable, still gutsy, but I do try not to be too witty at their expense. So that balances out the extra toughness.

There is a famous English actor, Alan Howard. His wife, or companion, is the writer Sally Beauman, who was a good friend of mine. Alan hates critics, but he liked me, partly because Sally liked me, and partly because he discovered that I was a human being and cared about theater as much as he did. Then he came to this country in a play called *Good*, which was anything but that. And to describe what he did in it, I said that at one point he assumed the stance of a man chasing after a runaway goose, which as criticisms or witticisms go is fairly mild. But for Alan Howard, that was the death. Sally called up in a mournful voice and said that we would no longer be able to see each other or communicate. One day, I ran into them on a street corner with their child. I recall exactly where it was and the oblique angle of the sun. It was close to Christmas; he said, "Happy Christmas," and those were the last words he ever uttered to me. I'm sorry. I liked him, and I was very, very fond of her. I think she had a publisher send me one of her books once. That's all she could do after all those years of friendship.

Or take the case of Maximilian Schell. As an actor, he is almost always good, but as a director he has his ups and downs. When I give him a good review, we are friends; when I give him a bad review, he doesn't know who I am. That comes with the territory.

INTERVIEWER

Do you ever regret writing something extremely nasty?

SIMON

Sure, sometimes. And sometimes I regret reviews that weren't tough enough. It can go either way. Usually, it's not so much that I was too hard on someone, but that I didn't think of the most effective way to say it. I'm writing for everybody who wants it, but I'm writing, first of all, for myself. I have to feel satisfied that I've met the challenge of this piece of work, whatever it is. That means that one is writing for the hardest judge of all. And if you can pass that test, you'll do all right by everyone else. After that, you also write for your readers, for the artists or nonartists or antiartists. You write both for the present and for posterity, if it will have you.

INTERVIEWER

You talked about writing for the future. What will people see in your reviews a hundred years from now, particularly when you're describing an ephemeral art like theater and they can't go back to the work?

SIMON

It depends. A really good critical essay does conjure up an image. In some ways it's less than a photograph, in other ways it's much more. If you read it fifty years later, you will say, "Well, I don't know whether I would have seen it that way, but I can see someone seeing it that way, and it does conjure up something before my mind's eye." A gutsy, passionate, individualistic, flawed but very human, very from-the-gut review, will always stand up in some way. It will be *a* truth, and *a* truth is always better than no truth.

INTERVIEWER

How would you assess your role in the drama criticism of the day?

SIMON

I see drama criticism as being either academic, in books and learned journals, which doesn't concern us here, or popular, in newspapers and magazines, which does. Now, popular criticism in this country is written mostly by fans, hacks or lackeys. The fans love everything they see, and are worthless. The hacks have scant education and knowledge, but can turn out fluent journalistic prose—only neither their style nor their opinions command the readers' attention. The lackeys serve the interest of their publishers, who want more theatrical advertising, which comes from generally favorable reviews, and greater readership, which comes with a sense of well-being in the theater. Or so they think. My function is not to be any of those three things.

INTERVIEWER

How have you managed to sell this position to a popular magazine?

SIMON

What made it possible is, I think, that I amuse some readers and get others worked up. Laughter and indignation seem to be marketable.

INTERVIEWER

How well do you think you have succeeded?

SIMON

That is for others—for time itself—to tell.

—**Davi Napoleon**

NOTES ON CONTRIBUTORS

DRAMA

Karl Kirchwey, a Guggenheim recipient and winner of the Rome Prize from the American Academy of Arts and Letters, directs the Unterberg Poetry Center of the 92nd Street YMHA in New York. His third book of poems, *The Engrafted Word*, will be published next year.

Martin McDonagh won the 1996 Evening Standard Award for Most Promising Playwright and the 1996 George Devine Award for Most Promising Playwright. *The Cripple of Inishmaan* premiered at the Royal National Theatre last December.

Doug Wright received an Obie Award in 1995 for his play *Quills*. His other plays include *The Stonewater Rapture*, *Interrogating the Nude* and *Watbanaland*.

POETRY

Mary Jo Bang's first book of poems, *Apology for Want*, will be published this fall. She is the poetry editor of *The Boston Review*.

Shelley A. Berger, a lawyer, lives in Venice, California.

Michael Burns recived an NEA poetry fellowship in 1995. He is the author of *The Secret Names*, a collection of poems.

Anne Carson is the author of *Eros the Bittersweet*, *Plainwater* and *Glass, Irony and God*. She lives in Montreal.

John Richard Reed received an MFA from the University of Massachusetts in 1994. His work has been published in *Poetry* and *Western Humanities Review*.

Edward Hirsch's most recent book of poems is *Earthly Measures*. He teaches at the University of Houston.

Stephen McLeod's poems have been published in *Southwest Review*, *Agni* and *American Poetry Review*.

Tony Sanders's poems have appeared in *The Gettysburg Review*, *Ohio Review* and *Grand Street*. A past winner of the B.F. Conners Prize, he lives in New York.

Richard Shelton is Regents Professor of English at the University of Arizona, Tucson.

Elizabeth Stein received an MFA in poetry from Columbia University. She lives in Somerville, Massachusetts.

Eleanor Ross Taylor is the author of *Days Going/Days Coming Back* and other volumes of poetry. She lives in Charlottesville, Virginia.

Robert Thomas's poems have been published in *Agni*, *Shenandoah* and *The Iowa Review*. He lives in San Francisco.

Frederick Tibbetts's poems have been published in *The New Republic*, *The Yale Review* and *Press*. He lives in Princeton, New Jersey.

Wyatt Townley lives in Kansas. Her most recent collection of poems is *Perfectly Normal*.

Susan Wood, a professor of English at Rice University, received a Lamont Poetry Selection in 1991 for *Campo Santo*, her second book of poetry.

FEATURE

Israel Horovitz is the author of *The Indian Wants the Bronx*, *Line*, *Park Your Car in Harvard Yard* and more than fifty other plays.

INTERVIEWS

Benjamin Howe (Sam Shepard interview) is an assistant editor of *The Paris Review*.

John Lahr (David Mamet interview) is drama critic for *The New Yorker*. His most recent book is *Light Fantastic: Adventures in Theatre*. The photo of David Mamet and Gregory Mosher appears courtesy of Gregory Mosher.

James Lipton (Stephen Sondheim interview) is dean of the Actors Studio MFA/School of Dramatic Arts at the New School in New York. He is the author of *Mirrors*, a novel, and the non-fiction perennial, *An Exaltation of Larks*.

Jeanne McCulloch (Shepard interview) is an editor of *The Paris Review*.

Davi Napoleon (John Simon interview), a contributing editor at *Theatre*

Crafts International, is the author of *Chelsea on the Edge: The Adventures of an American Theatre*.

Mona Simpson (Shepard interview) has received the Whiting Writer's Award, a Guggenheim grant and the Hodder Fellowship at Princeton University. Her most recent novel is *A Regular Guy*.

Laurie Winer (Wendy Wasserstein interview) is theater critic for *The Los Angeles Times*.

ART

Tony Walton is a designer for theater and film. His current Broadway productions include *Steel Pier* and *A Funny Thing Happened on the Way to the Forum*.

Robert Wilson was born in Waco, Texas. He has won numerous awards, including the Tony and the Obie, for his theatrical productions. He is represented in New York by Paula Cooper Gallery.

The Paris Review
Booksellers Advisory Board